Zoe Taylor

THE
Library
FOUNDATION

Enhancing the work of our library
libraryfoundation.org

WOMEN'S WORK

ALSO BY MEGAN K. STACK

Every Man in This Village Is a Liar

WOMEN'S WORK

A RECKONING WITH HOME AND HELP

Megan K. Stack

DOUBLEDAY  NEW YORK

All rights reserved. Published in the United States by Doubleday, a division of Penguin Random House LLC, New York, and distributed in Canada by Random House of Canada, a division of Penguin Random House Canada Limited, Toronto.

www.doubleday.com

DOUBLEDAY and the portrayal of an anchor with a dolphin are registered trademarks of Penguin Random House LLC.

Jacket photograph © Fuse / Corbis / Getty Images
Jacket design by Jenny Carrow

LIBRARY OF CONGRESS CATALOGING-IN-PUBLICATION DATA
Names: Stack, Megan K., author.
Title: Women's work : a reckoning with home and help /
Megan K. Stack.
Description: First edition. | New York : Doubleday, [2019]
Identifiers: LCCN 2018035800 (print) | LCCN 2018038585 (ebook) |
ISBN 9780385542098 (hardcover : alk. paper) |
ISBN 9780385542104 (ebook)
Subjects: LCSH: Stack, Megan K. | Child care workers—India. |
Child care workers—China. | Working mothers—Biography. |
Americans—India—Biography. | Americans—China—Biography.
Classification: LCC HQ778.7.I4 (ebook) | LCC HQ778.7.I4 S73 2019
(print) | DDC 362.71/20954—dc23
LC record available at https://lccn.loc.gov/2018035800

MANUFACTURED IN THE UNITED STATES OF AMERICA

1 3 5 7 9 10 8 6 4 2

First Edition

For my mother

Author's Note

The experience of motherhood was eventually to radicalize me.

—ADRIENNE RICH

I gave birth to my children in China and India. They are the sons of migrants, born into expatriation—Americans growing up in Asian megacities on the cusp of the Asian century. It wasn't my goal to have children overseas; it just happened that way. I got pregnant when I could and gave birth in the countries where I found myself at the time. I am a journalist and a writer. I didn't want to abandon my work for motherhood, and I didn't. Since my first baby was born, I've written two books. This is one of them.

I wanted to keep working, and I wanted to have my children. It seemed simple before it began.

But then the babies were born. My husband came and went for work, traveling the way I had once traveled, the way we had once traveled together—across the country, around the world, bringing back the grains of roads I'd never walked, the fading ghosts of spice and smoke rising from his skin. I stayed home with my children and my writing and the women who watched our children and cleaned our house so that I could keep writing. These women and I had little in common. They were poor women, brown women, migrant women. And at first I pushed them to the edge of thought. They were important to me, primarily, because they made me free. I wanted them to be happy. I didn't want to know the details. But that didn't work for long. The women were there. The women were here. We are here, together. I understood all too well the functional purpose of our arrangement, but I wasn't sure it made any sense.

Nor could I find the mess and nuance of our household reflected faithfully in any medium. Domestic workers are usually depicted in one of a few ways: essential financial investments made by guilt-free families; scrappy naïfs cruelly exploited by the heartless, clueless rich; or—most insidiously, I've come to think—"like family." Fundamental female experience is forever reduced to its crudest caricature. Childbirth is screaming. Periods are blood. Domestic work is a fairy tale: Cinderella under the thumb of a ruthless stepmother is finally living the dream when she becomes a benevolent princess with smiling servants of her own.

Gradually I realized that our house was an enclosed landscape of working mothers. That was the basic thing. The most important employees who worked for me—women who shifted my thinking and cleared the way for my work and cared most lovingly for my children—were migrants who'd left their own children behind to work in the city, and ended up in my house. We spun webs of compromise and sacrifice and cash, and it all revolved around me—my work, my money, my imagined utopias of one-on-one fair trade that were never quite achieved.

When I was a reporter, there existed this cliché about women who covered wars and other humanitarian disasters overseas. They used to say—and we used to say sometimes, too—that we were a sort of "third gender." We couldn't dream of being men, of course, but we were also exempt from some of the constraints that bound the women we wrote about. We could bare our faces in the street or sit with the men at a segregated dinner. Maybe a commander who would never talk to a woman from his own country might grant us an interview. We were bridges between the tacit maleness of the news organizations that had sent us and the women who were affected by the news, the grieving mothers and worrying wives. We ourselves were neither here nor there.

No matter how much time I spent with a subject, no matter how intimate the interviews became, a yawning space separated me from the people I wrote about. They had one kind of life, and I had another. I was tethered to the concreteness of the newspaper, and to the abstractions of journalism. The particular troubles faced by women did not affect me, nor did my own personal struggles have anything to do with the women I was interviewing. I was just passing through.

After having babies, after raising children in close quarters with women I hired to help, this necessary distance began to warp and melt. I couldn't maintain the sense that I was going along and everything was just fine. It didn't seem fine. Sometimes it seemed crazy.

The immediacy of domestic life and the desperation of small humans left few opportunities to question our choices in real time. We stumbled confusedly through a house that was also a job site, grappling with the intimacy of underwear, bathrooms, feeding children, and cuddling them to sleep. Our routines were disrupted by pregnancies, abortions, miscarriages, weddings, domestic violence, funerals, sick children, and school fees. Mine, theirs. The stuff of women the world over. We lived together in the space left by men who were temporarily elsewhere. Men who beat and loved; disappointed and disappeared. The promise of men, the threat of men, the uncertainty of men's actions.

We lived those years in China, a rising superpower, and India, an emerging economic engine. These places represent our collective future; they are the stuff of the world's dreams and nightmares. They are also places that have made statistical headway toward erasing women. Female fetuses are aborted. Newborn girls are murdered. Older girls are denied food. Female life is stifled before it can reach womanhood. This systematic erasure of women is not a government initiative, but a wildly popular and only semi-underground grassroots movement. And, of course, women participate.

Meanwhile, we—the women who occupied my house—were left to improvise, to endure what we could endure, to become as monstrous as we allowed ourselves to become. Our existence and interplays were literally intramural—between walls, among ourselves.

We were not unique. Our private problems are no doubt duplicated in households all over our planet. And yet housework is seldom considered as a serious subject for study, or even discussion.

This is an injustice on a grand scale, for housework is everything. It's a ubiquitous physical demand that has hamstrung and silenced women for most of human history. I'd love to believe the struggle for women's equality is concentrated in offices and manufacturing plants, but I've become convinced that this battle takes place, first and most crushingly, at home.

When we are saddled with disproportionate work at home—and studies show that virtually all of us women are, particularly during child-rearing years—we are too embarrassed to say so out loud. We don't want to complain. We don't want to tax our romantic partnerships. And, in the end, we stand to be blamed. The fact of this disproportionate labor is further evidence of our incompetence. We didn't choose the right partner (we are foolish), we didn't stand up for ourselves (we are weak), we were outmaneuvered in our own homes (we lack tactical skills). It is proof that we are not sufficiently devoted to our children or to our careers, depending upon who's doing the judging. It is proof—and there is ever more proof—that we ourselves are not sufficient.

Hiring domestic help is a stopgap and an evasion. The entire model does nothing for the middle class, since only women wealthy enough to pay for domestic help, or women poor enough to regard these jobs in terms of social mobility or survival, are affected. But for those who can afford it, paid domestic help takes the pressure off parents and marriage; off employers and society at large. I have seen online articles prescribing hired household help as a foolproof tonic for marital difficulties and even as the secret to life's happiness. Whether these arrangements provide personal fulfillment and marital bliss to the domestic employees themselves—this detail is never mentioned.

I think about all the houses I've known since withdrawing from the world to work at home. I remember the scenes and the stories. And I think, somebody should investigate. Somebody should write about all of this.

But this is my life. If I investigate, I must stand for examination. If I interrogate, I'll be the one who has to answer.

WOMEN'S
WORK

Prologue

───────

Dawn hadn't broken yet, and the dim caverns of the Beijing bus depot mumbled in drowsy din. Travelers staggered under their loads: mounds of clothing bundled and tied with rope; boxes of cheap toys; bulging sacks of grain. Exhausted faces hunted anxiously for the right bus. It was the Chinese New Year, and China's workers were going home.

It was just a few years ago, but that morning already seems like a very long time past. Another life, somebody else's life. I was still a foreign correspondent then. I covered China for the *Los Angeles Times.* I was traveling that morning with colleagues—a photographer and a translator—but we hardly spoke to one another. We'd done our jobs a thousand times before. We stalked and swung through the crowd like pack animals, eyes on the prey.

A construction worker named Li Guangqiang was our window into the world's largest human migration. We'd asked to document his journey home for the holidays, and proudly, ill-advisedly, he'd agreed. Every year, migrant workers pour en masse out of China's cities and industrial hubs and travel home to far-flung families. Billions of odysseys crisscross the land in a bewildering tangle of traffic and trains and humanity.

Li's eyes shot uneasily from gate to gate, but when he caught me staring he adjusted his posture into an imitation of ease. Short and stocky, he planted his feet and squared his shoulders with bullish determination. His smile was quick and true, but in repose, his features went grimly still and his eyes narrowed as if on the lookout for a trick.

He lived poor in the city, sleeping in a frigid shelter of cinder blocks and corrugated tin alongside a frozen canal. For his journey home he'd chosen clothes that gave no hint of hardship: dark jeans fashionably distressed, puffy down coat, and a black pouch slung over one shoulder.

Following Li, we tossed our bags into the belly of the bus, scrambled aboard, and elbowed down the aisle. The engine shuddered to a start and the bus roared through darkened neighborhoods to the edge of town, then spun outward on smooth freeways, a thread unwinding itself from the snarl of the city, stretching into emptier territories. Passengers twisted to click parting shots of the fading city lights on their phones.

"Are you sure we're on the right bus?" somebody asked.

"I forgot my luggage! Can we go back?"

"Get somebody to send it to your village, or get off right now," snarled the bus driver.

A cry went up: "Turn on the heat!"

"No," the driver yelled. "It's a waste of fuel."

China rolled past—factories, construction sites, cranes. Billboards screamed their dubious promises to replace desolate roadside with luxury condominiums. It was a landscape of advertisements and gambles and works-in-progress.

I like to ride on roads through big countries—Russia, China, India, the United States. I like the vastness of the land and the isolation of large spaces under endless sky. I imagined the Middle Kingdom unfurling around us: land rolling west into the Gobi Desert, east to the Pacific Ocean, south to the Yellow River, north to the ends of the earth. Watching the world approach and vanish behind glass, I let my thoughts sweep over days and years gone and the unlived time that yawned ahead. Maybe the dislocation of a long drive opens the brain, encourages our minds to skim our private panoramas of time and personalities. We are used to the illusion that the world sits there, still and docile, while we charge through the scenes. We are moving; the earth is static. It's a trick of perception, of course. Nothing is ever still.

I carried notebooks and pens that morning. I had a job that carved my path through life, prodding me into places and dictating what I should do when I got there. As a foreign correspondent I'd lived in the great cities of the world. I'd covered wars and natural disasters and moments that abruptly changed history. I'd given myself over to this work so young, and so completely, that I wasn't sure anymore what would be left of me without all the journalism. I didn't know, and I didn't wonder. The job had become who I was; it was my organizing principle.

But now I'd quit that job, and everything was about to change. I was only working out my notice. The journey to Li's village would be my last big assignment for the newspaper.

Beneath the padding of down jacket and scratch of wool sweater, my unborn baby curled and kicked. I was four months pregnant. I had begun writing a new book. A book and a job were work enough, but a book and a job and a baby? I knew it was impossible.

Job, book, baby: I'd forced myself to choose the one I loved least. It was a terrible choice, because I loved each of them.

It's true—I loved my job. The travel, the restlessness, the writing. I loved the careless confidence of knowing that, whether an experience was unpleasant or glorious, everything was always about to change. A new city, a new conversation, a new story. I lived in the flux, out in the world, and I liked it there. The rooms and the smells, the afternoons so heavy with duty you had to force yourself through them, running fingers over surfaces, making yourself try again, call one more time, take the chance, out among the pieces and scenes.

The hours of this last journey drained along. The earth rose into mountains and thicker trees, then flattened out into farming fields. I shot along the road in a shuddering chamber and remembered.

I had met Tom out there, out here, in the world. At the Baghdad airport, waiting for a plane to Amman, we sat side by side and stared at a departure board left over from the days of Saddam Hussein. Thin plastic letters advertised flights that never flew. Tom and I studied that defunct departure board together like it was a piece of art, with the war outside and Baathist dust fine as powdered chalk in the slanting light. Iraq had been invaded and its government overthrown. We were young Americans who'd come to document unthinkable things. Tom had a duffel bag and Dante. I had a backpack and American short stories. We met, we talked, we fell away. The world carried us off, washed us back together. Seasons, rooftops, mountains, fights in the street, kisses against walls. Beirut nights raw with rain, mountaintops in Yemen, bursting into the Moscow streets to feel the flakes of our first Russian snowfall melt on our faces. We were walking the canals of Venice when he asked me to marry him. A few weeks later we were driving north through South Ossetia, trying to reach the thickest fighting in yet another senseless war, when a Russian MIG fired a missile that only barely missed our car because Tom noticed the plane and hollered at the driver to turn. That night we sat on the floor of a hotel room in Tbilisi and booked a band for our wedding reception.

Then we were married and living in Beijing. It was just the two of us over a hot summer. Trained pigeons circled out from neighboring rooftops. Their passing, the tight music of their feathers and fleet shadows sliding over the grass, stirred our hair and prickled our skin. We ate red beans on crushed ice and listened to music from the bars on Houhai. Thunderstorms, shaved noodles, weeping willows. I was sure I had never been so happy.

I went to Australia for a book tour, and when I came back it was fall and I was studying Chinese and working and then I was pregnant. I crashed out of Mandarin class to puke in the language school bathroom. I fell asleep on my office sofa on winter-dark afternoons. I understood that I was going to quit my job, but I couldn't complete the act. I spent weeks crafting my resignation letter.

The day I finally pushed Send, Beijing stretched frozen and glistening under winter sun and I rode a taxi across town, past the skaters on the lake and the shabby, low-slung shops selling mittens and toys and the steaming stalls where workers and students queued for roasted chestnuts. And I told myself that everything might be better or worse from that day, but at least things were changing. I was having a baby, starting a new book. My teeth sliced the winter air; I would eat the future whole. I was ready even to savor a mistake, to lose everything for the pleasure of building again from scratch.

One thing led to the next, and the next had led me here, to this bus. This was my last journalistic journey for a long time. Forever, for all I knew. My last big story would not be a conflict or a corruption or a hurricane or an election—it was an extended domestic vignette, the illustration of one family. Li was one man, and his family was the story.

Households had never held my interest. Houses were everywhere—inside war zones, across from parliament buildings, along military parade routes. They were the background scenery of great events; their residents were bit players who crept onto balconies to peer down at the action on the streets below. A collection of walls and beds and things to eat. No big deal. They caught my attention only when their members met with violence or achieved greatness in the wider world.

I hadn't realized yet that households are life itself; households contain and enable the entire human landscape. The only household I had ever inhabited had been a place I'd yearned to escape. I'd worked adult jobs for years before I could bring myself to buy a couch, with its implications of a sedentary and stable lifestyle.

It was night by the time we reached our stop. Fireworks burst pinwheels in the sky. We newspeople clambered into the backseat of Li's cousin's van and muttered together. The photographer warned us to hang back when we reached Li's house.

"I need a good shot of the reunion with the wife," he said.

Li sat quietly in the passenger seat as we plunged into the country night, on rough roads that bumped through winter-dry fields of wheat and corn. At last we stopped before a darkened house. Last year's faded wishes for prosperity and happiness clung to the metal gate.

Shoulders hunched, fists clenched, Li stomped through the courtyard in a few strides, pushed open the door, and stepped onto the concrete floor. The sitting room was bone-cold and bathed in thin sulfur light. The photographer crept behind him, hands on the camera. The translator and I lurked outside, watching. Beyond the cotton curtain that led to the next room, a television flashed and flickered.

Li glanced at us over one shoulder. We stared back wordlessly. A cornered grimace passed over his face.

"Hey," he shouted gruffly in the direction of the television. "Come out here."

Ducking her head and staring at the ground, his wife swept reluctantly through the curtains. Her face was chapped ruddy from wind and sun. For her husband's homecoming she'd tugged her hair back into a bun and put on a padded cotton jacket printed in red swirls.

Li frowned and huffed, shooting his bride an impatient, unreadable look. I couldn't understand his annoyance. Maybe the appearance of his moon-faced wife had rudely smashed his city reveries. Maybe he was just nervous. She stepped closer, then stood uncertainly at his side. Shoulder to shoulder, they regarded us. No hand stretched, no smiles cracked, no arms opened. Nobody said a word.

The uneasy moment was diluted in cries of welcome as the neighbors poured in the door to greet Li.

The next morning Li's wife minced goat fat for stew, banging it over and over with a shining cleaver. Her breath hung like fog in the frigid kitchen. The frozen fat resisted the blade, and she rubbed her thick fingers on her belly for warmth. Her name was Sun Fengzhi.

"You know," she told me almost immediately, "I went away once, too. Look—"

Wiping the lard from her hands, she led me into the bedroom. On the wardrobe, in pride of place, hung a fading snapshot of Sun and three other women. They posed in factory smocks on the dock of a faraway harbor, smiling shyly for the camera. The woman in the photograph was so young and pretty I could hardly recognize her. The picture was only two years old.

That was the year Sun left the children with her parents and found a job at a DVD component factory in Qingdao. She was thrilled by the travel, stimulated by the new city, and happy with her friends at the factory. But her son grew unruly; his grandparents could not handle him. She returned to the village.

She was not satisfied, she told me, but she was resigned. She had hardly seen Li since their wedding. She knew how the story ended: Her children would grow up and find jobs elsewhere, and she would raise the grandchildren. The cycle would repeat itself.

"I'll end up here alone with the grandchildren," she said flatly as we wandered back into the kitchen.

I sensed the emotional slackening, the relief of a sympathetic stranger. Another woman.

"He went away, and I had to take care of everything," she said quietly. "It was really difficult for me. I had to take care of the kids myself. I used to hold them so long my arms were in pain. I had to be their father and their mother."

The women of her husband's clan lurked in the doorway, listening. One of them peeled away and raced through the neighboring houses to find Li. *Your wife is criticizing you to the foreigners!*

Sun Fengzhi's face clouded with coming tears. Her voice fell to a whisper.

"In the beginning, when he went away, he hired—" The word was in the air. *Prostitutes.*

Li burst into the room.

"Stop complaining so much," he hollered.

He lurched toward her and snarled in rage. She flinched away from him. Watching their eyes and bodies, I thought that he had hit her before, and would probably hit her again, for answering our questions.

"She has so many complaints," Li said to us, glaring at his wife.

Their son joined in: "Stop complaining," he shrieked at his mother.

She dropped her reddened eyes to the stew.

Li's quiet panic was obvious. It made me think he'd agreed to our project only in a muddled rush of incredulity and embarrassment. Perhaps he'd thought it would boost his status in the village. He hadn't expected us to write about his wife. He probably hadn't expected us to speak with her at all.

Now we hovered in his kitchen and followed him around like some ungainly Greek chorus, whispering among ourselves and documenting his every sneeze. Staring at him. Taking his picture. Asking everybody questions.

Well, not everybody. The next time we saw Li's wife she hardly looked at us. I tried to catch her eye, but she always managed to look elsewhere. She was a woman and so it was easy enough for her to disappear. When the men burned money for the ancestors in the graveyard, she stayed home and cooked. She gave the men the juiciest morsels. The women of the family fed themselves on scraps and leavings.

She was a woman, and so she could vanish into our midst. The world will always suggest that this is an appropriate thing for a woman to do.

When our time was done we left. Casually we took a very long and very expensive taxi ride to a distant airport so that we could avoid another bus trip. We ate noodles in the departure hall restaurant and drank coffee and then we flew back to Beijing. I was returning to a week of parties and folk festivals. I was flying back to my husband. I was flying back to myself, to the rest of my life.

I thought it was my last trip. But that's a trick that trips have: You don't even know where you've been until you're not there anymore. I didn't know where I'd been, and I didn't know where I was going.

I didn't know that, in the years to come, I would spend more time with women like Li's wife than I'd spend with my husband. I didn't know that my own family life was about to get enmeshed with the lives of migrant workers—women who left their villages and children to earn money in my home. I didn't know that the sensation of being flummoxed, of plunging into another family's private dynamics, would soon dominate my days.

I didn't know that I, too, was about to disappear.

PART ONE

HOW TO
DISAPPEAR

Chapter 1

It was a Tuesday morning, and Tom was packing to leave me. He was headed out into the hinterlands, to a small town in south China where the Communist Party was cracking down on rioting factory workers. This was Tom's kind of adventure—a trip out into the provinces, into The Real China, to witness a fracture in the power of the Party. A substantial assignment with a light dusting of adrenaline.

As for me, I was just trying to get comfortable. I experimented with pressing my spine straight against the floorboards, then raising my pelvis into the air. I sighed and groaned.

Rolling clothes into logs and stacking them upright in his backpack, Tom pointedly ignored me.

"Are you really okay with going on this trip?" I asked churlishly.

"Come on." He smiled at me. "You're not due for two more weeks."

"That means anytime from *right now*." With a heave I rolled over to my side, letting the heavy sac of water and child splash dully onto the floor.

"The doctor said you'll probably be late," he pointed out cheerfully. "I bet it'll be three more weeks."

"You don't know." No, that wasn't comfortable either. I pulled air into my lungs and held it, trying to push my ribs off my womb.

"There are flights every hour."

I sighed. The baby punched. He had to come out, somehow. My flesh stood in the way of his life. Tissue would tear, blood must flow, pain was a promise.

"I'm going to the airport straight from the office." Tom dropped a kiss on my hair. "Text me and tell me what the doctor says."

"Don't go." I was too hot to think straight. I begrudged him, in some confused way, the airports and adventures that I had relinquished. Maybe I sensed that our fates were about to diverge radically; maybe I was trying, clumsily, to make him share my inconvenience and immobilization. Maybe I just wanted a companion, my love, the baby's father. Maybe I was scared.

"Honey," he said. "I can't sit here for four weeks."

And he went.

————

"Your fluid is too low," the doctor announced the next day. "He has to come out right away."

"What?" She might as well have said I was pregnant with a kangaroo kid. The indignation I had unloaded on Tom was, at bottom, an empty flourish of spousal guilt. Never for a moment had I believed the birth was imminent. "Why is the fluid low? What do you mean, right away?"

"The fluid is low because he's not peeing. That means he's not getting nourished. This can happen with gestational diabetes. The placenta sometimes stops working."

I was numb, trying to follow. Then a spike of horror.

"He's starving?"

"He's not starving," she said gently. "But he does need to come out now."

"My husband isn't here. I mean he's traveling."

She squinted at the ultrasound report, pen on her lips. "Can he be here tomorrow?"

"Yes." Goddamn right he can. "Are you sure it's okay to wait?"

"One day is okay. Go home. Take a long walk. Hopefully you'll go into labor and we won't need to induce."

"So I'll have the baby tomorrow."

"If not tomorrow then Friday."

"But the baby is coming now. Like, this week."

"Yes." She was laughing at me.

I called Tom, too shocked to be smug. Then, alone in the apartment,

I started calling friends. *I'm having the baby tomorrow.* Repeating the words, I tried to make myself believe it was true.

I hadn't packed a suitcase. Most pregnant women pack for the delivery months in advance. Checklists clutter the Internet: soft pillow, relaxing music, favorite chocolate. But I, who had thrown together hundreds of suitcases for all manner of climates and crises, who had once kept a "go bag" stuffed into my office closet for the next suicide bombing—I had never faced the ritual of packing this one, particular bag.

The baby was coming. I wasn't ready. Tom wasn't here. The whole thing was slipping off track.

I can no longer remember why this seemed important at the time, but during my pregnancy I'd become obsessed with the idea of a natural birth. I wanted to push my baby into the world through the vagina and without drugs. I told myself that I was a writer and an artist, a woman unbound by fear and pain and convention. I wanted the undiluted experience.

I knew everything about birth, or so I thought. Of course, I knew nothing about birth then, and I know nothing now. I know only that nobody knows anything about birth except women who are in the act. Like all great pain, like every altered state, it can be apprehended only from within. It can't be anticipated or remembered.

I thought birth would be the texture of the soil; the color of the moon. I thought labor would be simple work. I thought pain would not be pain. In my imagination, it was like that.

I didn't stop to consider that a truly "natural" birth would consist of a teenaged mother facing a decent chance of death, nor that there had been nothing natural about my pregnancy so far. I'd staved off motherhood with birth control while I built my career, only to discover that I needn't have bothered. Pregnancy eluded me until I flew halfway around the world to undergo surgery for endometriosis.

A thirty-five-year-old frame stiffened and battered by decades of hard living and neglect, my body was not the youthful web of flexible ligament and muscle that biology would favor as its maternal vessel. "Advanced maternal age," the doctor had written across the top of my file.

Nor was my temperament suited to natural birth. I'm a runner and an insomniac, not a yogi or meditator. I'd distinguished myself as the least relaxed mother in the HypnoBirthing class I'd attended with Tom in tow. The midwife had rolled her eyes and clicked her tongue over my tensed shoulders, so I ground my teeth and tried *even harder* to relax. I tried, really I did, and somehow that was part of the problem. I didn't know how to stop trying.

During all this moony preparation, I hardly thought about the baby at all. This new human life was a misty idea, a blurred bundle of my own emotion wrapped in an impossibly fluffy blanket, which, come to think of it, I didn't own.

It was a lot to think about; it's always a lot to think about. Maybe this is how our contemporary psychology confronts drastic change. Couples drown out a fear of lifelong commitment by obsessing over iris-and-ivy centerpieces and the vocabulary of the vows. Who wants to think about diapering and colic when you can sip chamomile tea with beatific pregnant ladies and swap tactical advice designed to outmaneuver the dreaded obstetrician? ("They're *surgeons,* you know. They think it's their *job* to cut you open.")

I approached birth with the competitive, adrenalized mentality of hard-charging newspaper work. Labor was an arena in which I would struggle and—inevitably, eventually—triumph. I would do it. Me. Motherhood itself lurked out in the margins of an old map, scribbled with sea creatures. *Here be dragons.*

Tom struggled to get home. Thunderstorms raged in southern China that night. His flight lingered for hours on the runway. Hunched over his computer, dripping sweat, he hammered the interviews into a news story. Finally the plane took off into the night sky, carrying my husband north.

Harried and soggy and exultant, he reached our apartment at three a.m. I was lying in bed, wide awake.

Four hours later, we drank a pot of coffee and took a taxi to the hospital.

————

A cot with bars and perfectly white sheets. Instruments with dials and screens, steel tables, metallic skeletons and hooks, things that rolled away. A pullout sofa for Tom.

I kicked off my shoes and climbed onto the bed, but lying ther
like an affectation. Hospitals are for broken bones, surgery, stitc
Now I felt, obscurely, that I was making much of myself, swanr....g
around on a perfectly normal Thursday morning.

"What are we going to do all day?" I asked Tom.

I kept looking at him and thinking, *You should be at work!* I think I
even said it once: "This could take a while. I could call you."

"Don't be ridiculous," he said.

I hated the bars that made the hospital bed resemble a cage. They
delineated the man from the woman, the mother from the father. I
malingered in plastic and metal and hospital pajamas. Tom sat with
his exhausted complexion and street clothes. I wanted him to find it
strange, too, but he didn't share my agitation. When I fretted over the
bars, he frowned. "They're just for—you know, physical safety," he
said absentmindedly.

If he realized we'd been split from each other, he didn't mind.
Maybe he had been raised to expect it; maybe I had not. The memory
of those bars would stay in my mind for years.

The doctor came. The doctor frowned.

"The baby has not dropped," she said. "The head is not engaged.
Your cervix is closed."

She tucked her clipboard under her arm and looked into my face.

"This induction is not going to be easy for you," she said. "I know
you wanted a natural birth, but under these circumstances I recom-
mend an optional C-section."

This was precisely what the midwife had warned us to expect—the
doctor wanted to medicalize my birth!

"I don't want a C-section," I snapped. "But you said it's 'optional,'
right? I have a choice?"

"Ye-e-s," she said slowly. "I can't say it's imperative. Not yet. So, of
course, it is your choice."

"Then no," I said firmly. "No C-section."

"Fine," she said. "We'll start by trying to soften your cervix and
start contractions. Then we'll see how it goes."

———

The summer day pressed upon the hospital and the city, pressed upon my belly with an immobile and dull ache. We pestered and pressed the nurses for permission to go for a walk. Getting out of the maternity ward was like getting out of prison. Forms were signed; promises extracted; bracelets issued.

The drab side streets of northern Beijing offered no cheerful place to stroll. The sidewalk came and went in unhelpful patches. We passed faded dusty storefronts and stalls hung with crutches and stale bandages and flimsy wheelchairs folded like dinosaur skeletons. A chain Italian restaurant, heaps of fruit, laundry. All was pavement and towers and walls, all was mineral hard surface.

"Let's go in here," I said. "It looks like there's some kind of playground or park—"

"It's a workers' compound," Tom said. "They built these all over China. All the people who live here will have worked for the same factory or ministry or whatever."

Through a rusting gate we entered a constellation of brick apartments. Old men played mah jong at picnic tables, shuffling their tiles, cupping their hands over cigarettes. A sweaty day, sky clotted with smog, air thick with coming rain. The young and the elderly had fled cramped quarters for the cracked pavement and weedy beds of the courtyard. Clusters of women bent their heads together, and children roamed wild. There was a miniature amusement park with a tiny merry-go-round, sun-faded plastic animals, a trampoline. An old man took coins for the rides. Only one small girl had pocket money; she spun alone and serious, as if she'd done this ride before and it was never what she'd hoped. The old man hawked and spat. Soon her turn would end.

"We won't be able to get out this way," Tom warned.

"There must be a second gate."

"These compounds usually have only one way in and one way out," he said. "But we can try."

"Okay." I kept walking.

Our path was shrinking; the buildings closed around us. I led us down one alley, then another, but each one was a dead end.

Tom was right.

"You were right," I told him.

"It's not about who's right," he said.

Forward momentum hit the wall. We could only return, retreat, and go back to where we had started.

————

Back in the hospital room, painful contractions gripped and vanished in pointless rhythms. The hours dragged along, but the baby didn't budge.

A nurse tucked sheets over Tom's sofa bed. I crawled in beside him, sluggish and sick, and twisted in contractions until sunrise.

Morning brought breakfast trays and yellow light. Smog stood thick in the air. In the schoolyard behind the hospital, children sang their morning exhortations to rise up and build a new Great Wall and counted off their exercise drills. I had been in the hospital for twenty-four hours, and practically nothing had happened. Morning fell to afternoon and sunset clotted into black, but still the baby stuck high. Another night in wakeful limbo. Too much pain to sleep and yet I was desperate for more pain, enough pain to tear this baby, at last, from my body. In the morning the doctors urged me, again, to have a C-section, and again I refused. With grim, we-tried-to-warn-you faces, they hooked a sack of Pitocin to the IV and flooded my veins with birth hormones.

I had been stultified and swollen, but now my body began to shift around with excruciating speed. I distinctly felt my hipbones dragging themselves apart. The sensation reminded me of the rack, of hapless medieval lieutenants drawn and quartered, horses pounding in opposite directions to spill hot blood on stinking dust. Torture, execution, European history—God! I didn't want any of that in my head. I had expected some tearing and stretching, but this sensation was deeper and deadlier and unspeakably painful. My skeleton was being dismantled. There was nothing in my brain but gruesome images and a single mantra: *I am going to die.*

I was supposed to be thinking of other things. The midwife had trained us to meditate and "go to a place deep inside," as one of the hippie moms had described birth. But it wasn't happening. I had been awake for two days straight and my strength was blown, and that place inside of me, if indeed it existed, was not findable now.

The hospital room had disintegrated into its own drabness. I rolled far out at sea, in the fogged dark of night. The waves pushed and tossed and I couldn't keep my head above water. I'm here, I'm lost, let me go. Another life is buried within me. It is also my life. My own life must rip itself from my center and leave me dead. Let them take it. Let me go. His life, my life. Take it, do it. I can't anymore.

"Give me an epidural," I gasped when I could speak again.

The contractions were fast.

The needle was huge.

I couldn't have cared less.

"You have to stay still, even when the contractions are coming," the doctor warned. "If the needle slips you can be paralyzed."

Cold steel slipping quick oh God that's my spine. I was still at sea, but now it sloshed with the sweetness of nothing. I was too limp to talk. "I'll take a shower," Tom said uncertainly.

"You should," I agreed. He withdrew into the bathroom and I heard the slap of water on tiles. I luxuriated in nothingness.

But something was happening. Monitors beeped, buzzers bellowed, nurses raced in from the hall. Suddenly the room was crammed with people rushing, chattering, flipping pages.

"You're going into surgery," somebody shouted. "The baby's heart is failing."

"One, two, THREE!" They heaved me onto a stretcher. Tom came dripping and bewildered from the bathroom, and then he was running beside me, somebody had given him a cap and a mask, somebody had given him scrubs. I was losing moments. I understood what was happening and I understood that it was happening to me. It had already happened a very long time ago. It was a memory in real time.

The surgery was freezing cold and snappingly bright. Nausea rolled and curdled.

"I'm going to throw up," I whispered to Tom. "I don't know how—"

"We've already cut you open," a nurse barked. "No moving. I'll put a towel under your chin and you vomit there."

I did as I was told.

I heard a baby crying.

———

He was a boy; we named him Max. Isn't every woman shocked by her first baby? So many things I hadn't anticipated. His wizened face already carved with ancient griefs and nameless rages. The love he provoked—fierce and searing; a natural disaster; a bloody sweet tornado that demolished all that had been before.

"Feed him," the nurse said sweetly. "He needs to eat."

She arranged him on my chest, grabbed my breast, and scraped the nipple over his mouth. He chewed, sucked, smacked.

"Good," she said.

"He's eating?"

"Yes."

"Something is coming out?"

"Something will come."

I worshipped the nurses. I never wanted to leave them. Whenever I wanted to feed the baby I pushed the button by my bed and somebody appeared to smile and coo and arrange us into a nativity sculpture. I loved the button that summoned them. I loved their faces and their voices. Each nurse was sweeter and softer than the last. I wanted to stay in their care forever.

———

The baby's face was fixed in my mind long before his birth. He was a boy, and so I was sure he'd look like Tom: dimples, long lashes, and dark, soft eyes. A mop of chocolate curls, eventually, then glasses.

I was wrong.

I took my baby to my breast, expecting my husband. But—*Oh God, it's my father, it's my father dying of cancer again, the bones and the ears.* I had chosen Tom for new life and new family, new genes, new house, new world. I had taken Tom's name because mine clanked with the heaviness of a lonely childhood, of watching my father die with nothing resolved, nothing said, except finally *I love you,* because in the end there was nothing else possible to say.

It wasn't only that the baby resembled my father, which was undeniable. In those first wild days when Max emerged from starvation in the womb and the nearly fatal beating of uterine contractions, he looked exactly like my father on his deathbed. I cradled the baby in a maternity ward in China and hurtled back to a living room in Connecticut, my father in feverish madness, clawing for life and babbling in anger and sucking morphine from a sponge.

That's when I knew it was hopeless. I could give up my name and go all around the world, but I couldn't escape myself. I had given birth to my father in his moment of fatal torture and to my own younger self who had been disobedient and rebellious and faithless. I'd tried to break new ground, but the soil was me and my genes were full of ghosts. I was sorry for myself and sorry for this tiny creature, my baby, with his snapping round maw and emaciated face.

My baby was my father, and now it was my job to feed him and keep him alive. It could have been written by Freud. No, this was all wrong. It wasn't supposed to be like this. I had to keep him alive. How could I keep him alive?

Tom was at my elbow, face full of unshaven wonder and sleepless serenity. He went out walking and came back and said, "I could see his face so clearly. I never remembered anybody's face like that."

Like a puppet I said: "Yes, he's beautiful." Inside I was screaming. I couldn't eat or sleep. The nurses offered to take him to the nursery, but I couldn't stand to be apart. I lifted him onto my chest and nodded off to dreams of Spain, dreams of my father who lived in Spain, and my baby was an egg balanced on a checkered tablecloth, and then the egg rolled off and cracked and the yolk seeped out. The horror of Humpty-Dumpty, I had let my baby fall! I jumped awake in terror, but he was still there on my chest, swollen pink face pushed close to my own.

His bowels were a wreck; we changed his diaper dozens of times. We were sweating and panicked.

"Is it supposed to be like this?"

"How can I know?"

Then he fell asleep, and that was even worse. I stared at him in white terror. I could detect no movement in his chest and eyelids. Was he dying here, in a hospital bassinet, while nurses gossiped in the corridor and I sat watching? I laid one finger on his bony chest and felt it rise and fall. I woke Tom up and whisper-sobbed my fears.

"I don't know," he croaked. "He's not supposed to sleep?"

"He didn't sleep last night."

"Well, what do you want to do?"

"I don't know!"

"Should we call the nurse?"

"Am I being crazy?"

"Well, honey, I don't know. I think we're in the hospital, so if you think something's wrong we should call the nurse."

"He's sleeping!" I sniffled to the nurse when she came.

"Good," she said.

"No, but I mean, he's sleeping like nothing will wake him up. And he's never slept like this before"—as if I were speaking from years of maternal experience—"and it's scaring me. It seems like he's hardly breathing. I just have a feeling something's wrong."

"He's tired," the nurse said. "He need to sleep. Birth is very hard for babies. And your labor was very long. This make him tired."

"I don't know."

"He's okay! Don't worry." Her smile was sympathetic, and something more, as if I were being cute.

"Don't you want to do some tests?"

"Better not bother him."

"But—"

"Thank you. Thank you very much." Tom flashed her a significant look, giving her permission to go.

When we were alone he said, "Honey." He said, "Everything's all right." He said, "Why are you crying? We have our baby and, look, he's perfect."

He said, "You need to get some sleep."

And I said, "I *know*. Don't you think I know?"

I spent the night staring wildly into the bassinet. When the first thin light of dawn edged the curtain I called my mother.

"Mom," I said, "he's sleeping, and he won't wake up, and I think it's bad. Nobody else thinks it's bad. The nurse says he's fine, but I just don't think he should be sleeping like this. I mean newborn babies don't sleep all night, right? I mean, look, I really do know that I'm being crazy, but at the same time I can't stop myself. I'm just so scared he's going to die." I was sobbing, choking on tears, and I wanted to be small again, to bury my face in her lap.

"Sweetie," she said. "Babies sleep. They do that. He's probably very tired. And when they're so small it's hard to see them breathing. But you're in the hospital and I am sure that if something were wrong they'd tell you."

"Really?" I sniffled. "You think he's okay?"

Even from across the planet, she was the only person in the world who seemed reliable.

"Really," she said. "I think he's just fine."

And he was. He was fine.

"I've been awake four nights in a row now," I told Tom when he woke up. "I didn't even think that was possible."

———

I hated the hospital room. I hated the dreary light that fell through limp curtains and the anonymous walls which were stained with my own drastic emotions. I hated remembering the parade of doctors who'd urged me to have a C-section, and my own mulish refusal. I felt stupid and reckless and as if I had already failed at motherhood, having lacked both the physical ability to deliver the baby naturally and the common sense to change the plan. The room was full of self-loathing, and I was desperate to leave.

On the other hand, I was terrified to go home. How could they let us take the baby home? It was crazy; it should have been illegal.

"When do we have to bring him back?" I asked the nurses.

"Two weeks."

This was criminal, indeed. Didn't they know our ignorance and incompetence could kill him a thousand times in two weeks?

"Is there a number we can call if we have questions?" I glanced longingly at my bedside call button. "There are so many things we don't know."

They took pity on me and copied the direct line to the nurses' station onto a scrap of paper. All the way home my fingers kept burrowing into my pocket to make sure it was still there.

It rained in Beijing that day. Shrieking, crashing rain; monsoon rain in a city hot as an oven. Water pooled at the floor of the city, forced people from flooded homes and swamped the subway tracks. The city was drowning that day, but I hardly noticed. No hurricane, no plague, could have turned the streets more hostile than they already looked to me. Even the light was stabbing at us, everything moved and cawed and flashed, and how could I protect this baby? I hadn't slept in a week and I was out of my mind.

I sat in the hospital lobby holding Max in my arms while Tom hunted outside for a taxi. The doors were propped open, and the room sang softly with summer downpour. Industrial lights blazed and sweated. I couldn't believe there was still a world beyond the hospital walls.

On the opposite sofa perched a trio of blasé British club kids, students probably, two boys and a girl. I stared at them, and they looked back at me absentmindedly. We might have been watching one another on TV.

They looked at Max, and one of the boys said to the girl, "Actually I quite like babies."

"Do you want kids then?" She picked with exquisite fingers at her lower lip.

"Yeah?"

I sat regarding them as they muttered and moved. Beautiful twining creatures who spoke softly and smelled of tobacco and skin creams, they were emissaries from a world devoid of everything the baby and I had just undergone. People, real people, to whom babies were nothing but a passing whim. For a minute they distracted me from the terror that I would drop the baby, he would stop breathing, the rain would never cease, it would carry his father away.

Tom was back, flustered and sweating. "Let's go."

The baby was light and disorganized as chicken bones in my hands. He thrashed in his car seat and howled with fresh indignation when the wet air touched his face. Tires shushed and neon gleamed through the storm's unnatural dark in the month of light. The smell of rain seeped in through the cracks of the taxi; cold air huffed from vents. The baby was hysterical, and I had my face in his, whispering nonsense. *This is rain, this is weather, this is China, this is the world.* It was the first of countless times I would speak to my children and feel Tom listening, trying not to wonder, not to care, how I sounded to this man I had married. *We are all together in the world, and this is how it will be, and have you ever seen anything so good as rain? It goes on the fields and makes food grow.*

Inside I was screaming, *What have I done, how will I take him through, how will we protect ourselves?*

After a while he quieted and stared at the rain streaking in silver rivers down the glass, and the globular quiver of red and yellow and blue light, and together we sat and regarded the rain and the colors it threw, the great smear it made of a summer day in the city.

He blinked his weak small eyes and pursed his baby beak, and I knew if love could kill I would already be dead.

Chapter 2

The taxi pulled up to the lobby. We were home. Home-ish. We had no home, really. We had returned, that was all, to our rented apartment in a skyscraper. The lobby smelled like dried flowers and good perfumes, and the doorman was glad to see us. The apartment was stale and hot after days of abandonment. Rain glittered and writhed down the windows. We turned on lamps and air conditioners and sat within our cool, well-lit spaces on a wilding summer afternoon.

My stomach wouldn't calm. I could hardly sit on the couch.

"I'm nervous."

"Nervous about what?" Tom's eyes stayed on the baby.

"I don't know," I said. "That's the worst part."

Our apartment with its books and Spartan kitchen and breakable things was a museum to our past selves. Tom crashed through the rooms, reclaimed lost territories. Fresh sheets on a new crib, printed diagrams for swaddling blankets, drawers full of unworn baby clothes.

I hulked on edges—fat, swollen, bandaged, sweating. Home was unrecognizable, and so was I.

———

The baby is crying.

The baby is crying.

The baby cried all the time.

We patted and paced and rocked and cooed. We turned the music on, then off. We studied Internet videos about burping and *sssshhh-*

ing and draping babies tummy-down along our forearms. In the desperate hours after midnight we'd ride the elevator down through mute floors and carry him into the night. Architecture fell away and the summer sky bloomed over our heads, and for some unmeasurable pocket of time Max fell silent, agape at the mysteries of heaven.

Then he started crying again.

Whenever he erupted in tears, which was roughly every time he found himself out of my arms, somebody helpfully handed him back to me.

"The baby is hungry."

"He just ate."

"But he's crying . . ."

Who could argue? *For God's sake stop the noise, put your nipple in his mouth.* We knew no other way to quiet him. My nerves jangled and screeched until he settled against my ribs, and then the flow of milk shot delicious stupefaction fast and sure through my veins. The baby regarded me gravely. His eyes were young fat almonds, his tiny fingers curled and arched, reaching for the things of the world. Everything was all right then, every time. I whispered his name, shredded its consonants like a leaf in my hand, and wondered whether my mind and skeleton would survive this desperate new love.

––––––

The moment my mother stepped into the flat, the knots in my gut slackened. Had she ever riled my nerves, had we really fought, sometimes bitterly? I had even, in my pregnant naiveté, considered telling her to stay home. To give us space. To bond. As a family. This had been lunacy, I could see that now. She was a goddess and a saint. She had birthed three babies.

She sat next to Max on the couch and read liltingly from paperback murder mysteries. "It doesn't matter what you read," she trilled knowingly, "as long as you use a soothing voice." She ate take-out salads and hung our laundry to dry in the tiny sunroom and washed endless dishes.

I tried not to think about all the parts of my lower gut that were sliced when they carved the baby from my womb. In ancient times they cut mothers open only when they had already died or when their lives had been deemed irrelevant. I'd read about a Chinese emperor who slashed six sons from the womb and left their mothers for dead.

My mother fretted over the surgery. She had delivered all her babies naturally and had always suggested that there was no pain involved. Come to think of it, what the hell?

"You lied to me," I told her now.

"I did not," she insisted. "It wasn't painful. A strong sensation, but not pain."

"You don't remember."

"Maybe," she allowed.

"For sure, you forgot," I told her. "Nobody could go through labor and say it doesn't hurt."

I hoped my mother would tell me that she, too, had been weepy after giving birth and that the crying would soon stop. But she shook her head. She hadn't cried, she said, but then I should keep in mind the particular atrocity of the delivery.

"He almost *died*," she kept saying.

I accepted this silently. The words sounded wrong, like I was gathering sympathy under false pretenses. I knew countless women, especially my age, who'd delivered their babies by emergency C-section. I tried to recall a moment when I'd truly thought the baby might die. The images were murky and unreal, like radio music overheard while half asleep. I recalled pain, exhaustion, throwing up. The sensation of bones dragged out of place. I remembered thinking, *knowing*, that I was about to die.

But not the baby. Not from the delivery. His life would inevitably come into being. My body would have died to help him, with or without my consent. We had labored in opposition or we'd labored in concert; competed or cooperated. Both at the same time? Something like that? I couldn't recall. Already biology had scrubbed my mind. I didn't care. My baby was here, and so was my mother.

"We need *strings*," she said brightly when the baby cried, throwing a lazy arm through the air. "Or piano. Chopin's nocturnes."

"Drink a beer with the bedtime feeding," she suggested when the baby woke up too often. "That always worked with you guys."

"Try putting him to sleep on his *stomach*," she chided. "That always made you guys sleep longer."

Ridiculous advice, useless advice. But I liked it. She was telling me that it was okay to laugh and do things wrong, it was okay to come up with dumb, even deleterious, solutions to the confounding problem of the tiny baby.

She suggested—by being there, by being alive—that the conundrum of the crying newborn was not a horror, but an inconvenient facet of the most complicated blessing life can bestow. My mother was telling me that none of it, in the end, had to be taken quite so seriously.

Mostly I liked her terrible advice because it made me feel, even in China, that I was home.

———

It never failed: The crying erupted at four a.m. You could set a clock by it.

Every morning I crashed into predawn darkness, yanked rudely from a dreamless haze by the baby's wails. I carried the shrieking bundle of child into the darkened living room. He'd drink milk for a bit, then slip sobbing from my breast. After that, there was nothing to be done—he'd cry and cry and cry. I'd sling him over my shoulder while I banged around brewing coffee, stinging eyes screwed half shut, screams hammering my ears—my God!

Then I sat on the living room couch and held him in stupefied horror. He cried, and sometimes I did, too. I didn't know how to arrange my body, how to touch him, what to say or think or be. It was too foreign and too loud. One living room wall was nothing but a massive window onto darkness. The reflection of the ceiling light quivered in the pane. I was wrecked. Aerial bombardment had been easier for my nerves to withstand. Lord, somebody, deliver me into a fighting zone. Strum my adrenaline, shove me between life and death. Not half-awake-life-with-crying. Not this, please.

Fingers stiff as wood, I tried to massage him according to the photocopied traditional Chinese medicine worksheets the hospital had given us. These fumblings made his sobs only more desperate. I pumped his legs in the air as if he were riding a bicycle. I pressed his thighs into his stomach. Nothing helped; the crying had no pause, no dent.

Sunlight spilled over the horizon, glittering painfully off the steel and glass of towers. I was crazed and haggard, outside of myself. Light battered my eyes.

Three hours. Four hours. The crying went on.

I was not impassive. I lacked the experience to regard the crying as an objective truth, to let myself exist next to it, parallel and accepting. I hadn't learned that it is a mistake to join small creatures in their emotions. Instead I felt every sob and shudder in the knobs of my spine. I held him until I couldn't feel my arms. I didn't understand my son's misery, but I endured it; with panicked love I partook of it. And I kept trying things, anything, to stanch his grief, to discover the secret source of his pain.

Finally he exhausted himself; the crying stopped; silence came back.

Tom padded into the room, his pajamas clean and soft. The first few mornings he'd come racing, too, but soon he stopped. Even my mother claimed to sleep through the noise.

"What's going on with him?"

I couldn't bear to look at Tom.

"I don't know."

"What does the doctor say?"

"Colic."

People trickled back into shops and streets. Watching through the glass I let myself be bolstered by the dull certainty of an unremarkable morning. All these strangers had been babies once. Sure they had cried in the dark. Sure they had wept and wailed, but one day they had stopped, and later they hadn't remembered a thing.

One day the crying would stop. I would be the only one to remember.

———

Max was always eating. I must be doing something wrong. I had the impression that other new mothers did things, sometimes, aside from breast-feeding. He had been starving in utero, I reproached myself. No wonder he's famished.

At least, I thought he was famished. It wasn't like we could ask him.

My own mother, to my astonishment and disdain, couldn't remember how often babies ate. *How could she forget?*

I pecked searches on my laptop with one hand while breast-feeding. I often landed on the website of a pediatrician named Dr. Sears. His tone struck me as authoritative and condescending. He bitterly opposed feeding schedules and insisted the baby must sleep in our bed. He had eight kids. My grandparents also had eight kids. How do people do that? I wondered about Dr. Sears's wife. I felt positive she would be less fun at parties than my grandmother. I was pretty sure my grandmother forced the children onto schedules. They were all fine. Within shouting distance of fine. Alive. Most of them, anyway.

The kindly Dr. Spock, on the other hand, was amenable to feeding schedules, but maddeningly evasive about how or when to create such a thing.

I need specifics, Dr. Spock. I'm drowning, Dr. Spock.

Dimly I recalled that a chic and stiletto-heeled lactation consultant had materialized in my hospital room after birth. I'd sobbed uncontrollably throughout our discussion. She had watched fat tears soak my snot-slicked cheeks and asked, sardonically I thought at the time: "Are you all right?"

I loathed her for this question. I believed good manners gave her two choices: gather me, bleeding and bawling, into her lap, or pretend nothing was happening.

"I don't know what's wrong with me," I'd muttered hatefully.

She'd murmured something about hormones.

Later I'd tried to purge her visit from memory. But now that her job title sounded relevant, I tried to recall what she'd actually said. Oh yes: "Feed on demand." That sounded like the path of least resistance. It also described what I was already doing. My days were feedings punctuated by showers, snacks, and sleeps.

I understood, in a blurry way, that I was going about things the hard way, but changing course needed powers of concentration and investigation that had fallen out of reach. Having stumbled into a default routine, I was too bone weary and fog-headed to make any changes. I didn't understand the breast pump. I couldn't muster the wherewithal to untangle the tubes and cords, let alone figure out how it related to my body.

Wherewithal. That word floated constantly through my thoughts. *I don't have the wherewithal.* It meant energy, health, brains, optimism— in short, everything I'd lost when I gained a baby.

At no time in all this milky mess did I think to offer Max a bottle of formula. My time around the natural-birth mamas had given me the impression that, if I gave him a bottle, the sky would fall. One bottle and my breast-feeding days would be over. They'd stamp a scarlet *F* on my back and exile me to the edge of town with my soon-to-be-subpar offspring.

Besides, I was scared of formula. It hadn't been long since poisoned milk powder had gravely sickened hundreds of thousands of Chinese babies. Formula meant black market chemicals, corporate malfeasance, and dead children.

I Googled and I breast-fed and, one by one, the days slid past. My mother cooked, Tom cleaned, I fed the baby. We ordered takeout and watched DVDs. Every day was wild and provisional. Every time the baby grew one day older, my mother's departure loomed one day closer. This arrangement, which just barely delivered us from one hour to the next with some semblance of nutrition and hygiene, was about to dissolve.

And then, one fine and ordinary summer morning, a great upheaval rocked our household: Tom showered, buttoned himself into a collared shirt, and tapped forth in stiff shoes.

"Bye, honey."

He was going back to work.

"When are you coming home?"

"Well . . ." He straightened the kinks in his phone charger, then spoke with demeaning patience. "I don't know. It depends on what happens."

The door banged. He was gone. I had found him out in the world, and to the world he would return.

Max was two weeks old. My brain shivered like jelly. I had snatched a tiny creature—*our* tiny creature—from the edge of life. Where did Tom think he was going?

I had no reason to be surprised. I knew the nature of his work—it had, after all, been my work: cataclysms and eruptions, grabbing a suitcase and rushing off to the airport, tossing apologies over a shoulder. He couldn't do his job properly unless he did it full tilt.

I knew that. Who knew better than me?

And we needed his job. Our domestic existence was balanced on his job.

Who knew better than me?

Yet there I was, holding the baby among the dirty breakfast dishes in a domestic vignette straight out of the 1950s. It was atavistic, but it was happening. There we were, the son of a single mother and the feminist daughter of a feminist mother, re-creating the same old scene.

It wasn't until he vanished back into work that I understood: My husband would support me financially, but he couldn't save my book. My career would sink to the bottom of the sea if left up to him. Not because he didn't care, but because he simply wasn't *there.* He wouldn't be home enough to do half the housework. I couldn't, in clean conscience, ask him to stay up all night with a colicky baby and then sneak into a Tibetan village in the morning. He couldn't clear the time for my writing—I'd need to solve that problem on my own.

I was beginning to see the flaws in my plan to write books at home, but that wasn't the worst of it. The dread that had come upon me in the hospital was thickening instead of abating. In the secret corners of my heart, I was afraid I was going crazy.

"You gain access to emotions you never had before." That's what a friend told me after she became a mother. She made it sound like a wondrous discovery. And, in a way, it was like that. I thrilled to a love I never felt before.

But it was love like an oblivion, and it was full of terror.

———

Long mad mornings. Weird sleepless nights. Veins of summer lightning. Sleep bleeding to life bleeding to sleep. I was a shade; my baby was ancient; I had been breast-feeding forever. I slipped in and out of dreams, my head crashed and jerked, my neck ached. Max slurped himself to sleep against my heart. Together we woozed and drooled.

The dead children came back to me then. Small ghosts pulled themselves from the rubble of forgotten towns. All of the dead came back, but especially the children. They demanded a mourning I had not completed at the time of their passing.

Maybe it was sleep deprivation, or perhaps the shock of seeing my dead father's face on my newborn son, but death played in my mind like an unwanted newsreel.

My father was the first. I was twenty-three years old.

A few months later I watched an execution in Texas. The condemned man was strapped to a gurney and injected with poison. His family watched from one darkened room, and his victim's family watched from another. I can't remember, now, which family I joined, but I was there, too, a rookie reporter looking through the window with the kin.

After the man's heart stopped and the doctor called the time, prison officials shut the curtains on the death chamber. Families were led away, weeping, their paths carefully choreographed to avoid one another.

Back in the pressroom, my boss began his interrogation:

"How many straps? On the arms, on the legs? Above the knee, below? Which side of the room was the door on? Was there a speaker, a clock, anything else? Last words? Eyes open or shut?"

We were still in the death house, drinking cans of soda at a table. He asked me to draw a diagram of the gurney. I was new on the job; he was training me.

I drew the picture. I remembered every detail. I was impassive and my boss approved. I got the message: See everything, say nothing, and write it all down. Move through the world that way. Silently I agreed.

A few weeks later Texas executed another man. That time, I went alone.

Then I started covering war, and lost count of the dead. Afghanistan, Israel, Iraq, Lebanon. Bombardments from airplanes, suicide bombings, gun battles, extrajudicial executions. Bodies abandoned in cars and on roadsides.

It seems to me, now, that my father's death was a gateway. I threw myself into work to numb the grief, but work kept pushing me back toward death.

But it wasn't until I sat alone and fed my tiny baby, who looked just like my dead father, that the faces and smells came rushing back. Dead small bodies. Dying small children. Dying small children who moaned for parents who didn't come because they were already dead. Caked with mud, crackling with dried blood, bodies jutting at unnatural angles—or simply frozen still, and absent from their flesh.

I had not been cavalier. I had felt those deaths, but I'd also suppressed them as fast as possible. I was counting bodies, scribbling quotes, finding somewhere to file, making the deadline, doing the edits, and going to sleep so I could wake up and do it all over again in the morning.

I'd known that dead children were a particular obscenity. On the other hand I considered all civilian deaths obscene and unforgivable.

Maybe breast-feeding was the first chance I'd had to sit quietly and think. Maybe I looked for the bodies and dug them up, driven by the superstitious fear that witnessing so many dead children would mean that I . . . couldn't finish the thought.

So I sat in the dark and remembered. I remembered their homes and families and dolls and the clothes they wore the day they died. I sat in the dark and roamed back in my mind, down forgotten roads into morgues and hospitals and homes. I sat in the dark, milked by my baby, and cried heavy silent tears for children whose deaths I had covered and forgotten years earlier. I cried for their mothers and my father and myself and for my perfect unsullied baby who could only be ruined by this world.

———

In the bathroom, brushing my teeth, a scrap of song drifted through my mind: *They can't take that away from me.*

Scrub-a-dub-dub, three men in a tub. Whatever else happened—or didn't happen—that day, I had polished my enamel. Rinse and spit;

victory smacked of mint. Tooth brushing, once done, could not be undone.

The way you sing off-key . . .

Now. Where was I? Oh yes, my holdings. I had to take stock of my holdings.

My first book: Its day had dusked. Fast, fast it slipped into the past tense. Soon it would be as if it never were.

My second book: A mess of an unfinished manuscript.

Job: None.

Husband: Check.

Thanks to husband's job: enough money, good health insurance, and a sun-washed apartment on the twenty-third floor of a skyscraper in Beijing's business district.

No problems, right? Right, no problems.

Still it felt like I had a problem. The cold reality of my gender was dawning on me. I'd known enough, already, about harassment and domestic violence and pay differentials and the incessant, exhausting focus on how you look and laugh and talk. But it had all been basically manageable—not ideal, certainly, even enraging, but navigable—right up until the baby came.

It was motherhood that forced me to understand the timeless horror of our position. The obvious, hidden-in-plain-sight reason women had not written novels or commanded armies or banked or doctored or explored or painted at the same rate as men.

The cause was not, as I had been led to believe, that women had been *prevented* from working. Quite the opposite: we had been doing all of the work, around the clock, for centuries.

Somebody, after all, must wash and feed and train the kids and get the food and clean the house and care for the sick and elderly. That work is physically depleting, logistically daunting, and relentless. It is not a job, but a constant gaping demand for labor. It's a ceaseless work that has gobbled up our energy and stamina, eroded our collective health, and starved our communal mind of oxygen for generations.

We did the work, taught our daughters to do the work (assuming we survived their births), and then we died. That was it. Domestic toil had ground us, one after the next, to dust. We had not been educated because then, naturally, we might balk at the work. We might have the audacity to point out that we were doing all the work. We might ask the men to do some of the work, themselves. And they didn't want to do that work. Nobody wants to do the work, if they can escape it.

Still we go around thinking that our primary problem, the essence of our position, is that men explain things to us or that we make less money for the same job.

But, most basically, it's the work—the work that we still, somehow, have not managed to escape. It is the work we pretend doesn't exist.

Only after giving birth did I internalize the reality of having quit my job. I'd slaved and slashed and elbowed to maintain that job, but in the end I'd let it go like a balloon, rolling in my mouth the rare flavor of a bold gamble. Retirement it was not. I was pregnant and I was quitting, but in my mind it was the opposite of "opting out." The time to finish my second book was coinciding with the arrival of a baby. I imagined long, silent afternoons in spotless rooms, typing clean lines of prose while the baby napped beatifically in a sunbeam.

Something like that. The assumptions I'd made, the foggy mental images of life with a newborn, were so idiotic I couldn't conjure them anymore.

For one thing, there was Tom. In my imagination he was there, too, at every critical moment. I never thought about his job. I assumed that, to the extent that our lives would be exploded, the disruption would be evenly shared. That was the expectation of my generation; an equality we had been encouraged to anticipate even as our mothers—draped in legitimate amnesia or, perhaps, motivated by the loving desire to spare us the truth of our disruptive origins—consistently downplayed the physical and emotional rigors of bringing a child into the world. They gave no answer for that part. Their revolution was elsewhere. When it came to the children and the housework, they had no solution to suggest.

I hadn't factored in the child himself, not in a realistic way. His emotions, my emotions, our symbiotic state. I had imagined a baby as a modification to an existing life, like an extra room built onto a house. Now I learned that babies wipe away all that preceded them, remaking the family with love and violence and the smug inarguability of biology.

I hadn't factored in sleep deprivation, or my shredded psyche, or the primal cravings to be near the baby, to smell and hold him.

But most of all I had not understood that, once the baby comes, the house is full of work that must be faced.

In the United States, the average maternity leave lasts for three months. I'd assumed, therefore, that three months must be a magical milestone beyond which babies' needs winnow down to accommodate a forty-hour workweek. American families coped. Women went back to work. Single mothers pulled it off. I never internalized the brutality of U.S. paternity policies until I was in China, trying to fathom how I would avoid insanity if I had to return to a job when my baby was three months old.

And yet. Maybe, I thought now, I'd quit too hastily.

A maternity leave would have ended—painfully but clearly—back at the office. It would have held my place in the working world, the world of deadlines and transactions and politics and money. The world of men.

Come to think of it, I'd been warned. *They won't fire you now that you're pregnant,* a few battle-hardened working mothers had counseled. *And then you're entitled to maternity leave.*

You're walking away from free money, a single mother had told me bluntly.

I'd dismissed the advice as cynical, its logic beneath my dignity. If I wanted a job, I'd get one. No need to laze around growing a belly and collecting a paycheck.

Calm down, I told myself now, peering gravely into my own eyes. *You were done with that job, anyway.*

It was true: I wanted to write books. I'd written one and I wanted to write more. I had an agent. My book had gotten good reviews and been a finalist for an important award. It was natural that I could, would, should write more.

Now things had gone crazy, that much was undeniable. Maybe I had gone crazy, too, and maybe I would get better, or maybe I wouldn't. Either way, the days were sliding past. Time's a-wasting, my mother always said. I had to get a grip and get back to work.

My manuscript malingered deep in my computer files. The baby turned in his crib. I wasn't sure whether it was morning or afternoon.

But there was an obvious answer to all of this. I was an American in Beijing, remember, a woman of means in a city teeming with rural migrants who'd come to hustle for work as nannies and cooks and cleaners.

Help is affordable. That phrase rang in my ears.

It was a euphemistic phrase. It meant "Human beings are cheap here." Foreigners said it all the time. I never heard a Chinese person say "help is affordable."

Cleaning ladies were nothing new. I hadn't cleaned my own home for years—I'd traveled so incessantly I hardly occupied whatever place I was renting at the time. When we'd lived in our courtyard home in old Beijing, a bespectacled grandmother biked to our gate every morning to brew a pot of coffee, cut a bowl of fruit, and slosh through the rooms with a mop. When we moved across the city— trading our picturesque-but-falling-apart cottage for the responsible conveniences of centralized heat and endless hot water—she'd politely declined to keep the job. The commute wasn't worth her while.

We'd meant to hire a new *ayi* before the baby was born but hadn't found one. And now here we were, living in disarray when, as any parent in China would have immediately understood, this was an unnecessary and self-imposed martyrdom. Help was all around. Ask and we would receive.

"You're lucky you'll have your baby here," Beijing friends had enthused as my pregnancy swelled, "because *help* is so affordable."

Help!

Chapter 3

I looked at her. She looked at her hands. The dining table stretched between us.

This person was not what I'd had in mind when I'd called the housekeeping agency. I'd envisioned a jolly grandmother, shabby and staid, a village old-timer in worn sweaters who'd brew noodle soups and know absolutely everything about babies.

This woman was young, perhaps too young—all sinew and spring; pointed chin; sharp elbows. Her black eyes flashed and fell beneath a stylish fringe of bang; the bones of her face were strong; thick hair swung almost to her waist. She was dressed in some sort of acid-washed denim and a T-shirt printed brightly with garbled English.

Fact: The best people I've found in life look all wrong at first glance.

"Do you have any children?" I asked.

A pause, her mouth popped open, and her eyes flew to the agent—was she allowed to answer? An almost invisible nod. She turned back to me.

"Yes."

Soft, sweet voice. Too soft, too sweet. Oh no, that would drive me crazy. Thirty years old, and she couldn't look me in the eye.

"One daughter," interrupted Yulanda, the agent. "Three years," she added before I could speak, tapping the sheet of paper she'd slid before me when the interview began.

Oh yes, right there, along with her province of origin (Hebei, a prized birthplace for Beijing nannies because the Mandarin is reputed to be pure there, and heaven forbid the babysitter should pollute the toddler with some bunk twist of Chinese), height (tiny), and weight (ditto).

I smiled at the agent, whose grin hadn't quivered since she walked in the door. I worried her lipstick would soon crack and crumble like terra-cotta left to bake in the sun.

"Is your daughter—is her daughter—" I didn't know who to address.

"With the grandparents," Yulanda said firmly. "In Hebei."

"You—she—are you—here with—"

"Husband."

"And where does she live?"

[Unintelligible.]

"How long would the commute be?"

Almost two hours with a bus change, but she was willing to do it.

"I need help with the cleaning. With the cooking and laundry," I explained, seized by a fluttery impulse to justify myself. "I don't need help with the baby. Maybe when the baby's older. When she and I have gotten to know each other better." I spoke first toward the top of the younger woman's head, then into the unchangingly amiable face of the agent.

Yulanda cracked out a few lines of Mandarin, then turned to me.

"Okay," she announced.

"You understand?" I asked the younger woman.

"Okay," she echoed meekly.

"Well—" I paused, unsure how to get them out of the house. "I need to check her references. Can I call . . . ?"

Yulanda whispered to the candidate, who clattered up and chirped, "Thank you." Scrambling her feet into sandals, she disappeared out the door.

"What you think?" Yulanda's voice was all sugar, but the *ayis* cowered before her. Her teeth gleamed like a shield. *The better to eat you with, my dear . . .*

"Her English isn't so good."

"She understand. Try her."

"Is there anybody else we can meet?"

"Now, no. Full time, no. Summer, always difficult."

I was desperate. I would give this woman—what was her name again?—a chance.

To verify her references, I phoned a former employer who'd since moved to Singapore.

"She should be good enough," said the faraway woman in a clipped accent that made me imagine enormous rooms bleached to immaculate white. "I trained her myself. I had her managing the whole place by the time we left."

Struggling to envision the shrinking waif I'd met as a crack manager, I repeated this endorsement to Tom.

"Sounds good to me," said my husband, eyes on his phone.

We told the agency to send her over.

————

The very next morning she marched into our house, put down her bag, and picked up a broom. By noon the floors shone, the kitchen reeked of fake lemons, and we could see our faces in the faucets.

She was businesslike and quick. Squat, stand, bang the doors, march down the hall, out with the trash, in with the towels. She scrubbed circles around me while I breast-fed the baby, lulled by the sensation of chaos righting itself with minimal demand on my body or brain. When our gazes crossed by accident, she smiled. She came every weekday, arriving at eight in the morning and staying until six at night. She'd come on Saturdays, too, for overtime. We paid her less than five hundred dollars a month.

Ayi, a catch-all designation for female domestic workers across China, literally means auntie—significantly, the sister of one's mother. But this lady didn't want to be my aunt.

"No, please," she giggled. "This is for old woman."

"What should we call you?"

"How about Xiao Li?" *Little Li.*

Typical: I'd gone looking for a grandmother, and ended up with a younger sister. Still, from that very first morning, I felt better when she was in the house. That's the plainest truth: Xiao Li came and I felt better.

Well, anybody feels better in a clean room, especially if they haven't slept. And there's a terrible something I've noticed about houses—they always feel cleaner when somebody else has done the cleaning. Xiao Li couldn't scrub away my existential dread, but her presence somehow softened it. Anxiety and darkness still stretched perpetually beneath every moment with my baby and husband, and hung like a backdrop beyond my ambitions and ideas. It had become my subtext, the ground on which I stepped. It had been there ever since my baby was born. I felt it, but I didn't know how to explain it. Not even to Tom, especially not to Tom.

"Maybe I have postpartum depression," I said one day.

"I think you just need a good night's sleep," he replied.

He hummed along; he checked in. He advised sleep. He didn't, however, offer any suggestions for how such a thing was to be gotten.

I hated the night. Tom tumbled into his flesh, leaving me alone in fitful consciousness. I dipped in and out of dreams with the cries of the baby. In my mind I swam deep midnight seas thick with snakes, or skirted a bleak and lightless landscape, stalked by grave robbers and wolves.

Morning brought light and coffee and sometimes it brought visitors, but, most important, it brought Xiao Li. She was sane and orderly and sweet. I was still tired and scared, but the terror wasn't quite so sharp.

It took only a few days for me to realize her importance.

———

Xiao Li brought lunch in plastic boxes, hot water in a thermos. At noon she scarfed her food on a rigid, straight-backed wooden chair we'd shoved between the counter and the inlaid microwave in our tiny kitchen. Then she'd bend her neck into an improbable twist, rest her cheek on the countertop, and fall asleep.

The first time I saw this torturous resting place, I was appalled.

"Xiao Li." I nudged her awake. "Please, lie down and rest on the couch. Or the guest bed."

She blinked and blushed, but stayed put.

"I like it here," she said simply.

Later, I tried to reason with her.

"You can't sleep there," I said. "It's not comfortable. Why don't you eat at the table and then take a nap on the couch?"

"I'm comfortable," she insisted.

One day Tom happened to be home; he was even more unnerved than me. "Why is she sleeping in that chair?" he hissed.

"She won't move," I said. "I tried."

"Xiao Li, please," I heard him say. "This looks very uncomfortable." She laughed.

"I'm okay!"

One day a friend brought a sack of Japanese takeout for lunch. She was also a new mother, but she'd gone straight back to her reporting job after her baby's birth. Now we dunked sushi rolls into soy sauce while she regaled me with her reporting adventures.

She'd recently visited a Beijing garbage dump, she told me, and profiled an old woman who rescued infant girls from the trash.

"People just throw baby girls into the garbage," she muttered, lowering her voice so that Xiao Li wouldn't overhear. "Can you imagine?"

"Don't worry," I whispered. "She's sleeping."

"By the way," I added, "will you please look at how she's sleeping?"

She tiptoed to the kitchen door, peeked inside, and, with a grin, returned to the table.

"It's driving me crazy," I said.

"She probably likes it there," she insisted. "It's her own little place."

"It looks," I said, "insanely uncomfortable."

"Chinese people," replied my brilliant and compassionate friend, "have a totally different sense of physical comfort."

Those words stuck in my head. I remembered them in a sick rush, months later, when I picked up Julia Boyd's book about denizens of Beijing's foreign legation in the years leading up to the Boxer Rebellion. The foreigners regarded the Chinese people of Beijing as "entertaining, challenging, occasionally frightening but ultimately unreal," Boyd writes.

"By convincing themselves that the Chinese operated under different criteria, the foreigners were able more easily to accept their suffering," she continues. "It was clear that the Chinese did not feel physical pain as acutely as Westerners."

———

Xiao Li ran clothes through the washing machine and hung them to dry in the sun. She tucked fresh sheets over the beds. She bought vegetables and rice and noodles and meat and eggs and cooking oil and spices. She fried our dinner every night, poured the steaming food into our dishes, and arranged the plates on the dining room table.

It wasn't enough. Xiao Li hungered for the baby. She hovered over him and whispered into his face. He smiled at her. She caught her breath with delight. The more I tried to discourage her interest, the more sweetly insistent she became. One day she blocked my path as I carried him toward the changing table.

"I do it," she announced, stretching out her hands for the baby.

"No, I will do it," I snapped, surprised by the hardness of my own voice. "You can watch," I added more gently. "So you learn."

"Okay."

Her eyes twinkled with smothered laughter. It was a kind laugh. She was not unsympathetic to my madness.

"Okay."

One afternoon I rushed home from an unexpectedly prolonged bank errand. My heart was flopping like a fish thrown to land. Max, I was sure, was howling for his mother, believing in his tiny brain that I had abandoned him. I imagined he was hungry and afraid and lonely. I couldn't endure the anxiety of imagining his anxiety.

I burst into the apartment—into a scene of serenity. Xiao Li cuddled the baby by the window. She sang to him softly in Mandarin, turning him gently back and forth in a shaft of sunlight. He stared at her face in rapture. She turned to me and grinned, as if to say, "See?"

Looking at them I understood that, if I was serious about getting back to work, I had to encourage this bond, not squelch it.

I began to hand Max over to Xiao Li at least once a day. Chattering and crooning, she carted him through the rooms. She laid him on the couch and sat on the floor, her face level with his, and amused him with a singsong monologue. She pointed out the sun and clouds and a faint stain of daytime moon. She read aloud from bright board books, tittering when she caught me eavesdropping on her clumsy English. "Feet in the day, feet in the night," she'd squeal, and tickle his toes.

I will never forget the way she said his name. The delicious anticipation of the *M*; the long-savoring relish of a drawn-out *a*; the strong *x* like the surprise of a smacking kiss. Exclamation point every time. *Max!*

As if the name itself tasted delicious.

———

"You want lunch?"

I had plumped down in my usual spot, on the beige armchair next to the bookcase—back to the kitchen, face to a window full of sky. I was staring at the autumn afternoon, sipping coffee with milk and trying to cheer myself up. And there was Xiao Li, ready to feed me.

"I don't want to eat," I told her gloomily. "I'm still too fat."

"No," she said politely.

I sighed. "I can't wear my clothes. They are too small."

"Okay," she said warmly, waving a dismissive hand. She didn't have the American inclination to convince me the fat was a figment of my imagination, but she was generous enough to insist it didn't matter.

"Your baby is still very small," she said. "After my daughter, I also was very fat. Like this—" She blew out her cheeks.

I laughed. "I don't believe you."

"Really. Even after one year, I was fat. After that, okay."

"How old is she now? Your daughter?"

"Three."

"Oh! Big girl." Compared with my infant, even one-year-olds loomed like freakish gargantua.

Xiao Li nodded agreeably.

"She's in your village?"

"Yes, she used to be here with me, but it was too difficult," she said. "Now she is with my parents."

"Your husband is here?"

"Yes," she said.

"He's working?"

"Yes."

"What does he do?"

I wasn't politely feigning ignorance. All of this was news to me. I'd heard these details when Xiao Li interviewed for the job but had forgotten them immediately.

"He is building."

"Construction."

"Construction," she agreed.

"Interesting." I smiled and let the questions drop. I didn't inquire after the child's schooling or caregivers. I didn't check whether it was Xiao Li's choice to get a job, nor dwell on the unsettling knowledge that her daughter had been deposited in a village with grandparents because (this went without saying) Xiao Li could not, herself, afford childcare. I made no effort to discover whether her lifestyle was a grand adventure or heartbreaking drudgery, or some combination of the two.

Those questions lined themselves up in my thoughts, but I left them silent. They lit too starkly the discrepancy in our positions. That I had money and would not have to leave my baby behind. That she was poor, she had not been educated, she didn't have choices.

I had the vague idea that my silence was magnanimous. I told myself I was sparing her from embarrassment. It hadn't occurred to me yet that I was the one being spared.

Anyway, we couldn't communicate very well. My rudimentary Chinese and her broken English gave us only a small vocabulary of baby- and household-related nouns and verbs.

But I also failed, deliberately, to use my imagination. I did not envision the faraway room Xiao Li shared with her husband, or her life beyond our apartment: the lengthy bus commute, the cooking and shopping and cleaning she did for her own family.

This line of thought was dangerous. If I found out too much, if the facts were too grim, then I might conclude that my domestic arrangement was fundamentally unfair. That was my formless and underlying fear: that if I understood too much, I might have to rip apart the status quo. I could either drown or I could wear Xiao Li as a life vest. There was no third choice.

———

"I'll take Max outside?" Xiao Li suggested one afternoon, tilting her head and brightening her eyes.

"Um," I said, obscurely annoyed.

My gut reaction: *Absolutely not.*

I glanced around the clean, empty apartment. It was a Tuesday afternoon. There was nobody here but me, Max, and Xiao Li; Tom wouldn't be back until the end of the week. I thought of my long-neglected book manuscript. In order for Xiao Li to make sense, she needed to do things like take the baby for a walk.

I knew that. I absolutely knew that.

This is what people do, I reminded myself. *This is what everybody does, everybody you know.* They put their faith in babysitters, nannies, day cares. They research the characters of the caregivers and the policies of the facilities, but there's no avoiding the inevitable moment of turning over a helpless child to near-strangers.

It felt crazy. It felt awful.

This must be crazy and awful.

No, I'm the one being crazy.

"It's okay?" Xiao Li prodded at my silence.

"Okay."

I seated Max in the stroller and reached for the straps, but, with a sidelong glance, she gently took the plastic buckles from my hands and fastened them. She wanted to show that she could do things right.

"You have your phone?"

"Yes."

I heard the ding, swish, and clank of the elevator.

They were gone.

What have I done?

Left alone, my mind flashed with disaster scenarios. Years of journalism have permanently seeded my imagination with all manner of sinister human possibility. *What's the worst that could happen?* is my least favorite rhetorical question, because I always have an answer.

Take now, for example: Human trafficking. Xiao Li had struck a deal with a kidnapping gang. Max was a perfect baby, lacking defects, brand new. He was worth a fortune. They could be waiting in a car downstairs. He couldn't talk, he would never remember me. Why had Tom insisted on using that agency? They were probably involved. I never liked that agent with her wolfish teeth . . .

No, stop it, stop! A thing so simple, I chided myself, *this should be okay—a babysitter takes the baby for a walk in the stroller. Try—just try!—to be normal.*

No, it's not right!

What was I thinking, letting this unknown woman in a foreign country take my baby? My mother would never have done such a thing.

No, she left us alone with random teenagers; that's worse!

I am a worthless mother.

I am out of my mind.

I tried to reason with myself—a white baby would be tricky to pass through the Chinese market. Surely my son would be more trouble than he was worth.

But—the Russians!

Oh God. The Russians.

We lived a short walk from the surreal hustle of the Russian district, a few square blocks of seedy karaoke bars and wild nightclubs and shady cargo depots. Groaning, rusting trucks panted into town off the long dusty highways to Central Asia to unload their crates into heavily guarded warehouses.

She could sell my baby to the Russians!

I hovered at the living room window, squinting into the midday glare, trying to distinguish the baby's red stroller and Xiao Li's yellow shirt among the crowds below. There were trendy boutiques, cafés, dry cleaners, beauty parlors. Paved paths snaked up grassy slopes dotted with pomegranate and ginkgo trees. It was a cheerful, busy place, utterly devoid of street crime, bustling with a steady smattering of business commuters and couples and schoolchildren, watched over by a small army of security guards. It was hardly a place that suggested danger.

There! Xiao Li pushed the stroller in lazy circles, pausing to chat with other *ayis* who chaperoned charges of their own. She bent into the baby's face, adjusted his sunshade, then wandered along the sidewalk, staring in the shop windows. She parked him for a time in the shade and sat companionably on the curb at his side, then rose and walked some more.

It was fine. I was ridiculous.

When she brought him back I snatched up the warm small body and breathed the sweet cream smell of my own, unmistakable baby. He gave me a grin as if I were the best thing that had ever happened to anybody, and nuzzled against my cheek.

I flushed with euphoria. My baby was back, and I had glimpsed a way forward. Xiao Li had taken the baby away and then returned him safely. Here she was, humming and cheerful and ordinary. Perhaps, then, this was indeed a woman I could trust.

And so it was, at first: the relationship with Xiao Li was transactional and strategic and terrifying.

Everything that was most precious to me—my work and my child— was bound up in the behavior of a woman I hardly knew.

The reality was simple and relentless: If Xiao Li showed up for work, I could shut the study door, sit at a desk, and write for an hour or two. Her absence—an attack of flu, a family crisis—collapsed all hope for writing on that particular day.

And so I enmeshed myself in a web of women's work—as worker, employer, and beneficiary, all at the same time. My own work rested on the cornerstone of another woman's labor. My writing was a commodity. My time was a finite raw material. The choice to hire domestic help was an investment, and therefore a gamble.

Like Apple computers or Goodyear tires, I reaped the benefit of cheap Chinese labor. But unlike those companies, I lived in my own factory, and spent more time with the cheap laborers than I spent with my spouse.

And, too, I fretted over the condition of my soul.

A friend called from Hong Kong one day: a mother and human rights activist.

"How are you doing?" she asked.

"I'm having a postmodern feminist breakdown every single day," I told her. "But otherwise okay."

She laughed. "Join the club."

It's true: I was in good company. The most brilliant and socially conscious female professionals I met around the world—the human rights workers, entrepreneurs, artists, journalists, diplomats, and wonks—enabled their careers by hiring impoverished women to care for their children.

That was the underbelly. That was the trade-off.

There was no other solution in sight.

———

Tom got tired of Xiao Li's cooking.

Even I, her fondest ally, had to admit a sameness in the stir-fried meats, greens, and eggs; mounds of white rice; cucumbers in vinegar. Any mouthful we didn't eat reappeared at the next meal as a side dish. Tom shoved these dingy leftovers aside, but I was too ashamed to instruct Xiao Li to waste the food. Instead I'd crumple the remains into paper towels and sneak them out to the garbage chute after she left.

I could feel Tom's silent irritation swelling. I knew an outburst was coming, and my outrage grew in anticipation. How dare he fuss over food when I was clinging to sanity by my fingernails? It wasn't the most innovative cuisine, but it was serviceable and nutritious and infinitely better than anything he or I was in a position to prepare. Couldn't he just eat dinner and shut up? Silently, I dared him to bring it up.

And, of course, he did.

"This is terrible." Tom pushed his chair back one night with a clatter.

"No, it's not." I knew an opening shot when I saw it.

"I can't eat any more stir-fry."

"I like it! These garlic shoots—"

"Can't you teach her how to make something else?"

"In all my spare time?" There was a warning in my voice.

"I'm going downstairs to the Italian place."

"What about me?" I said.

"You said you liked it," he spoke with fake patience. "So eat it. Or, if you want, you can go out when I come back."

I brushed past wordlessly when he returned. I'd lost my appetite, but there was principle at stake. In the Japanese restaurant down-stairs, I ordered a bottle of beer and drank it very slowly, staring out the window. Childless couples rushed through the darkness, stylish and conspiratorial, passing in and out of the streetlights.

By the time I got home, Tom had gone to bed.

———

I was stuck in my shrunken world. I tried to call forth another.

I found memories, sounds, smells, and followed them back to Moscow. Then, from a remembered Moscow, I softened the cityscape, let the buildings quiver and reform themselves as a fictional Moscow. A city that had been real to me, home to me, must now be rearranged in imagination. Truth had to exist inside the fakeries of manufactured details. To make fiction that was true, that was the trick. If the sentences didn't all but conceal the truth in a way that was palpable but not overt, then it was plain garbage. But somehow if you tried, you failed. There was a blindness to it, and a freedom. I had to let myself go, follow the words, reel myself out knowing it might be a sea of mud and the line might fray and snap. Go now. This is my chance. Go.

The computer was white. The page was white. The great empty sky in the window was white. The white of a Moscow winter. The white of a summer sky. White nights. St. Petersburg. Tired images. Postcards. Something somebody else would write. Not mine.

Turn the white space to snow. Fill the void with language. Find something true and put some words on top of it.

I was too tired. The fatigue was not wild and suggestive, but empty. Moscow had fallen out of reach. Instead I wrote:

You think about the 1950s. You think there is perhaps some value in repression and bottling things up. You think it might be more palatable, at least more honest, to live with some Don Draper, an unabashed sexist who does not labor under the illusion that he leads a progressive and egalitarian lifestyle. You wonder what happened to the man who said we'd never outsource our childcare. You think about the competition between short-term needs. You think about compromises. If you speak up angrily, he says you are acting crazy. If you speak up sadly, he says you are making yourself into a victim. You try not to speak, but that makes you sadder and more crazy. If you don't speak up, nothing will change. If you speak up, nothing changes. You become unable to take seriously any feminist who hasn't had children in a heterosexual relationship. You have learned that's where the bloodiest, hardest most intractable battle lies, and that it lies there mostly hidden because millions of families balance on the silence.

My head rang. I was tired. I'd fought again with Tom. We fought over all the new things there were to fight about—chores and time and sleep and responsibilities. We fought because we were both exhausted and secretly convinced the other one had the better end of the deal. We fought because we were neurotically careful not to fight in front of the baby, and that meant we almost never got a chance to fight at all, and by the time we fought the annoyances had fermented to a potency that obscured altogether their original cause. We fought because we used to baby each other and now nobody got babied but the baby.

As for me, I fought because I was reeling in shock, and because Tom was hardly there at all. He had slipped easily back into his old life while I had been bombed back to some prehistoric version of myself. And I was angry that he had accepted this superior position, this lesser disruption, as a sort of birthright. And so I fought with his absence.

It felt, in sudden flashes, like we were on the brink of collapse. But, then again, every new parent I knew was having some version of the same argument. And that made it seem safer—like a head cold or a developmental phase, something that would pass with time.

When we weren't fighting, Tom listened with interest. I told him how I'd been changed and humbled; described the things that had happened to my body and mind.

"You should write about all of this," he told me.

"All of what?"

"Becoming a mother."

"No!"

This suggestion made me furious. It seemed to me that every college-educated woman with a laptop, a baby, and a sketchy grasp of grammar had reinvented herself as a "mommy blogger."

Not that, no way—not for me. I had fought too hard and too long to go down like that. Never would I absent myself from the broader world and its serious abstractions like politics and economics. I had beaten the boys before and I wouldn't stop now. My writings would not be set among refrigerators and cribs; would not smell of rubber ducks and diaper creams.

True, I was adrift in that world. I was suffused with maternity, plumped and drifting on streams of milk and hormones—but I would not allow myself that fecundity, that dissipation of clean living, which made me think of a spot in overripened tomatoes where the skin disintegrates and the fingernail sinks into caving flesh.

That could not be me.

That's why I needed Xiao Li.

Chapter 4

Six perfect pastries glistened under glass. The kiwi seeds twinkled like tiny chips of onyx. They would never be eaten; the slender customers who frequented this bakery did not traffic in lardy sweets. The bakers, with their exquisite aprons and heavily Chinese-accented French, were guards and props in this museum to rarified dough.

I was drinking tea with a pair of friends. One was the mother of two small children. The other friend, after months of baggy blouses and soda water with lime, had finally copped to her long-suspected pregnancy.

"My husband is all ready to change diapers," the pregnant woman said smugly.

We laughed at her.

"You won't even care about the diapers," I said.

"Then what?"

We locked eyes. How frank should we be?

"Well, there's the sleep—" I began carefully.

"And the breast-feeding—" the other mother said.

"Right," I agreed. "God!"

A heavy pause settled over the table.

"For a while, like maybe a year, your husband will be an alien in your household," the other mother finally said. "It will feel like he doesn't even live there anymore."

I stared at her.

"That," I said with wonderment, "is exactly how I feel."

This mother-friend of mine had managed, in a few simple lines, to diagnose the malady of my own domestic life.

Tom had become an alien in the household.

———

"Are you getting any writing done?" Tom asked a few days later, dragging his eyes from his computer with the air of a disgruntled student forcing himself to contribute to the class discussion for the sake of his final grade.

"Some." I tried to sound light. "I'm still struggling to find the time."

"Maybe we need to find somebody better than Xiao Li," he suggested idly.

I stared at him in horror.

"What are you talking about?"

"It doesn't make any sense that we pay a full-time maid but you still have to deal with all this work."

From all corners of my brain, different strands of objection reared up and raced at once toward my mouth, where they collided and collapsed in a hopeless snarl of converging verbal attacks.

"The thing is—"

What to say, where to begin? Tom had no concept of the working hours required to maintain our tidy, properly supplied, and salubrious status quo.

He interrupted: "Well, honey—"

"Wait," I snapped. "Just wait a minute."

I covered my eyes and pressed as hard as I could.

Xiao Li was supposed to make me free, but she's turned into a trap.

In truth, Xiao Li and I both worked full-tilt. We shopped, cooked for the adults, cooked for the baby, cleaned, washed clothes, and, of course, there was the ceaseless time commitment of the baby himself.

If Tom and I were willing to live in a messy apartment, or to eat more takeout, then the addition of Xiao Li might have signified an easy path back to my writing desk. But we're both neat freaks and Tom is a picky eater, and since Xiao Li had started working for us, he didn't see any need to accept an unkempt domestic existence.

I had failed, yes, but not in the way Tom assumed. I had failed to properly communicate my daily reality to my husband. Now I had to try, but it was late and I was indignant.

"It's not that Xiao Li isn't doing her job," I finally said, tugging on the reins of my voice, which bucked and threatened to charge into a scream. "It's just that there's a lot to do. Like if she's cleaning the house, then of course I am with Max."

"What about his naps?"

"I have to, like, shower sometimes." Spikes of hatred, shards of sentences: *Picking the hours apart—I have to explain—and who is he to ask?—where is he all day?—if he takes a walk in the park, if he goes out for coffee—how dare he interrogate me like this—I would never—*

I wanted to throw a plate at his head.

"You don't understand," I finally said. "You're not here all day and you just don't have a realistic sense of how much work goes on."

"No, I guess I don't," he said meanly.

Now I was murderous.

"You should take my word for it. You should trust me," I exploded. "Because I have done your job. I know exactly what your day is. But you have never done this and I bet you never would."

Tom stormed off to the bedroom, and I sat reviewing my position with horror. Xiao Li had given me crucial scraps of time and valuable hope for my career, but I had paid for her presence in currency I was only beginning to understand. Now I saw that, if I pressed Tom to do more housework, he would call for Xiao Li to be fired. His estrangement from the housework would be recast as failures on the part of me, the manager, or Xiao Li, the "full-time maid."

He always used that word, *maid*. It made my skin crawl. There were accusations embedded in this word with its suggestions of opulence. I was an exploiter feeding on the flesh of the poor. I had turned into the kind of person we never wanted to be.

Tom, of course, was still at large in the world. He stuck up for the underdogs. He interviewed dissidents and human rights lawyers and Tibetan monks. He had become a parent and kept his career without making any degrading compromises. He didn't count his minutes and hours the way I did, with desperation, like a beggar reviewing a dwindling pocket of coins.

On the occasion of our baby's first Christmas, we gave him toys from IKEA: plush animals and wooden trains and puzzles. Things-that-were-not-plastic, imported from Scandinavia.

We were afraid of China. Not afraid of its streets or its people, but terrified of Chinese chemicals and plastics.

Not for nothing: Poisoned fog hung in the air, the water was filthy, and people died by the hundreds from tainted drugs and food. Black markets and counterfeit scams thrived, so you could never be sure you were buying what you thought you were buying. The scandals of a polluted land were incessant, each revelation more nauseating than the last: The "lamb" that was really dog meat soaked in goat urine. Human hair culled from hospitals and barbershops then melted down into "soy sauce." Cooking oils dredged from sewers.

The toys for sale in the shops of Beijing smelled like turpentine and kerosene and rubbing alcohol. One sniff sent the nervous system flashing and recoiling. The toys contained heavy metals and illegal dyes and phthalates, plasticizers widely banned in the West.

On Christmas Eve, Xiao Li burst into our apartment with apples in her cheeks and a wrapped present for Max.

"Merry Christmas," she told our baby sweetly. "I love you."

She helped him rip the paper, revealing a hard plastic duck with a round bottom. It chimed tinny songs and bobbed upright when knocked sideways.

Max loved the duck. He knocked and spun and guffawed. Next to our drab offerings of wooden contraptions and stuffed animals, Xiao Li's duck was shiny and loud, and he liked it better than anything he'd ever received from anybody. He batted and gurgled at the clattering creature, and Xiao Li glowed with pride.

"We have to get rid of that duck," Tom whispered as soon as we were alone.

"What are you talking about?" I knew exactly what he was talking about. "We can't."

"Honey," he said. "If he puts it in his mouth . . ."

I knew Tom was right. The duck was unhealthy and our baby was tiny.

But I also knew Tom was wrong. Chinese children played with such toys. Must we always dangle our child aloft, letting him see the world but not partake? We wanted China to enrich but not poison him, and sometimes, I thought, the line between the two evaporated.

And then, of course, there was Xiao Li. It was the only sort of toy her daughter would ever have. How could I dismiss it as a kidney failure waiting to happen? I might as well announce that her life and its contents were too cheap, her country too disgusting, our baby too precious for her offerings.

I tried to think of a way to subtly disappear the duck. But Max didn't have many toys, so the duck's absence was sure to be noticed and interrogated. It's not easy to hide anything from the person who cleans your house.

I tried to make everything all right with everybody, and it was a project.

I buried the duck in a pile of sweaters on an upper shelf. I never explicitly told Tom I'd thrown the duck away, but I allowed him to assume as much. When Xiao Li hunted for the duck, I'd shrug distractedly and make a mental note to put it back the next day—once Tom had left for the office. I always remembered to hide it again before Tom came home from work.

I shuffled the duck around, stretched the time between its appearances, and waited for everybody's memory to fade.

I needed camouflage, so I expanded Max's holdings. Now he had a shape shifter from America, a puzzle from Australia, a keyboard from Germany.

One day, of course, I slipped. Tom discovered Max with the duck.

"Why is this duck still here?" he cried in dismay.

"Oh," I feigned surprise. "I dunno."

"I thought we got rid of it."

I started to say *Me, too*, but stopped myself because this was technically a lie. "Yeah," I said. "We should throw it out."

I watched my husband yank the duck off the floor and stomp out of sight. Patriarch and protector, vanquisher of toxic fowl! I heard the steel door of the garbage chute creak open and then crash shut, swallowing the bird whole.

Max whimpered. I scooped him into my arms and carried him into another room.

A moment later, he had forgotten.

As for Xiao Li, if she ever noticed the duck's disappearance, she kept it to herself.

———

I counted once, and counted again. I rifled the other hip pocket, and the back pockets. Yes, for sure, cash was missing. The wad of bills I'd stuffed in my pocket was short a few hundred yuan. I was positive.

Well. Almost positive. Maybe I'd spent it and forgotten. Maybe I'd taken less money than I thought. I stood dazedly in the laundry room, jeans dangling from one hand, trying to relive the morning.

I'd set out to buy slippers for Max, shoving the bills deep down into my pocket. I'd made my way on foot along bright, hard winter streets and pushed through the weighted plastic curtains into the dim warrens of the Silk Market: stretches of stalls and booths piled high with all kinds of clothes for all kinds of people, every imaginable knockoff and piracy and grotesque synthetic creation haggled over by a rowdy pack of merchants and buyers and tourists and vagrants.

My quest was specific: the January drafts were keen and the floors were cold and Max needed thick wool socks, the kind with plastic beads on the soles so he wouldn't slip. I hunted and prowled and pawed and soon found the sort of slippers I had in mind. A quick negotiation, and I was headed home.

All that time, the clump of bills sat snug and deep in my pocket, pressed against my thigh. A knee-length coat, in turn, covered the pocket.

I had been bumped and jolted a bit, true, and ridden on packed escalators. Still, I was certain nobody had sneaked a hand up under my coat and down into my pocket. I'd stopped in the deli for coffee, spilled the coffee on my jeans, rushed upstairs, and changed clothes hurriedly at the bedside. The bedroom, then, was the likeliest place— the cash could have fallen to the floor. But the money was nowhere to be found.

"Xiao Li." She paused in the kitchen, eyes turned over the rim of her hot water thermos. "Did you find money?"

Blood flew into her cheeks.

"No," she said. "How much?"

"A few hundred."

"Ohhhh . . ." She frowned. "You went to the market—"

"It wasn't the market," I interrupted.

"But many pickpockets are there," she protested. "And they are very good at taking money. You won't feel it—"

"Will you help me look?"

Our hunt turned up no cash. Meanwhile, I had picked apart my memories until they were meaningless. I'd constructed a dozen plausible explanations and false recollections—handing money to a beggar, absentmindedly dropping change onto a pile of merchandise—and one of them might be real. It was nothing. Maybe it was nothing. Probably.

Or maybe I'd been losing money steadily for weeks, months, who knew? Maybe Xiao Li was a nefarious, snickering stranger who'd been ripping me off all the while, preying on my sleep-deprived psyche.

As if she'd read my thoughts, Xiao Li's search became desperate. She turned out the pockets of coats I hadn't worn in years and scrabbled in disused shopping bags. And she kept telling me that I must have been robbed, these thieves are very clever, I wouldn't know . . .

I was uneasy, she was uneasy, and soon Max would be awake from his nap. I hadn't accused Xiao Li or even hinted of suspicion, but the suggestion of petty theft loomed between us. And maybe, I thought in annoyance, the suspicion was legitimate. Maybe in exhaustion and desperation I'd invited a clever con artist to plunder my home.

So what if she steals some cash? I suddenly thought. *Maybe I should look the other way.*

But nastiness clumped at the root of that thought, too. As if Xiao Li's poverty excluded her from the norms of human interchange; as if she were not a woman in full standing, but some wretch whose misdeeds should be expected and overlooked.

Besides, I had to consider my own conscience. If we weren't paying her enough to feel firmly that we didn't deserve to be robbed, then obviously her salary ought to be raised.

We paid her plenty, I reminded myself. More than most, I reminded myself.

We were paying the agency, though, that was the catch. The agency offered protection for all involved: It covered Xiao Li's health insurance and would place her in a new home if we fired her. But this arrangement cost us all more than the going rate because someone from the agency showed up every month to demand their share of Xiao Li's salary.

All of these thoughts churned past, one suggesting the next, as I searched for money I hadn't earned in rooms I hadn't polished.

Tom, of course, had no doubt.

"She took it," he pronounced, interrupting before I'd even finished the story.

The easy certainty of this accusation filled me with fury. It was one thing for me to entertain fleeting suspicions. It was quite another for Tom, who'd so casually detached himself from the household, to accuse Xiao Li.

"You don't know that!"

"Come on," he said. "Look how much money we're burning through. We never spent so much before."

"We didn't have a baby."

"He barely eats any food!"

"He changed the whole economy of our house."

"Changed the whole economy—?"

"Look," I said. "I keep telling you, you don't understand this house anymore. So you should just—shut up! Because I am not a moron, and I am here all day."

I paused. Tom said nothing.

"We buy diapers. They are imported, and they cost a fortune."

"This is not diapers—" Tom interrupted.

"And wipes," I interrupted back. "And diaper creams. And fancy moisturizers and organic shampoos and stuff like that. And on top of that, we used to skip meals and eat out a lot. Which was somehow cheaper than buying groceries."

"The places we ate were not cheap!"

"Sometimes they were. And besides, now I buy organic milk and organic vegetables and fancy farm meats and all of this, because Max is here and I'm breast-feeding him and now he's starting to eat food too—"

"Fine. I can accept everything you're saying," Tom said. "But I still don't think that adds up to what we're spending. You should look at the bank statements."

"I'd be happy to." We both knew I was lying. I didn't want to look at bank statements.

"Anyway—" he began, and I braced myself.

Now it would be time to discuss my irresponsible financial behavior. I ran the household in cash. I didn't track expenditures or save receipts. I emptied cash from my pockets onto tables and counters.

"You've got to stop leaving cash around the house," he said now.

"I know." I sighed in defeat. "But it's never a lot of money. And I trust Xiao Li. Trusted her. Trust."

"But it's not fair to her," he argued, and now his voice was kinder. "That money means more to her than it does to you. You shouldn't test her in that way."

I understood that he was right. Not about everything, but about this one point. Yes, fine, he was right.

We never found the missing money or discussed it again. But the memory of its disappearance stuck.

———

Every morning Xiao Li opened the door with her copy of the key, slid off her clicking flats, and set down her faux leather purse. Then she picked up the jeans and T-shirt and flip-flops from her cubby by the laundry room, and headed to the bathroom to change herself into a domestic worker.

She dressed for the bus in slacks, blouses, neat turtlenecks, and dress shoes. She could be mistaken for somebody's secretary or an entry-level bureaucrat. I assumed that was the point: to camouflage herself in the crowd, drop her identity, answer to nobody.

Anyway, that's what I imagined. I never embarrassed her by asking about her clothes. Besides, I was in no position to talk about fashion.

Pregnancy fat still clung to my frame, but I refused to buy bigger clothes. I wore stained maternity dresses, baggy tops, and frayed pants that had once required a belt. My shoes were scuffed and split. The busted seam of my favorite leather shoulder bag hung agape.

"Geez, if only we lived in a city full of skilled craftsmen who work supercheap, maybe you could get that bag fixed," Tom said bitingly.

"Meg, seriously," he said another day, touching my bare elbow through a hole in my sleeve. "Will you please—please—buy some clothes?"

No, no, no. I would not.

I was desperate to lose weight, and buying a larger wardrobe would be a capitulation. I was also paralyzed over money. I physically cringed whenever I recalled my status as a nonearning member of the family. From Tom's salary we lived and saved with disposable income left over, but I hated depending upon my husband's job. No matter how many silent pep talks I gave myself about the importance of being with Max and the long-term investment in my writing career, I couldn't convince myself that I had a right to spend money when I wasn't actively earning.

Meanwhile, I looked terrible. I knew it, Tom knew it, and, perhaps most of all, Xiao Li knew it. The baby was the only member of the family who didn't consider me an embarrassment.

One afternoon I made for the grocery store wearing a Blues Brothers T-shirt I'd owned since college, now featuring a torn neck and indistinct mustard-colored stains. Before I reached the door, Xiao Li stepped firmly into my path.

"You will wear that?" She pointed at the shirt.

"Why?"

"It's very bad," she erupted.

"It's not that bad." I was surprised, and a bit wounded.

"Yes," she insisted. "It looks very bad."

I understood that, in her eyes, I wasn't doing my job. We had a nice respectable baby and a nice respectable flat; my husband put on his nice respectable clothes and went off to his nice respectable office. I was the note of discord. I should be shopping in boutiques and visiting the hair salon. That was the kind of woman Xiao Li would like to serve.

Xiao Li no longer reminded me of a kitten. Her shyness had fallen away, and I'd seen the dignity she could summon in moments of reflection or duress. She was short, but she stood straight and slim as a ballerina, head erect and eyes appraising.

I imagined that, if she were in my position, she would run the house with glamour and aplomb. Already she carried a nicer phone than I did—hers a counterfeit iPhone; mine an old black Nokia. She was more stylishly—if cheaply—dressed.

I was pretty sure she thought that, given my considerable privilege, I should be doing more.

———

Winter darkness came down early. I was alone in the apartment.

Xiao Li had taken Max walking in the stroller, but a bitter cold had hardened over the streets and I wanted them to come home. I called her over and over again; no answer.

Anxiety clawed up the back of my throat. Something had happened. Somebody got hurt. A car in the darkness, a motorbike, a kidnapping. Headlights scrambling the twilight, rushing crowds blinded by hoods and hats. Gone, my baby was gone. I paced the floors and made myself swallow some water.

Finally I heard the elevator ding on the landing and the scrape of a key in the lock. They were home.

Xiao Li was flustered. She flitted up and down the length of the kitchen counter, twitching her hands among the utensils, eyes averted. Max fussed, cheeks blown bright pink by the cold.

"Where were you?"

"I went to the bank."

"What? Where?"

"Just here," she said. "It's close."

"Please don't take Max for your personal errands." I rubbed his frigid cheeks with my own face.

"Sorry," she said.

"And you have to answer your phone. You have to!"

"It was very loud in the street—"

"I don't want this to happen again."

"Okay. I'm sorry."

"This cannot happen again," I said coldly. "Do you understand?"

It was as close to threatening her job as I could bear to come.

"I understand."

I felt that something had happened, some information had been lost. This incident was such an obvious aberration of our normal household routine that I hardly knew what to make of it.

But there was nobody to explain. Xiao Li and I had reached the outer limits of our communication. As for Max, only the cold in his cheeks told a story. I held him tight and whispered nonsense bits of love and told myself, because I thought it was true, that nothing bad had taken place.

I knew I would fire Xiao Li if she scared me again.

———

Max and I sat alone on a grassy slope, letting the early spring sunshine soak our skin. The cries of children rose up from below; their shadows flew along the pavement; the glass of shop windows winked in the light. We pushed our fingers into the grass, and the loamy smell of thawing earth came into our noses.

We were waiting for Xiao Li. Once she finished cooking dinner, she'd come and hang out with Max in the fresh air while I worked upstairs in the quiet apartment. In the meantime I'd climbed the hill because I didn't know where else to go.

Mothers, nannies, and toddlers milled in the open air. A group of mothers of school-aged children drank wine and roared with laughter at a sidewalk café. Their hair was blown smooth; they were slim; they talked too loud. "This is like a scene from *Sex and the City*," I heard one of them bellow. Back among the children, a fight had erupted over a plastic shovel. A nanny scolded her sobbing charge.

I felt a wave of fatigue and confusion: Now that I had a baby, did I have to take part in this? It looked awful.

I remembered my own childhood, inching onto the playground, unsure how to make friends. The other children were daunting and exotic and sure of themselves. I wanted desperately to join them, but I didn't know how.

I'd been good at talking, in the end. I'd grown up and moved to new cities and made a lot of friends. Half of my job had consisted of chatting with strangers. But I didn't think I had anything to discuss with these women. And I was discovering, painfully, that people are considerably less interested in conversing with a pudgy new mother who claims to be writing a novel than they had been in chatting up the bureau chief for a well-known newspaper.

At a recent dim sum brunch attended by writers and journalists and intellectuals, I had sunk down on the ground of the courtyard to breast-feed the baby, for there was nowhere else to go except the bathroom. There I crouched, cross-legged and disheveled, bound like a peasant woman to breast and baby and earth as the adrenalized banter of my past life sailed off into bare branches overhead.

I didn't fit into this group anymore. I no longer traveled to the cities they mentioned; I didn't interview the people they discussed. I told myself I didn't mind, but it was a lie. I minded terribly.

Now, lingering awkwardly outside the crowd of babies and care-takers, I felt that the destruction of my social ego was complete. I'd gone around the globe only to end up where I'd started—awkward at the edge of a playground. Worst of all, I had my baby in tow. He would have to learn from me, and that was a dead end. I propped him up against my side and braced him with one knee, feeling sorry for both of us.

Then I caught sight of Xiao Li. She scrabbled up the hill, an arm flung to the sky, grinning at the rush of spring air.

"Why here?" she demanded in Chinese. "Here there are no little friends!"

"The sun is good here," I offered weakly, but Xiao Li hadn't waited for an answer.

She scooped Max up, toted him back down the hill, and plunked him down among the children, calling out greetings to other *ayis*. She cooed hello to another baby, reached for a toy, and introduced Max. She wove a web of chatter and giggles and light. She knew how to socialize him, she knew how to surround him with friends.

I wandered off dazedly into my sudden freedom, grateful that Max was in the thick of things, where I had always longed to be.

And not because of me, but because of Xiao Li.

Thank God for Xiao Li.

Chapter 5

Night had never been good, but now the nights were getting worse. The baby and I drifted through a landscape of dark stumbly halls and gloomy rooms and ashen sky in the windows. Day was a bright quick flash between the long drag of sleepless hours.

Instead of sleeping longer stretches, the way other babies seemed to do as they matured, Max began to wake up more often. I couldn't find any method to get him back to sleep except to feed him milk, and since the milk came exclusively from my body, I was stuck in a crazy and lonesome loop.

We told ourselves he must be teething. We cursed our luck. Tom was struggling to function at work, so I decamped to the guest room, next door to the nursery.

"This is insane," one of my closest friends, an American doctor, erupted over email when I described my schedule. I felt like she was reaching through the computer to shake me by the shoulders.

"You're going to have a nervous breakdown," she scolded. "You need to sleep train. Now. Tonight."

My mother agreed. So did some corners of the Internet—although others suggested we were dabbling in child abuse.

At last we tried the solution that everybody kept suggesting: We left Max alone to cry himself to sleep. To do this, I had to override every flashing emergency instinct in my mind and body. Neglecting to answer my baby's cries unleashed a hormonal and emotional hurricane in my depleted self. I must have wept three tears for every one of his.

And then something truly dreadful happened: Max's sleep patterns deteriorated even more. He began to wake up with frantic regularity, and became so nervous in the vicinity of his crib that he refused daytime naps altogether.

Horrified, hating myself and everybody who had encouraged us to sleep train, I abandoned the effort.

"My nerves are shot and my heart is broken," I emailed my doctor friend reproachfully.

I hadn't slept more than four hours in a row in the nine months since Max was born, and now I hardly slept at all. We were up six or seven times a night. Before sunrise I gulped down pots of coffee to stay sentient. Caffeine slamming through my veins and hammering in my heart, I could never manage a nap. Sun up, sun down; lather, rinse, repeat.

There was a madness to this lifestyle, and a madness in me. Whenever Max slept, day or night, I hissed and glowered, trying to impose silence on the apartment—on Xiao Li and Tom and, of course, on myself. I disciplined myself with a thousand neurotic tricks:

I could recognize every creaking spot in the floorboards by the graining on the wood, and sidestep them in the dark from memory.

I knew precisely the degree of pressure required to release every doorknob without clicking the latch.

I stifled coughs and pushed my finger into my upper lip to stop sneezes.

I learned to cushion my steps lest my knee and ankle joints crack.

I observed, through careful study, that clattering dishes and clanking cutlery were the loudest sounds in the house, audible through the thickest walls, but that televisions and ringing phones didn't carry.

I lived in terror of waking the baby, and I shared this terror with deliverymen, houseguests, and anybody else who made the strategic error of existing in the vicinity of my sleeping child.

Tom, naturally, was the most egregious offender. I harangued him at barely audible decibels when he dropped a bowl too loudly into the kitchen sink or turned on the television or opened the bathroom door before the toilet flush stopped running. When his rubber flip-flops pocked and squelched across the floor, I ground my teeth and pledged to divorce his unruly ass as soon as I regained my faculties.

"You have made the atmosphere in this house crazy," he protested.

"*You* are making it crazy." The best defense is a good offense.

"How am I supposed to *live*," he shrieked in the whispery way we'd adopted, "without *making—any—noise?*"

I admit: I stalked the darkened rooms like some weird and wild-eyed Lady Macbeth. I can see, now, that my paroxysms of muted rage when my cousin blew his nose in a closed bathroom were, okay, yes fine, disproportionate. And that it wasn't very hospitable to kick a pack of girlfriends out into a chilly January night for the crime of laughing too loudly. And that, most likely, my mother-in-law was trying to be silly, and not maliciously mocking me, when she crept on exaggerated, mincing tiptoes while somehow, still, crashing her feet loudly to the floor.

Guilty. I plead guilty.

In my humble defense, I was tired beyond all reason. I was not feigning desperation; it was real. Sure, I thought resentfully, it was easy for everybody else to come around and make noise. They didn't have to deal with the consequences.

It did not occur to me that I was, myself, turning into a consequence.

———

Nighttime socializing was the agreed-upon prescription for all that ailed me. My friends, Tom, Xiao Li, my mother—everybody pestered me to "get out."

Whenever I was accosted with some evening plan, I smiled a forced smile and pretended to agree that it sounded like fun. Which is to say, I pretended that I still subscribed to a concept called "fun." Privately, I thought it sounded terrible: an ordeal of strangers I didn't want to meet and conversations I'd rather not have and friends who would pity my unkempt psychological state and still-fat-after-all-these-months figure.

Most of all, it sounded like hours of lost sleep. Just thinking about getting any more tired was like sliding slowly and nauseously down the walls of a carnival Gravitron that has just stopped spinning.

But, like most people on the outer edge of sanity, I wanted desperately to pass as normal. So I played along. I made plans with my mouth while, in my secret thoughts, I crafted the excuse I would deploy by text message at the final hour.

When I did go out, I'd spend the night obsessing miserably over how late I'd reach home and how achy and ancient I'd feel in the morning. Max would be awake in two more hours, then again two hours after that, then up for the day three hours after that. *I'm fucked, I'm so tired, I want to die. Why can't people just leave me alone?*

Meanwhile, all the mental machinery that had once sorted out "interesting anecdotes to share" from "information to repress because it is too personal, too unflattering, or too biologically specific" had stopped working. Talking with anybody but a trusted confidante became the social equivalent of leaning against an expected railing only to pitch into bottomless air. I'd overhear myself answering with full and unadulterated honesty any question posed by any acquaintance of any gender. Dim awareness that I was saying too much, coming across as strange, making people uncomfortable, or, worse, feeding their raptorial hunger for tawdry details—nothing shut me up. I was so sleep deprived I might as well have swallowed a truth serum.

One Friday night Tom shooed me out of the house to meet a few friends for dinner. We were four women journalists: one who'd vowed to stay childless; two mothers; one woman pregnant with her first child.

Conversation, inevitably, turned to the effects of children upon career. Insert horror stories: the ones who mother too much and the ones who don't mother enough.

"Tell me again why this is supposed to be something I want?" Our resolutely childless friend's eyes gleamed with candlelight and schadenfreude.

"But there are so many good sides," earnestly interjected the other mother.

They turned to me—how about you? And, as usual, I heard myself begin to speak without any clear idea what would emerge from my mouth.

"I feel like I've disappeared from the world," I heard myself say.

"Like I've sunk way down to the bottom of the ocean and there is no way I'll ever manage to swim to the top again."

Silence sat at the table for a minute.

"But this image of being sunk down," said the other, earnest mother, wrinkling her nose. "It makes it sound like you're depressed."

"I guess so," I agreed. "But I'm not conscious of being depressed. I'm not sad. I think I'm just exhausted."

That night I went home and started an essay called "How to Disappear."

"You disappear in layers, falling softly through the silt. Vanish first from the workplaces, from the hotel lobbies and press conferences and luggage belts. Next you disappear from dinner parties and cocktail parties and house parties. You are still in doctors' waiting rooms; you are full of rolling baby; you are serene and smug. You're too tired, anyway; you'd rather fall asleep at home; and then it gets too heavy, too hot, and then you just don't care, you are overcome, wrestled to earth by biology. But even then you are in the shops, on the sidewalks. Later you will be nowhere but darkened rooms. Later you will creak through Facebook like a ghost, brushing past the other people who don't exist anymore anyplace else. The others who have disappeared—mothers, mostly, and the unemployed, the ill."

I never finished.

———

I went to the vagina doctor to discuss my existential dread. It felt awkward, but I could think of no other remedy.

Imagine a murk of anxiety. Imagine you are so tired your face feels like permanent putty and you cry at the slightest provocation and, in general, you are about as raw and crumbly as the flesh of a pale white mushroom with its skin rubbed away. My head rang and chimed. I slipped into waking dreams and semi-hallucinatory states. I heard echoes of sounds from hours earlier. I wandered into rooms only to forget what I'd been looking for—this happened over and over again until I'd burned an hour pacing back and forth, and then I'd weep in sheer frustration. I found myself walking down the sidewalk with no idea when I'd left the house or where I was going.

But the worst part was the lingering fear. I was scared all the time, scared to my bones, scared every single day. I was scared of the fear itself—that it would soon block out my rationality and reason and I would end up in a Chinese mental hospital where, on top of being crazy, I would be unable to explain myself. I was so afraid of getting locked up and separated from my baby that I hid from everybody, even Tom, the extent to which I'd lost control of my faculties.

I asked my mother why I felt so awful. *Sweetheart, I just don't know,* she said. *It's so different from my experience,* she said. *I'm so sorry,* she said.

I asked my mother-in-law. *The children were always my bright spots,* she said. *I never expected it to be easy,* she said.

Every new mother I knew was tired and worried. I didn't know how to tell the difference between normal-bad and bad-bad.

With nobody left to ask, I turned to the oracle of excess and exaggeration, transformer of scratchy throats and bad moods into cancer and mental illness. In other words, I submitted my troubles to Google. Women should visit their gynecologists if they suspected they might be suffering from postpartum depression, Google replied.

That sounded odd, but far be it from me to know who helps new mothers with anything. After all, I reasoned, the root of *hysteria* is "womb." There is a special kind of low-grade insanity that has historically been linked to the female organs. This idea feels, all at once, misogynistic and unpardonable and, just maybe, I now thought, true.

Sitting in a plastic chair by the gynecologist's desk, rubbing my hands nervously under her quizzical gaze, I told her I was feeling anxious, fighting dread, and that I wasn't getting any sleep at all.

From her fumbling half sentences and bewildered pauses, I inferred that I shouldn't have come to her with my emotional troubles. I was embarrassed. Damn those websites! This doctor could read ultrasounds and interpret labs and deliver babies. She offered birth control and Pap smears. My psychological state was beyond her expertise.

Still, she tried. She told me that she also had an eldest child who didn't sleep. He was now some horribly advanced age (six? seven?)

and still cost her many nights of rest. Having raised this demoralizing specter, she wrote a referral to a psychiatrist for postpartum depression screening.

"Just to rule it out," she added encouragingly.

Unlike the immaculate white main building, with its cappuccino bar and whimsical indoor tree and cascades of sun through the skylight, the hospital's psychiatry unit was an ill-lit and dilapidated brick building resembling the segregated schools I'd written about in Louisiana. Shatterproof windows protected the receptionist from maniacal patients such as myself. The waiting room was musty and mournful, with cracked chairs and a few dirty magazines.

The doctor was a dowdy-looking man in his latter middle age. I told him I hadn't slept in months. I explained that I didn't know whether I was sleep deprived or depressed or even whether there was any difference.

The doctor labored to follow my language. I repeated, slowed down, and reworded.

"I do not understand," he finally said. "You have your husband and your baby. Your husband is working. You live a good life, in a nice apartment. You have an *ayi* to help. You are not"—he gestured in the air—"on a mountain somewhere, alone with your baby."

This declaration took my breath away, for I had, coincidentally, been tormented by precisely this image—the baby and I alone in the dark, in a mountain cave, wind whipping our backs, wolves sniffing after our blood. Having to keep him alive by myself, in desperation, in the wilderness . . .

"But that's exactly how I feel," I cried. "In my brain, logically, I know it isn't true. But I can't get rid of this feeling. And it's so terrible."

I was choking back tears. I hated admitting to all the ugliness in my mind while he stared at me blankly.

The psychiatrist pulled from a desk drawer the oldest, thickest laptop I'd ever seen. He clicked some buttons and produced a computerized card game. I was incredulous, but obedient. I played on the computer for nearly half an hour. The game involved matching or memory—I can't remember anymore.

Afterward the doctor studied my scores and frowned.

"Your mental function is very seriously impaired," he announced. "This result, uh. It does not correspond to a person of your professional background."

"I told you, I haven't gotten any sleep—"

"I think you have postpartum depression," he continued. "I am seventy-five percent sure. To be one hundred percent sure I need to see you again. I cannot make the diagnosis in one meeting."

He told me to come back in a week. He prescribed an immediate course of psychotropic drugs and sleeping pills.

"But you said you couldn't make a diagnosis yet," I said.

"That's right."

"Then how can you prescribe me these pills?"

"The sleeping tablets will help you," he said.

"It's not that I can't sleep. It's that my baby wakes me up all night. Besides, I meant the other pills. These antidepressants."

"They will make you feel better," he said.

I'm not opposed to antidepressants. But I'd never taken them before, and their appearance now felt too quick.

I'd come to the psychiatrist, of course, knowing drugs were the most likely outcome. I'd steeled myself to accept the diagnosis along with all suggested treatments. I knew I was in a terrible predicament, and so I'd warned myself to shut up and take the pills. But when the time came, I couldn't do it. The prescription came without explanation, discussion, or alternatives. There was no mention of side effects or options.

I didn't like it. I didn't like it so much that a sluggish shadow of myself, languishing half dead under the rubble of my broken brain, stirred itself back to life. I walked out of the psychiatrist's office without saying good-bye. I kept walking out of the crummy brick building without stopping at the front desk to make another appointment. I walked all the way out to the street and put my arm up for a taxi and rode home. This rusty but real defiance grew a little stronger with every step.

It wasn't the drugs themselves, but the slipshod carelessness for my psyche that I couldn't accept. The admission that there was no diagnosis, but anyway just take these pills. *No,* I told myself. *Not like that.*

By the time I got home, I was angry. Something about this middle-aged man who had squinted through his glasses at me like I was a rare zoo creature had stirred me to fight. Our linguistic gap, in the end, felt like a metaphor for his remove. He couldn't hear my words, he couldn't catch my meaning, he couldn't diagnose me.

But he could quiet me with pills.

"There has to be another answer," I stormed to Tom that night. "This can't be the answer."

"What do you mean?" he said.

"If a woman is in an intolerable situation, the answer is not to drug her so that she can tolerate it. The answer should be—*should* be—to change the intolerable situation."

He nodded sympathetically.

"I hear you," he said. "So what are you going to do?"

"I'm going to find another way."

And I did.

———

Maybe, I decided, I was looking at the problem backward. Perhaps my tortured mental state was, in fact, a normal response to a traumatic birth followed by an unendurable lack of sleep.

I turned my attention to Max. If I wanted to clear my head, I needed to sleep. And if I wanted to sleep, he had to sleep. Sleep training had been a bust, but maybe there were other options. I did some research and found a pediatric sleep specialist in Beijing—an Australian Chinese doctor who ran infant sleep clinics and was preparing to write a book on baby sleep. People said she worked miracles. I booked an appointment.

After that, it was appallingly easy. Two quick appointments and everything changed.

We learned that the baby needed more solid food during the day; he was waking up from both hunger and habit. We also learned that there was a third way, a sort of commonsense middle path in between sharing a bed (which none of us, including our light-sleeping baby, wanted to do) and making Max "cry it out" alone until he passed out from exhaustion. She gave us a foolproof method of comforting the baby when he cried, then putting him down awake to fall asleep unassisted.

"The thing is," the doctor told us, "you really have to buy into this, or it's not going to work. You have to do everything exactly the same way, every time. But, if you do, I promise you it will work."

And it did. It worked. Max learned to put himself to sleep.

The doctor also brought Tom into the nursery, encouraging him to put the baby to bed and respond to his overnight cries. "You're depriving your baby of an important source of comfort," she said. "His father."

Within a few weeks we had the mythological baby who fell contentedly asleep in his bed at seven p.m. and slept straight through to seven a.m. Once the worst sleeper in the building, our baby was now the best.

It was hard to digest how easy it had been to fix, and how close we'd been to help all along. I was relieved, but I also felt stupid. In fact, other mothers had advised me months ago to seek the advice of this particular doctor, but I hadn't paid attention. I'd been disillusioned by silly books promoting useless theories, sticky gripe water, and cumbersome white noise machines. I'd grown cynical of anything that advertised sleep solutions.

Maybe I'd embraced the misery of early motherhood as some sort of penance—the inevitable price that must be paid for a child so perfect and a love so full. Or maybe I was just too exhausted to distinguish a helpful doctor from a snake-oil saleswoman.

The first few nights of Max's unbroken sleep, I bolted awake at odd hours to cries that weren't there. But gradually my nervous system unwound itself and I, too, began to sleep. Then I slept like I had never slept before. I crawled into bed, sometimes, before the sun had even set.

After a few nights of solid sleep, I felt so energetic I upped the ante. I joined a gym and resumed the hard, sweaty runs I'd dropped when I'd gotten pregnant.

Slowly my head cleared. The thrum and clamor drained from my ears. And, most important, the dread dissipated.

One morning I rode my bike through the sunshine to buy fresh fruit at the farmers' market and felt the first warm wind of summer on my face. At a literature festival I said something quick-witted and a little bit mean and realized, with an adrenaline rush, that my personality had not been lost forever.

It was still there. I was still there. Still here.

I had my baby, and I was still here.

But it had taken the better part of a year to get there.

Chapter 6

I baked a cake of carrots and raisins and frosted it with cream cheese, cut dripping chunks of watermelon, and tied a helium balloon to the arm of Max's high chair. I did these things eagerly, thinking that just as romantic love spends itself in sex, this maternal love sought physical expression in the icing of cakes and scrambling of eggs and straightening of covers. I worked at other things so I could make money to pay others to do these tasks, I mused, only to snatch them back again in random spasms of love.

We lit a candle and sang "Happy Birthday" to our first child, for the first time. Max sat straight, glancing from face to face and resting his plump forearms on the high-chair tray with leonine majesty. He didn't understand, but he liked it plenty. He approved of the guests—his three favorite people. He crowed over the leaping candle flame. He gobbled watermelon until his chest was sticky with rose-colored juice.

Tom crouched and hovered, taking pictures from every angle.

When the time came to blow out the candle, I held Max's dimpled hand and whispered his wish into his ear. We had been one flesh, we had lived and almost died and gone crazy together, and now I wished on his behalf because he had no words.

I blew the flame away. Max clapped along for company.

The birthday was finished; another year opened before us. Tom rushed off to work. I laid Max down for a nap. Xiao Li swept up the crumbs and stored the leftover watermelon in the refrigerator.

While Max slept off the revelry, I picked up the camera and flashed through the pictures. That's when I realized that Tom was missing from every frame.

It happened fast; nobody was paying attention. At least, I wasn't paying attention. Maybe Tom had hoped I'd seize the camera and shoo him into the frame, or that I'd ask Xiao Li to snap a few shots of our family, battered but joyful, posing behind the birthday cake.

But I hadn't. The pictures depict me, Max, and Xiao Li. This makes them awkward. We never framed them. The images were not planned, nor what we particularly wanted, but in retrospect they contain a certain documentary truth. That first year, in my memory, was populated by me, Max, and Xiao Li.

She wore a T-shirt and cutoff jeans that day, and gamely stuck a sparkly party hat on her head. While Max smeared cake over his cheeks, she squatted at his side and giggled. She beamed with a simple, obvious happiness—not her baby, but a baby she had tirelessly tended, had reached a milestone.

And Tom—his face is not captured. He was there and not there. Making it all happen, but absent from the action.

———

After that, I started angling my camera to crop Xiao Li out of photographs. I'd always balked at posting pictures on Facebook or emailing them to family if they depicted Xiao Li. I was embarrassed to admit she was there. I didn't want to advertise the fact that we hired other people to do our housework, that we didn't clean up our own messes, that we lived in neocolonial comfort with a locally hired domestic underling. Nor was I keen to admit that I was, perhaps, not a fabulously competent artist and mother who managed to do it all—when you factored in Xiao Li, you could argue that I was hardly doing anything.

What's more, Xiao Li's presence diminished my newfound sense of commonality with far-flung friends and family. My adult life—the travel, triumphs, and traumas—had mostly been alien to the people I loved. I couldn't discuss with my cousins or childhood friends the maddening campaigns to get an Iranian visa, or the weirdness of getting drunk on a winter morning with a killer in the Caucasus, or the crushing loneliness that filled my gut when I woke up in a hotel room and couldn't recall what country I was in.

I could, however, chat happily for hours about the constipating effects of applesauce on infants or the travails of flying with toddlers. Parenthood had furnished me with something I hadn't even known I'd been missing: a major life experience in common with my loved ones.

Except there was Xiao Li, making it—making me—weird all over again.

As I began to exclude her from the photographic record, I realized that most of the families I knew seemed to do the same: my former colleagues, my neighbors, the parents I befriended through our apartment's baby group—none of them showed off pictures of the nannies.

They all said things like "Xi Ayi is like a member of our family." That sounded cozy and loving, as if the *ayis* were not laborers, but blood relatives or volunteers. But pictures don't lie. If you want to see the ambivalence that pervades domestic labor, check the photographic record.

Check it on both sides, too. Because there's something else I've realized: the nannies exclude their bosses right back.

————

Xiao Li and the other neighborhood *ayis* liked to take their charges to the indoor playground across the street. This was one bit of childcare I was delighted to outsource. I hated the cocktail of boogers and hand sanitizer and drool slicked over contraptions of plastic and rubber, the wild screech of lisping nursery rhymes from mounted speakers, and the pressure to act nonchalant when some hulking seven-year-old clawed Max's face or pushed him off the slide for sport.

Xiao Li at least pretended to enjoy the experience. Max was sincerely pleased by the place. And I certainly relished the empty apartment. Everybody won.

Upon their return Xiao Li would proudly pull out her phone and flash through the photos: Max belly-down on a water bed, studying fake fish through translucent plastic. Max, who could not yet jump, perched in puzzlement upon a trampoline. Max laughing helplessly as balloons flew around his head.

She couldn't send the pictures to me. She didn't have email, and I didn't have a smartphone. But she carried them around with her, this growing dossier that documented my son's days. These were memories snapped out in the world and away from me—or at home, when Tom and I were gone.

I never knew why she took so many pictures of Max. Did she look at his picture at night or on the weekends? Surely not. I mean, surely not, right? Maybe she was just playing or passing the time, or giving herself some insurance in case she was asked to justify the hours or prove her devotion to the child.

I wondered whether she showed the pictures to her daughter or husband, or displayed them to her family when she traveled home to Hebei. These questions were idle and unanswerable. Every nanny I've known has taken endless pictures of the children she tends and the rooms where she works. Whenever I'm handed a phone to look at a picture of my child, I realize it's one of hundreds in a long chain stretching off in both directions.

Other pictures are clearly not intended for the boss's eyes. I've seen selfies of nannies posing in their employers' bedrooms; throwing parties in their bosses' homes during vacations; borrowing their clothing—posing, always posing. The employers themselves are perpetually absent from the pictures.

We take pictures of everything except for one another.

I guess there is fantasy on both sides. The nannies pretend they live in these comfortable homes and mother these plump babies. Perhaps they sometimes allow themselves to play dress-up—not only with the clothes and the rooms, but with the children.

We employers pretend our polished existences are the natural result of our work and excellence—not the fruit of another woman's labor. The rooms are clean because somebody else cleaned them; the kids thrive because there's an extra adult around the house. It takes a village, and damn it, we've hired one. But nobody wants to say that, not straight out like that.

We all want to pretend it's not a job, it's not about labor and cash and schedules. The employment relationship is the only reason we coexist in these rooms, and yet we treat it like an inconvenient, even nasty, truth—the first thing we'd like to crop from the picture.

I was leaving Xiao Li outside the frames, but I didn't feel good about that, either. I didn't like pretending that she didn't exist. Her stories and songs and smiles are planted in my child's mind forever—how could I bleach her physical self out of existence?

How could I lament my own disappearance—only to erase another woman?

———

All the while, I was uncomfortably conscious that I'm not the sort of person who is supposed to have these kinds of dilemmas. These are rarified problems of the ethereal elite, and by breeding and temperament I'm a peasant. I have a posh British friend (at least, I understand she's posh because other British people always use that word behind her back) who once tried to explain to me how, in England, class has nothing to do with money but is easily recognized by such clues as schools and the way one treats servers and staff. Well, first, it seems to me that schools and staff have everything to do with money, and second, she was unable to coherently describe the difference in how people talk to servants, and I've been wishing for specifics ever since.

As for me, I'm an American crossbreed of servants and supervisors. Status is a question of who may command and who must obey; who barges through and who steps aside. But my family is white, and so that difference was not carried in our American genes. Status is a circumstance external to ourselves, a thing we gained and lost from one generation to the next. We white Americans are superstitiously and secretly preoccupied with its getting and keeping. I believe that's why we are so tiresomely obsessed with our "experience" as customers; why we tip with the seriousness of penitents sacrificing on the temple of a fickle god; why we insist upon a veneer of egalitarian friendliness at all times. Maybe, too, that is why we've fought so bitterly against any suggestion of equality with black Americans—we are afraid to accept as part of our national identity a blood that historically mandated the fate of lower—or nonexistent—status. We say, *Our nation was built by immigrants.* We don't like to say the truth: *Our nation was built by immigrants and slaves.*

I mean to say that the events in my household are not new, nor are they specific to me and Xiao Li, or to Asia, or to this moment in time. Between Xiao Li and me seethed an ocean of difference so vast we couldn't perceive each other clearly, even when we were in the same room. And yet it was always in the back of my mind that I come from people who did the same work as Xiao Li. I could trace the reversals of fortune that elevated and abased generations of women in my family. I knew these changes were tied to movement, to uprooting oneself and crossing seas. And we had done that. Xiao Li and I existed together in rooms that we'd traveled to reach. So maybe anything could happen. Maybe Xiao Li or her descendants will end up rich in the United States. Maybe I will end up poor.

My great-grandmother was a Hungarian teenager brought along— imported, in a way—to the New World as somebody's servant. She was a nanny who crossed the Atlantic taking care of an opera singer's child. She reached America and kept going: jobs and reinventions and peregrinations around the Midwest; a wedding to a fellow immigrant; the birth of American children.

And then—just like that, within one generation—her daughter was back in Europe, having married a man who rose through the ranks of the U.S. Army in World War II. That daughter, my grandmother, oversaw a showpiece household in bomb-chewed Vienna while her husband sorted out the fates of the "displaced persons," which is a sanitized way to describe the survivors of concentration camps.

Daughter of a village girl, daughter of a servant, daughter of an immigrant. But she was the lady of the house now, replete with nannies and cooks and maids, pearls on her throat, and one pregnancy after another. It must have seemed to her, then, like a perfect completion of her destiny. It must have seemed so good. But life was just getting started.

There are various points to all this, and here is one: I am not the first woman in my family to fight about the housework.

Eventually, of course, my grandmother found herself back in

America with a big house in the D.C. suburbs and five children—but no more hired help. She pressed the kids into service in the house, but gradually they got busy and grew up and moved out. My grandfather hired a maid; my grandmother fired her in a pique. Disgusted by an increasingly disordered home, consumed by his extraordinary success as a lobbyist, my grandfather spent less and less time at home.

My grandmother lost herself in charity work and music—playing the organ at church, teaching piano, writing an opera—while her house slid into filth and, eventually, her marriage collapsed.

Having gotten divorced, my grandfather was free to date younger women and play golf and hobnob around Washington. As for my grandmother, she spent the rest of her life playing music in public and destroying her home in private. She never accepted the divorce. She murdered the house by suffocation. Rooms were filled to the ceiling with stuff until they became impassable and were effectively erased from the geography of the building. A bathroom was given over to the many cats who twined and mewled through the detritus—layer after layer of soiled newspaper, a sickly tower that skewed up toward the ceiling.

I want to say the destruction of the family home was a metaphor, a sort of proto-feminist protest, a final fuck you. I want to believe that my grandmother elaborately disrespected the house because it was the only way to explain her fate: domestic life had been a trap and a dead end. I believe there is truth in that.

But the house was filthy and sad and I know that, when you peel away the metaphors, my grandmother's illness has a name: She was a hoarder.

These stories hang over me. They were always there, but now I consider them anew. Having disappeared into my own household, I meditate on the fates of the women who begat me, on the unknowable alchemy of chores and cleanliness and husbands and sanity.

My own mother would not be bogged down. She said good-bye to all that, and she married a man who was nothing like her father, and they moved together to a forest-side house in New England that was old and ramshackle and drafty. The clanking radiators couldn't keep the place warm in the winter, and in the summer the walls sweated and I stuffed my cheeks with ice cubes to sleep. But there were broad trees overhead, and vegetable and flower gardens, a strawberry patch, raspberry bushes, an apple tree—and the woods, fragrant and shadowed and crawling with life.

My mother was an activist with the League of Women Voters, using the hand-cranked mimeograph in our basement to print manifestos in wet, acrid streaks of black ink. She bought us, her daughters, T-shirts: "A woman needs a man like a fish needs a bicycle." Barbie dolls were banned lest they spoil our body image.

Before marriage she was a news reporter who successfully sued her bosses for paying her less than they paid men who did the same job. As we grew up, she ran for town council and became a reporter at the town's weekly newspaper. She was a force to be reckoned with and, eventually, she took over as editor in chief.

At home she taught my sister and me how to do all kinds of things. How to sew and iron clothes; bake cakes and boil up homemade cranberry sauce; knit and crochet and embroider and quilt; polish silver and set tables to Emily Post standards.

My brother was largely exempt from the traditionally feminine domestic arts. He was not expected to cook. His chores were different: lawn mowing, snow shoveling, leaf raking. We girls had cross-stitch kits; he had model airplanes.

My mother's feminism didn't have a private sphere. Behind closed doors, in the house, things went along as ever they had. Maybe, for her, it wasn't very important. My father's housework contributions compare favorably to most young fathers I know today, which can either—depending upon how you want to look at it—serve as an indictment of our lack of progress or a laurel on the memory of my father.

My mother educated me impeccably to make my way in the world. When I read *Lean In* I was mostly confused: Who were these women who didn't speak at meetings or take their seats at the table? It never even crossed my mind that I should keep my thoughts to myself or hover at the edge of the action. And that is because my parents never gave me even a shadow of suggestion in that direction. They didn't even introduce the possibility to dismiss it.

But now I was dabbling in a realm for which I had not been prepared. Now I was waging the only battle I'd been warned to avoid.
When I got married, my mother flatly advised me against squabbling
over chores.

"You have to ask yourself," she said, "'Is this the hill I want to
die on?'"

————

"My husband wants another baby," Xiao Li said one day. "He is talking about it all the time."

So was she. Family planning was on her mind, and I could see that
she sought a more fulsome reply than the blandishments I'd murmured so far.

"It's illegal." I stalled.

That was true. China's infamous one-child policy still, at that time,
limited births to one baby per family. (It has since been abolished.)

"That doesn't matter," she said.

"What do you mean, it doesn't matter?"

She shrugged.

"Do you want another baby?" I pressed.

"No," she said. "I don't want."

"Why?"

"I don't know." She shrugged again. "It's too hard."

I couldn't guess whether she was speaking frankly or telling me
what she thought I wanted to hear.

"You mean—"

"The pregnancy. The small baby. It's so hard."

"That's true," I sighed. "But still," I added gamely, "I think you
would be glad afterward."

This was not sincere. I had no idea whether she'd be glad or not. I
was talking out of embarrassment. I hated the thought of our house
without Xiao Li. And I didn't want her to think I was involving myself
in her family planning; I could hardly manage my own.

For her part, Xiao Li was not so shy.

"You should have another baby," she told me.

"Not right now."

"This time, girl," she said, guileless as a child asking for a doll.

I laughed nervously. "I don't know."

"Yes," she said and giggled. "Babies are so cute. I love babies."

———

"Do you have a picture of your daughter?" I asked Xiao Li one afternoon.

"Here."

Mischievous eyes, round cheeks, body twisting with legs splayed. Two fingers for the camera: peace and victory. Mouth screwed into an insouciant half smile.

"She's beautiful," I said lightly.

Xiao Li wrinkled her nose and shrugged.

"She's ugly. Like my husband."

"No!" I was sincerely shocked.

"Yes," she insisted. "She looks like my husband."

"Well." My Western etiquette floundered stupidly in the face of a mother who glibly declared her daughter ugly. "I think she's cute."

Xiao Li made a small noise in her throat, twisted her mouth, and flipped to the next picture. This one showed the girl inside a small bedroom that contained practically nothing. A window in the background, a mattress on the floor. The girl perched on the low bed, grinning proudly into the camera.

"This is Beijing?" I asked.

"Yes, here."

This must be Xiao Li's room, then. The place where she and her husband slept. I scrolled through more pictures of the little girl, then stopped again. I recognized the brick pathways and pruned hedges of our apartment's courtyard.

"This is Xin Cheng Guoji?"

"Yes," she said.

"You brought her here?"

"Yes."

"Oh." I tried to pass off my confusion as regret. "You should have told me. I would like to meet her."

I tried to imagine introducing this small girl, this child-stranger, to the foreign boy who greedily soaked up her mother's time and work and love. I pictured myself trying awkwardly to communicate. I should have a present for her, if such a meeting were to happen. But what would she think, and what would I say? *Your mother leaves your house to make mine nicer. She leaves you and spends the days with my child while I am also here.*

And Tom—what if Tom were home? I wasn't sure I could forgive him if he behaved toward this small child with anything other than immaculate warmth and kindness. If he grunted into his phone or walked out of the room abruptly or committed any other small rudeness, I would be enraged.

I pushed the phone back, like it was dangerous; like it might burn my hand if I held on to it too long.

Chapter 7

The table was spread with cold eggplant, spiced noodles, and duck cooked in tobacco. Iced beer bubbled in squat glasses. I'd come by bike to the restaurant, swinging free through the sun to meet a friend and her family for lunch. She was a Malaysian writer of detective stories—sharp and fast and funny—and she was traveling with her husband and adolescent kids. We were drinking, laughing, the lunch was rolling along . . .

The phone squalled. I glanced down to silence the ring, and saw the name of the caller: Xiao Li.

This could be nothing but bad news. Xiao Li never called.

In the frantic gap between accepting the call and raising the phone to my ear I could hear, muffled but unmistakable, the hysterical howl of a wounded baby.

My wounded baby.

Xiao Li was crying, too—crying so furiously I couldn't understand her words.

"What? Slow down." I jammed my finger into my free ear. "What?"

From the storm of wails, a few phrases emerged: *You come. Max nose broken. Too much blood.*

I surged to my feet, nearly toppling the table, and gasped some garble about a broken nose.

"Go, go, go." The parents took up the ritual chant. Their impassive adolescent children roused themselves from laden plates to regard this crisis with sleepy-lidded interest. "Call me, tell me, I hope . . ."

My friend's voice fell away as my feet pounded down the stairs toward the street.

Blindly I fled, shoving the door, bursting into day, wrenching my bike lock so hard I shredded my fingernails. Straddling the bike, balancing on toes, I paused to call Tom.

"Max has a broken nose!"

"What?"

"I don't know! Xiao Li called! I'm out—"

"I'm headed home right now!" He hung up.

Buildings, sidewalks, and trees smeared into shapeless color as I careened through the day. I pedaled so fast I had the sensation of coming unhinged from everything around me. Adrenaline pounded down into my toes, pulsed in my earlobes, threatened to burst my fingernails clean off my hands. Dimly I registered horns, shouts, brakes. But no car hit me; I didn't fall. By some miracle, some mad grace for desperate mothers, the city opened a path for me where there should have been none.

I careened to the lobby door, pounded the elevator button, scrabbled for the key, and tumbled into the house.

Max lolled in dry, sullen silence in Xiao Li's arms. Gently I carried him into the bathroom. Smears of fresh blood covered the lower half of his face. I sat him down on the sink and sponged his face with a washcloth.

"His nose looks all right," I told a sniffling Xiao Li, who had followed. "It's his lip. Max, sweetheart, look up, look at the ceiling, honey—"

My voice shook; my heart roared.

I pried open his mouth and peered inside. The upper lip was split from within, his front teeth had slammed into the soft flesh. *Heads bleed*—my mother had always said that. *You can't hurt an Irishman by hitting him on the head.* That had been my grandfather.

I picked Max up and cuddled him. I kissed his hot wet cheeks and smelled his hair.

"He'll be okay," I told Xiao Li. "What happened?"

Xiao Li slapped her hands over her face and began to sob in earnest. Her thin shoulders trembled in her tank top; her keening cries echoed down the hall.

"What's wrong?" I cried. "What happened?"

"He was walking! He fell! He hit his face on the side of the bed."

"Well, that happens."

She kept sobbing.

"I mean—he falls down all the time," I said.

"I am not good," Xiao Li wailed. "I can't take care of him. I will find another job."

I felt my back stiffen.

"What?"

"I don't want Max to get hurt," she sobbed. "I can't."

"But babies get hurt," I pointed out, rubbing circles on his back with my palm. My child restored to my arms, I had calm to spare. "He gets hurt more with me than he does with you. I know you are very careful!"

This was true. Xiao Li hovered and caught much more assiduously than Tom or me; the rate of injuries on her watch put us both to shame.

But Xiao Li couldn't gather herself. And as her sobs grew louder and Max stirred uneasily in my arms, something in my gut hardened. If I, the child's mother, could keep my cool, then surely some equanimity might be expected from the nanny. She had lost her head and made that crazy phone call; she had sent me racing across the city with images of a mangled face. *I could have died,* I thought now. I had a wild urge to shake her or slap her across the face.

"You need to calm down," I said coldly. "You'll scare the baby."

But she was lost, beyond the reach of sympathy or anger, adrift on currents of her own sorrows. She was crying so hard I thought she must be grieving, in some oblique way, for herself. I tried to remember how old her daughter had been when Xiao Li had left.

Max mewled in my arms, burrowing his head into my neck to escape the wails of his nanny.

"Please go to the bathroom and calm down," I told her, trying to soften my voice. "This crying is not good for Max."

She went, and through the closed door we heard the sounds of running water and stifled cries.

Tom burst into the living room.

"Max—"

"He's fine!" I'd just locked one hysteric into the bathroom, and here was a fresh eruption of Sturm und Drang. Tom swooped down and lifted Max from my arms.

"So he didn't break his nose?"

"It's just a split lip."

"Where did you get the idea he broke his nose?"

"That's what Xiao Li said when she called."

"What happened?"

"He just fell down. He was walking and he lost his balance. You know. He banged his face on the bedpost. At least that's what I understand—"

"Where were you?"

"I had that lunch with Shamini."

"Oh right." He dropped kisses over the baby's face. "Max! You okay, buddy?"

He turned to me: "Where's Xiao Li?"

"She's crying in the bathroom."

"What? Why?"

"I don't know."

"Did you yell at her?"

"No, I was very nice." I realized that Tom's line of questioning sought, from all angles, something for which I might be blamed.

"I was annoyed about all the crying," I admitted. "Anyway, I want to call the doctor and make sure we don't have to bring him to the hospital or anything."

"I thought he had a broken nose . . ." I could see in Tom's slackened posture the same confusing flare and drain of adrenaline that had wrung out my own nerves.

"Me, too," I sighed. "But thank God he doesn't."

The doctor told me to ice the cut, and when I explained that the baby fought fiercely against ice, she immediately suggested a cheerful alternative: ice cream.

So we carried Max downstairs to a sidewalk café, where we presented him with his first-ever taste of ice cream: a soft-serve vanilla cone from the Japanese bakery. While Max earnestly slurped and smeared his face with sweet, cold cream, Tom snapped pictures to send to our mothers.

While we ate our melting treats, Xiao Li stayed inside, out of the sun, cleaning up after us and getting ready for the night.

––––––––

By the time we landed in Phuket, Max was lost to sleep. He lay unconscious in my arms, head jerking and lolling, mouth gaping, feet dangling. I carried him straight through the ill-lit cacophony of swindlers and drivers and porters; the drunk and the drugged; hawkers and touts. Tom struggled along, tugging the suitcase. I carried Max out into the warm, wet night and into a hotel car frigid with air conditioning and finally into a lobby where our necks were draped with jasmine garlands.

I breathed the frangipani and the fresh salt breath of sea and listened to the distant pounding of the surf and blinked around at terraces of fountains and pools lit by candlelight—and I began to realize the vacation was going to be all right. Maybe even better than all right. Maybe—did I dare to allow this possibility?—even good.

The trip to Thailand was Tom's idea. I'd agreed reluctantly. I didn't believe that the slow restoration of stability and sleep in our home was a function of Max's growing up. I'd cobbled our family back together with tape and rusting nails and pure willpower, as far as I knew, and I fought even tiny fluctuations in the routine because I feared they would prove its undoing. A birthday party that clashed with a nap, a later-than-usual dinner, or a minor variation in the thermostat temperature were enough to send me into quiet panic. I was always on guard against the misstep that would upend our household routine and shatter Max's ability to sleep and lead to sickness and exhaustion and, eventually, insanity.

It boiled down to that. I was terrified of being pushed back out to the edge of sanity. I'd been in those woods before, and I didn't want to go back.

There was nothing precarious or even particularly adventurous about this trip. We'd booked ourselves into luxury resorts in one of the world's most tourist-friendly nations. Still, I fretted and fussed over the luggage. I stayed awake until dawn the night before we left, stomach churning. I resented Tom for forcing this point, for obliging me to take this vacation.

"We haven't gone anywhere since Max was born," he'd said.

"I know."

"We spend all our time trapped in the house."

"I know."

"What is the point of being here if we don't explore together?"

"I know."

I couldn't argue. On paper, he was right. Still I believed he was wrong. The trip was reckless; we'd regret it.

But our days in Thailand were perfect. We picked our way slowly through that fragrant, jungled landscape like survivors of some painful fever. Our arms and legs were hollow as tubes of paper; we touched things carefully; we were easily pleased.

We strapped Max into a bicycle seat and pedaled dirt paths through rice paddies and fields, to fish restaurants on the beach. We were blessed by Buddhist monks in the mountains over Chiang Mai. We bought painted paper parasols, and when the afternoon rains pounded the hotel lawn we sat in lounge chairs and ate fat black raisins and watched the drops splash into the waters of the pool.

In a hotel in Bangkok Max let go of everything and walked alone across the floor for the first time, and it felt like a miracle.

We were happy on that trip, and all the more happy because we had almost come to believe that happiness was not for us. Other families would enjoy their vacations; we were destined to flounder and wallow and turn desperately against one another in the glass and plaster walls of our skyscraper.

We had traveled to Thailand to swim in the sea, but the sea was not available. Red flags snapped along the beach. The ocean seethed with a riptide that snatched even experienced swimmers straight out to eternity. I wanted to ignore the warnings, in a way, because I always feel tempted to ignore the warnings. Tom convinced me the danger was real.

So I held Max by the riptide. I sank down to the sand and wrapped my arms around him and held him tight against the tug of singing waves. The sea stretched to the sky. The sky was full of light, and the sea was full of danger. We could only look at the rise and fall; the flash of light and the splinters of dark below, the churn and crash that covered the secret life of the salt ocean.

I wanted to dip him into the sting of the sea, I wanted him to smell and taste and bathe in all the waters of the world. I wanted to wash him in the ocean with its mineral grains and eerie vegetable growths and unknown animals. But I waited. Maybe there was no real rush. I held on to him just a little bit longer, and together we waited.

Chapter 8

There was trouble with Xiao Li, but she wasn't talking. Not to me, anyway.

She had always been scrupulous about confining telephone chats to her breaks, but then, all of a sudden, the calls became constant. She stood with hunched shoulders, face turned into the corner of the laundry room, phone behind a curtain of hair. She whispered and sometimes she shouted in a voice that was harsh and scratched, which made her sound like a stranger.

Sometimes, after hanging up, she bustled back to work with flushed cheeks and averted gaze. Other times she stood by the washing machine and looked at the city sky pale with pollution and cried.

I paused and fluttered in doorways. I didn't want to pry into her private life. I didn't want to ignore her distress.

"Are you okay?" I'd ask.

"I'm okay," she'd reply.

And I'd turn away.

At last, she stopped me in the kitchen. Looking full into her face, I realized she looked terrible. Her eyes were shot with blood, and her cheeks looked as lifeless as pinched wax.

"My daughter is sick," she said.

"What happened?" I thought of flu, fever, bronchitis. Some childhood ailment, maybe a difficult one, but nothing too drastic.

"It's her heart," Xiao Li said.

"Is it serious?" A dread so intense it felt like giddiness.

"Yes," she said. "She is in hospital now three days."

I reached for Xiao Li, then stopped. I wanted to touch her, but I saw the warning in her eyes. She did not want to be pitied or hugged. My hand hovered, hesitated, then patted her upper arm awkwardly. She looked at me miserably.

"She's in—?"

"Hebei."

"Do you want to go?"

"I don't know," Xiao Li said. "No. It's okay."

"Who is with her?"

"My husband."

"Oh," I said. "Well, that's good."

"Yes."

We both lacked conviction.

"Do they know what's wrong?"

"No," she said. "They don't know."

"Was she sick?"

"Yes," she said. "She got very sick."

The girl lay in a provincial hospital near the village. Her heart was making a strange noise; there appeared to be some defect. The doctors ran tests but failed to reach a diagnosis.

The next day Xiao Li said she wanted to go to her daughter.

"Good," I said. "You should go."

I wondered, in a wordless flash, whether she'd have planned the trip if I hadn't suggested it the day before. I knew that some domestic employees didn't get personal days or family leave, no matter the crisis. Fleetingly I congratulated myself for being superior to those other, nefarious bosses.

"When will you be back?"

"I don't know," she said.

"But you are coming back."

"Yes!" she said quickly. "I'll come Monday."

"You'll come back to Beijing on Monday, or come to work on Monday?"

"I'll come to work on Monday."

This interrogation had evaporated any illusion of moral superiority, which I quickly scrambled to retrieve.

"Do you need money?"

"No," she said. "I have."

"Call if you need more time."

"Okay."

In truth, I knew she wouldn't ask for more time. I'd just pressed her to resolve her family crisis quickly. I felt guilty, but I didn't know how to undo the impression. Or maybe I didn't want to. Selfish though it was, I wanted Xiao Li to come back quickly. Her sick daughter was a horror I hoped would simply blow over.

———

It was September now, and a taste of ice sneaked into the breeze. Schoolchildren marched through the mornings in pressed uniforms. In Ritan Park the ginkgo leaves mellowed to brilliant gold, and gray-headed scavengers squatted in flickering shadows to gather the stinking nuts.

In the park I held Max aloft. He stretched his arms hungrily to the branches, traced the joints of twigs, and ran his fingers on the edges of leaves. I thought of Michelangelo's God touching Adam; this child who had so often pined for the light of the sky was seeking now the solid fruits of the earth.

I told myself to enjoy the long autumn afternoons with my baby. I tried not to worry about Xiao Li or her daughter or my book manuscript, which once again sat neglected. I fed myself with "it will all work out," "be here now," "all in good time," and any other suitable platitude.

Xiao Li came back the following Monday, but the news was bleak. Her daughter was too weak to get out of bed. Her heart still wasn't beating properly. The doctors were uncertain. The tearful phone calls continued, and when Xiao Li asked for another leave, I agreed.

"Get the agency to send somebody while she's gone," Tom suggested.

"I don't think she told them she's been gone," I said. "I don't want to get her into trouble."

"That's not your problem," Tom said.

"It is, though," I said.

"It's not. Don't make it your problem."

"Still," I said.

In the absence of constant cleaning, the rooms lost the fresh whiffs of bleach and wax and took on, instead, the discouraging smells of our carnal selves—dirty laundry, morning breath, diapers. I couldn't slip away to the gym or meet a friend for coffee, let alone write. Tom played with Max in the mornings until I'd showered, brushed my teeth, and shrugged into clean clothes. After that, I could last until evening without another moment to myself.

As ever, the biggest problem was work. When could I yank my eyes off the baby and borrow back my brain to get some writing done?

Naps, that was the obvious answer. But dishes rotted in the sink and pureed plums smeared the high chair and the washing machine chimed its smarmy wet clothes jingle. I'd rush through the rudimentary housework only to find the time had run out, the baby was awake again!

Desperate for an outing, I'd bundle him into his stroller and push him around to the butcher, the grocery store, the bakery, gathering slabs of meat and loaves of bread and vegetables, pausing eagerly to chat whenever we came across anybody I knew even tangentially.

I took him to playdates with our neighbors. And since I wasn't rushing back to my very-important-work at the computer, I finally slowed down and talked with the other mothers. It was out of desperate loneliness at first, but to my surprise I ended up liking them.

We cracked jokes over sugar-free muffins and bottomless pots of tea, and I shamefacedly realized I'd unfairly written these women off as dullard housewives. They turned out to be bright and witty career women who made me laugh and shared advice and erased my loneliness. I hated to remember how harshly I'd judged them, especially when, in reality, I was one of them.

Back at home, Max played with toys on the kitchen floor while I cooked dinner. By the time I'd bathed him and put him to bed and cleaned up the dinner mess, I wanted only to collapse in front of the television.

This existence wasn't bad. I knew that. I was still drifting away from my work, and so I had no peace. But when your mind is haunted by images of a child in a hospital cot with a mysteriously fading heart, a day alone with a healthy child is no hardship. My baby pointed out the early crescent moon in the sky; he tugged my earlobes; he said, "Mama."

Please God, do not ever let him hurt. Please give his hurt to me instead.

Visceral prayers. Inevitable. No good in the end. My parents didn't own my life; I don't own his. They couldn't spare me and I can't spare him. One day I, too, will loom in my child's imagination as a foreigner who thinks she has a right. One day he will shout, *I hate you.* He will shout, *I didn't ask to be born.* And he'll be right, all right, he'll be right like I was right . . .

I know all of that.

But still, but really, please God please, spare him . . .

Heavy thoughts while frying sliced pork, steaming broccoli, boiling noodles.

Xiao Li came and went throughout the fall, back and forth on the bus. She played quietly with Max. Her giggles no longer rang from the walls. She locked herself in the bathroom, but there was no rush of water in the pipes.

She had vanished into a quiet so perfect it made me shudder.

———

"How's your writing going?" Tom asked one of those evenings.

"Poorly," I said. "Not at all."

"Sorry, honey."

"Why are you even asking?" I could see the end of this argument before it began, and I knew it wasn't good, but I couldn't help myself.

"You must know that if I'm cooking and cleaning and taking care of Max, I'm not also writing," I said coldly. "Are you trying to make me feel bad about it?"

"Not at all," Tom said, raising his eyebrows over his glasses. "I'm sorry. I really don't know what goes on all day."

"Then stay home for a day and try it, and I'll vanish off somewhere and get some work done."

"But don't other parents, like back in the U.S., manage to have kids and also work from home?"

"Yes. Yes, they do." My anger collapsed into perfect calm. "They have messy houses and they don't complain about dinner. They buy baby food at the store and it's not poisonous. Their kids watch TV and play with iPads. If I plunk Max in front of the TV all day, I'll get plenty of writing done.

"Or!" I couldn't let him get a word in. "Or—you could stay late in the mornings and do some housework, or come home early and make dinner, or grocery shop on your lunch break. I can come up with plenty of solutions."

"This is crazy," Tom replied with an infuriating lack of emotion. "We have a maid."

"The *maid*"—I lingered hatefully on this word—"is a *person* who has a family crisis."

"So fire her," he said. "I'm tired of this."

"You think she should be fired because her daughter is sick?"

"I think she should be fired because she's stopped coming to work."

"Are you a psychopath?"

"Come on, Meg. Be serious. She's not doing her job anymore. We can give her a nice severance—"

"No! I can't—I mean—what if Max were sick and my boss fired me for going to the hospital?"

"Obviously," he said unrepentantly, "I would be furious."

"But you'd do it to somebody else."

"Because I have to worry about our family. And we are not a welfare state."

"I know, but—"

"Xiao Li has become a problem for us."

"Because she's missing work?"

"Not just that. Honestly, the bigger problem is that she has this weird hold on you."

"What are you talking about?"

"I can't even ask about what she does all day because you get so defensive. I feel like you have gotten so emotionally entangled with this—*maid*—that you're not seeing things clearly."

"I do feel solidarity. And I think firing her is wrong and I'm dead against it and I won't do it. I won't."

"Listen to yourself," he said. "I'm just trying to help you get back to work."

"It was really hard this past year, and she was here when you weren't," I blurted. "I know it's her job and she didn't do it out of love, but I feel grateful to her and I feel loyal to her."

"You feel loyal to the maid."

"Yes. I do. Stop calling her that!"

"That's what she is!"

"But the way you say it is so—nasty!"

"I can't talk with you about this anymore," he said. "It's too crazy."

"You're the one who sounds crazy to me!"

We thrashed our way through the same argument many times that fall. Neither of us backed down. The disagreement festered like some rotting thing caught in the trap of our personalities.

I admit: Tom was right. Xiao Li did, indeed, have a hold over me that transcended the technical boundaries of our employment relationship.

Plainly put, I loved her. My emotions toward Xiao Li were not sexual or romantic; neither platonic nor familial. But love it was, all the same. It was a love of gratitude and recognition and dependence; a love that tempered the madness and desperation of my love for Max into a survivable emotion. It clung to the plastic spoons, teddy bears, teething rings—but especially to the dimpled elbows and fuzzy skull and warm milky skin of the baby we passed back and forth.

In those fragile, wild months after Max was born, I'd lived in a dreamscape of darkened rooms and feedings and, most of all, terror. And just as surely as Tom could not understand this existence no matter how I tried to find the language to evoke it, Xiao Li intuited my state without a single word. I never had to explain to Xiao Li. She knew, the knowledge was in her face and hands, tactful and gentle, and I loved her.

I believe this love is inevitable and biological, weaving itself among women over the heads of newborns. I believe that the discovery of a woman's place in a constellation of other women is the new mother's consolation and best hope for happiness. I believe it evolved as a method of species survival. I haven't seen a study, but I will forever accept this as truth.

I didn't even know her full name, and I don't think she knew mine, either. She called me Excuse Me. Our relationship was inherently transactional. But I associated Xiao Li with sanity and health, with my escape from sleeplessness and depression. She was a trail of bread crumbs I'd followed out of the loneliest wilderness, and now I understood why bread crumbs figure in this ancient tale of children lost in untamable forest: because bread crumbs are domestic and comforting, they are the very stuff of survival, broken into bits.

Tom's intuition was correct. My attachment to Xiao Li had turned into an irrational dependence. And he didn't even know the extent of my treachery.

In those days I sometimes imagined Xiao Li, Tom, Max, and me adrift in an overcrowded lifeboat. Somebody had to be thrown overboard. I knew Tom would have to go; I would pitch my one true love into the waves. That is how deeply I had come to depend upon Xiao Li.

I repeat: I envisioned sacrificing my husband in favor of the nanny. And then I was surprised, even indignant, when he expressed unease over our family dynamics.

But I was also right. Xiao Li was in trouble. The doctors and tests were expensive; the agony of a sick child was acute; the implications for her family's future were bleak. I was correct that only a truly evil boss, some ghoulish overseer from the heartless factories of a Dickensian melodrama, would fire Xiao Li at that moment.

Could I, a mother, tell another mother she was not entitled to care for her sick daughter? Should I tell her to abandon her own child and hurry back to mine?

I could not.

Did I secretly, fervently hope she would do that anyway?

Some days, I did. I wished she would do whatever it took to arrive at my doorstep in the morning. I wanted her to go to the very edge of the not-horrible. I wanted her to allow me the illusion that her family's hardships were not so severe.

Tom was saying, forget her, save yourself, pay attention to our family's needs!

And I was saying, I can't forget her because her problem is also my problem and it has to stop somewhere.

We both had some truth on our side.

One afternoon I poured out the situation to a friend and former colleague. I was sure she'd take my side—she was a free-thinking single mother who had raised her son in tandem with a nanny. But her answer overturned my expectations.

"You should get rid of her on principle," she said. "Anybody who is causing this much trouble between you and Tom should not be allowed to stay in your house."

————

The child's health improved and then worsened. She left the hospital, then went back. Doctors prescribed a month of medication followed by another round of tests. She came to Beijing to be examined at the Children's Hospital.

"Who's taking care of her all day?" I asked.

"My husband."

That made sense. Xiao Li earned more money than her husband.

"She's not in school?" I asked.

A beat.

"No."

Thousands of years of mute maternal emotion embedded in pauses, sent across in looks, threatening the foundations of our homes and jobs.

"I'm sorry," I said.

Now that her daughter was just across town, maddeningly close, I wondered how Xiao Li could stand leaving home. I studied her for signs of impatience or fatigue, but she kept her lips set and her eyes clear.

I've spent my adult life immersed in the vocabulary and the study of language, but it was Xiao Li who made me see starkly that communication is not strictly an affair of words. There is something beyond speech and writing, some ephemeral compatibility. Xiao Li and I shared fewer than a hundred words in a common language, but suggestions and plans ran between us unspoken.

I understood her far better than I did many a native English speaker.

———

"Excuse Me."

I had been waiting for the coffee to boil up through the espresso maker when Xiao Li called. She leaned in the door, looking unusually calm.

"I want to go to the doctor."

"What happened?" I was geared for disaster.

"I think I'm pregnant."

Silence was wrong. I had to say something.

"Really?" That was no better than nothing.

"I think so."

"Are you—? How late?"

"I don't know." Her hands flapped, fingers stretched, and I realized that her calm had been a thin facade. "My daughter was sick and— I wasn't paying attention. Two weeks, three weeks."

"Late?"

"Yes."

I was trying to track this.

"Are you happy?" I blurted. That sounded bad, so I tried again. "Do you want another baby?" That also sounded bad.

"I don't know." She blinked, and tears pushed through her lashes.

"Don't worry." I rubbed her arm awkwardly. "You should take a test."

"I want to go this afternoon to the doctor."

"Okay," I said. "Fine," I added, trying to sound enthusiastic as I said good-bye to yet another afternoon of work.

A doctor at the neighborhood clinic said she was indeed pregnant, but that the pregnancy wasn't viable.

"What are you going to do?" I asked.

It was the next day, and we were back in the kitchen. Xiao Li had drawn a diagram of reproductive organs to explain the diagnosis.

It was the first time anything had felt so crucial and impossible to explain that we had resorted to drawings.

"I will—" She slashed a hand across her stomach.

She had scheduled an abortion.

"I'm sorry."

"It's okay," she said plainly. "It's better."

I looked at her face, trying to understand if she really thought so. Then I worried that I was taking liberties with her privacy, so I looked away. Her phone rang, and she excused herself for another huddle by the washing machine.

I wandered into the living room, mulling. What I had said was true. I was sorry. At the same time, I was relieved. Our status quo—my status quo—was safe. Xiao Li would not have to leave her job. I would not have to go forth without Xiao Li. At the same time, I was horrified at the easement of my panic. How malign I had become, I thought, to take relief from another woman's abortion.

Before I could finish excoriating myself, Xiao Li was back.

"Excuse Me," she said. "I talked to my husband. He made an appointment at Chaoyang Hospital. Just to check, before—" Again, she made that slashing motion across her lower gut.

"Okay," I said. "Of course."

We could see the red lettering of Chaoyang Hospital from the elevator landing. A dignified block of glass and steel, it promised a quality of medical expertise unavailable in a neighborhood clinic in the hinterlands of Beijing.

"Do you have pain?" I asked.

"No," she grinned dismissively, and went back to work.

A few days later, she returned with her diagnosis.

"At Chaoyang Hospital they said the pregnancy is okay," she announced, slapping a manila folder of reports down on the counter.

"What?"

"Yes!" She grinned. "It's okay!"

"Wonderful," I remembered to say. "But how?"

"I don't know. That other doctor—" She gave a dismissive jerk of the chin.

"So you will have a baby!"

"Yes," she said. "I will try. We'll see."

"Wonderful," I said again.

I stopped myself from asking about the job.

I already knew the answer, anyway.

Chapter 9

Xiao Li would quit her job and go. There remained only the question of time. Ever since I'd gotten pregnant, it seemed as if absolutely everything were nothing but a question of time.

"My husband wants me to stop working," Xiao Li told me.

"What do you want?"

"I want to finish this year."

"So you'll work until January?"

"Yes."

It was already October. I wasn't sure why she wanted to work those two extra months, but I was glad for the time. Xiao Li was the only tried and trusted babysitter I had.

"You need to develop a network," scolded a single mother friend who'd somehow flourished as a globe-trotting diplomat while raising her son. "You need at least three babysitters on rotation."

This advice sounded reasonable and yet utterly detached from my reality. I couldn't imagine where I'd find three distinct babysitters. Come to think of it, I'd never heard anybody in Beijing use the word *babysitter*. There were family members, if you were Chinese, or there were *ayis*. The idea of hiring a near stranger to keep an eye on the kids for a few hours—nobody I knew did that.

I had grown fond of some of the *ayis* who worked for friends, but it was a breach of unspoken protocol to ask another family's *ayi* to babysit. I'd be expected to first consult the mother of the family, and even if she agreed, she would secretly resent the favor. She would think I was trying to poach her nanny; she would be irritated to think of the *ayi* wasting her energy on another family. The situation would force her to confront her own submerged sense that she held a claim over the life of this woman—and she would resent all of that.

"It's too late now," I told my friend crossly.

"No, it's not," she insisted. "This will happen to you over and over until you set up a good network."

"Maybe."

"Seriously, I've been through this." She pushed ahead with surety and briskness. "You need to think in terms of networks instead of focusing on individuals."

"Duly noted," I grumbled.

Let alone three, I could hardly face the prospect of looking for one *ayi*. I dreaded having to replace Xiao Li.

"You should have changed earlier," a Japanese mother from our building said bluntly. "I read if you want to change nanny you should do it before the baby turns one. After that, they are traumatized."

My life seemed to have devolved into a maze of faces pointing out my mistakes and failures and shortcomings—usually when it was too late to change course.

"Noted," I told her sourly.

"What?"

"I get it," I said, "but it's too late."

"I'm just saying."

As for Tom, he couldn't get Xiao Li out of the house fast enough. As far as he was concerned, she was nothing more than her technical identity: a worker sent forth by the agency, quickly found and easily replaced.

"We should all move on," he said. "Start looking for somebody else."

"I don't want to find somebody else."

"Are you serious?" he said. "Why? We'll find somebody better."

"You don't realize how good she is."

"I have confidence that we can find any number of great nannies in this city of millions of people."

"Max loves her," I said.

"All the more reason," he argued. "The longer she stays the harder it will be to separate them."

"I'm working now," I finally told him plainly. "And once she leaves, I don't know how long it will be before I can work again. I want to hang on to this status quo for as long as it lasts."

He said nothing.

"Can you understand that?"

"Okay," he said.

It had all, somehow, gone wrong. Xiao Li was hired so that I could peel some attention from my child and reapply it to my work. That had happened, but only in precarious flashes. A nanny, I was learning, was not a day-care center. She was not a village. She was not a gadget who showed up and simplified life without complication. Xiao Li was a human being, and her problems had become my own. Maybe, as Tom kept saying, this entanglement signaled a lack of professional boundaries on my part. *But it couldn't have been otherwise,* I thought, *unless I lacked all human emotion.*

Every woman who hires another woman for childcare must struggle along this continuum. Emotion is injected and then removed from these relationships in a constant and nonsensical flux. At the whim of the employer, family sentiments are first amplified, then denied. Housekeepers and nannies who too aggressively assert the rights of the formal employment relationship tend to be harshly criticized. My thoughts rang with remembered voices of friends. These conversations boiled around me all the time. With the mothers in my building. With the women in our baby group. With my working mother friends.

It's just a job to them.

You treat them like members of the family, but you should see what happens when they leave. Suddenly all they care about is the reference letter and money.

I thought she cared about us. I mean, the kids. They cried. And suddenly she was like a stranger. Her whole face was different. She walked out the door like it was nothing.

It reminded me of a joke one of my Russian colleagues used to tell: *I thought it was love, but she asked me for twenty dollars.*

The punch line is the same: Even if love appears incidentally, that was never the point. It's survival. But when children are involved, it's hard to see things dispassionately. Who wouldn't like to enjoy the benefit of familial love without the inconvenience and inevitability? A family you can hire and fire?

We delude ourselves.

In those final weeks with Xiao Li, these uncomfortable ideas pinched at my thoughts.

"I would love to have you come back," I'd assure her, "when you are ready."

"Yes," she'd agree. "I also want."

This exchange had the sheen of sugar icing. There was no deal, no negotiation, no promise on either side.

Meanwhile, we lived with the inconvenience of new life. Clatters of falling brooms, furniture shoved aside, feet slapping down the hall. And then the explosion of a door; the splutter and retch of vomit. She still slept with her head twisted down onto the kitchen counter, neck bent like the stem of a stomped flower, but now the naps stretched longer.

Watching her, I remembered my own early pregnancy. Sickness had roared through my veins, congealing into a nausea every day more stubborn and strong than the day before. Thin swallows of water tasting of rust, lumbering like a wounded bear in the subway, miserably smelling every foul whiff of sewage and trash and cooking oil. Throwing up into traffic medians, behind buildings, in public toilets.

I still had my job then, but I had found small ways to get relief. I confided my condition to colleagues, slept on the office sofa, gave myself permission to produce a little less work.

In pregnancy I'd discovered one of those biological truths of womanhood that hide in plain sight: morning sickness is not a punch line or a plot device, but a severe illness that aches from the roots of the hair to the marrow of the bones.

For the first time, I wondered about all the women in the world who have no choice but to endure this sickness and keep working. Farmers and factory workers; women whose jobs were manual and grueling. Even white-collar women—who could at least sit down much of the day—suffered this crippling sickness in secret. Almost every woman I knew commiserated with my nausea because they, too, had been dreadfully ill, and yet there exists no employment protection for this stretch of early pregnancy.

We must do the essential work of the species in sickness and in secret. I guess I shouldn't have been surprised: We are still children when we learn to conceal the pain and blood of menstruation. We understand that the denial of our physical shell is the price of admission. We can join the men at work so long as we leave our bodies behind, or pretend that our bodies are just like their bodies. There is quiet sympathy from other women, but you must hide these things from the men because, as soon as they finish nodding gravely and sympathetically, they will remind you that this biological discrepancy was their point all along, and they will show you the door. Biology will be twisted into a rope and used to bind you.

Now here I was. Xiao Li was pregnant and puking, and I was her boss.

"You want to lie down?"

"No."

"You want to stop working? Stay home?"

"No."

"Are you sure?"

"I'm okay."

I turned back to my computer. I left it alone. I picked up her slack with the housework so that Tom wouldn't realize she wasn't physically able to do the job anymore. I encouraged her to rest whenever she wanted. I promised myself I would not pressure her or add to her load, and I didn't. At least, I don't think I did. The best I can say for myself is, I could have been worse, and she wasn't expecting anything better.

Meanwhile, I prepared for her departure.

"Xiao Li isn't going to come every day anymore," I told Max. "But she will still come sometimes."

"Why?" Max asked.

"She's going to have her own baby."

"What baby?"

"Her baby. Her own baby."

"I also want my own baby," Max replied.

"Maybe," I said.

Months are really just a few weeks. Nothing, really. The time dwindled away and then, on the appointed day, Xiao Li gave Max an extra-long hug and a kiss on his forehead. She looked into his eyes and said good-bye.

"Zaijian," he replied cheerfully.

"I love you," she said. "I will see you again," she said. "Okay," she said.

We had agreed to keep the parting quick and unemotional. We would not conceal from Max what was happening, but we would avoid a dramatic scene. Xiao Li picked up her purse and walked out the door and stepped onto the elevator.

And then she was gone.

She'd taken her work flip-flops, I realized with a start. Staring at the square of blank floor, I had the crazy sensation that I'd been tricked.

Well, of course she had taken her shoes, I told myself. *They were her shoes, perfectly good shoes.*

But she'd taken them surreptitiously. She'd waited for a moment when I was distracted to tuck them into her bag.

Looking at the empty floorboards, I knew that Xiao Li was gone. And I knew that gone was final.

Chapter 10

Next came a parade of *ayis* who didn't last.

The dour woman who scared Max. The young, pimply woman who kept the dirty dishes company while gossiping on the phone. The one who lied. The one who stank. The one who was so perfect she was whisked away to London.

"Do you think," said Tom, "that you're subconsciously looking for Xiao Li?"

"Maybe," I said. "But I can't help it."

"You should stop," he said.

"Good help is hard to find," I swanned.

I wanted him to laugh. He didn't laugh.

By the time Cheng Ayi arrived, I'd given up hope. I figured I'd spend the rest of our years in Beijing pining for an *ayi* who never came.

But Cheng Ayi was ideal. Her face had been beaten by years of sun and wind, but a quick smile punched deep dimples into her cheeks. She'd worked with the same family for seven years before coming to us, and immediately I could see why: she was energetic, intelligent, and good at everything from baking pies to inventing silly games with Max.

In truth, she was a better employee than Xiao Li had ever been. The house was shinier, the air fresher, the food tastier. Xiao Li had babied Max, but Cheng Ayi engaged him: the howls of Max laughing over Chinese riddles filled the halls.

Max still asked, from time to time, where Xiao Li was.

"Home," I'd say. "With her own babies."

"Okay," he'd agree.

My son's understated reaction surprised me. Max was an effusive toddler who hurtled across rooms to throw himself into his father's arms after a few hours apart. But Xiao Li was gone, and Max hardly reacted.

But then I noticed something: He didn't cuddle with Cheng Ayi. He didn't clamber into her lap or stroke her cheeks or giggle while she cooed into his face. All of the physical intimacy he'd shared with Xiao Li, the pantomime of a familial bond—he neither initiated nor accepted such tenderness. He rambled with Cheng Ayi through parks and chased through rooms and sang nursery rhymes with gusto. They were rambunctious together, even uproarious. Max was always delighted to see her—but never particularly sorry to say good-bye.

I wondered whether Max had learned to keep his caretakers at arm's length. Maybe he'd felt something when Xiao Li left our house that he didn't want to feel again.

I could sympathize. I was deliberately keeping Cheng Ayi at a friendly but firm distance. I hired another woman to clean and cook on the weekends. This cleared more time for family, and also gave us a potential replacement if Cheng Ayi abruptly left. I discreetly assessed the *ayis* working for my neighbors, especially foreign families due to leave China soon. I was constantly formulating backup plans and preparing for the disappearance of Cheng Ayi.

Max and I had learned, in tandem, that nannies are transitory figures. We wouldn't get too close a second time around.

———

"How's your book?" Tom asked.

We sat at a shaded sidewalk café table near our apartment, eating an early lunch before Tom headed to the bureau. Twenty floors overhead, Cheng Ayi cleaned our house while Max napped.

A few days earlier, we'd been jangled awake at dawn by a phone call from Ethel Kennedy. She had informed a startled Tom that he'd won the Robert F. Kennedy award for human rights reporting for a series of stories called "China: Living Under the Yoke." He would travel to New York to be feted.

And now here he was, asking about my book. The book I had hoped to finish before Max was born. The book that was constantly getting shoved aside while I attended to domestic crises. The topic of work—of my work and his work—remained raw. We could easily slip from this question into a bitter argument.

I took a breath and carefully stifled all of the defensive barbs clamoring for release. I took a time-buying slurp of espresso.

I'd learned a trick: Pretend that somebody else is asking. Not Tom. A friend in a café.

"It's hard to say," I began. "I'll try to explain—"

His eyes flickered; his mouth twitched. But he was just a friend in a café, so I tactfully ignored these signs of regret.

"Before I had Max, I thought the book was almost finished. You may have noticed, I always underestimate how long things are going to take." I tried to toss off an airy laugh. The man at the next table craned his neck around to see if somebody was strangling.

"But now I'm back in the swing of writing," I continued. "Finally, I can sit down almost every day and work uninterrupted for an hour or two. Do you know how huge that is?"

"I do." Was that a smirk or a smile? "That's great."

His tone was final. He was ready to change the subject. But I wasn't done.

"Now I've reached the most terrifying place yet. How can I explain?"

His fingers twitched in the direction of his phone. *Don't do it—*

"You know what it's like? It's like—"

His fingers slid and enveloped the phone; he peered into the screen.

"—eh—" I gargled air, gave him a minute to realize his rudeness. But his eyes stayed on the phone; his thumb prodded and tapped.

Pretend he's a friend in a café.

"It's like I've been trying to swim across the ocean. And now I've swum so far I can't go back. But I can't really see where I'm going. It's like that line from the Bible. We walk by faith, not by sight."

He said nothing. He was writing an email.

"So that's what . . ." I trailed off. "Are you even listening?"

"I'm listening! I get it! You feel like you're in an ocean and you don't know how the book is going to end."

"No, I do—it's not—never mind."

"Do you mind if we get the check?" He'd already tucked his blazer over his arm. "I've got to get to work."

"Yeah," I said bitterly. "Me, too."

———

It was still like that, but basically we were happy. It was hard not to be.

The seasons swept along, Max chattered and chirped and we caught ourselves laughing. We had a beautiful small boy who spoke Mandarin and English and made our hearts sing with every smile. We had excellent childcare in the form of Cheng Ayi. I reveled in an era of unprecedented productivity and contentment. I was fit and alert from running interval sprints at the gym. I was writing. I was working. The book was taking shape.

We left Max with Cheng Ayi and went out to eat and drink with friends. On the weekends our family of three picnicked in ancient parks and hiked the Great Wall and visited the zoo.

At Chinese New Year we feasted on soup dumplings and sesame-studded greens and vinegar cucumbers. We followed the lion dancers as they snaked and meandered through the neighborhood. We let Max stay up late to watch fireworks splash and fade over the rooftops.

We were finally enjoying China as a family. Life had become fun again.

Too much fun.

By the time the Year of the Snake broke over Beijing, I was pregnant again—I just hadn't realized it yet.

———

"I wonder what this one will be like."

"It's really hard to imagine."

"What if it's another baby just like Max?"

"What if it's totally different?"

"What if it's a girl?"

"What if it's another boy?"

A new baby! A new love! We were thrilled. We were terrified.

"At least this time," I said tentatively, "we know the hard part passes. It isn't endless."

Tom pushed his glasses up and rubbed his eyes.

"Please," he finally said. "I can't think about it."

"Everybody says the second baby is easier."

"I don't want to get our hopes up."

"Well, it can't be harder," I said. "That would be impossible."

"Let's stop talking about it."

The nausea had faded, and the rest of the pregnancy looked smooth. Max was thriving, Cheng Ayi was brilliant, and I would finish my novel. I was close now. I couldn't see how I could fall short. What could happen?

Something happened. Tom was offered a job. He'd work on investigations and projects, report to an editor he adored, and make more money. I knew he had to accept. This was the proverbial offer too good to refuse. I knew if I convinced him to say no, the untaken job would shadow us for years to come.

But there was a catch: The job was in New Delhi.

Slowly, sickeningly, the truth soaked into my mind: I wasn't going to spend the pregnancy finishing my book.

I would spend it moving our family to India.

———

Xiao Li came over one last time to say good-bye. She was waiting for me in the lobby when I biked home from the farmers' market. Her face had pillowed into softness; her stomach was firm and round. As the elevator climbed through the floors, she turned to me abruptly.

"You have my reference letter?"

"Oh. Of course. Yes." Had the letter been her only reason for coming?

Inside the apartment, she and Cheng Ayi exchanged polite greetings and appraised each other with cold curiosity. Max marched Xiao Li to his room to show off his books and toys. I could hear them chattering in Mandarin down the hallway as I printed and signed the letter.

She had brought him a present: a yellow T-shirt with some garbled English about mustard, and a pair of gray shorts with a monkey's face printed on one leg.

"Here you go." I handed her the letter.

"Thank you," she said. "I'll go now."

"You don't want to stay for lunch?"

"No, thank you," she sang sweetly.

Max came behind me and wrapped his arms around my legs, staring gravely at Xiao Li.

"Say bye-bye to Xiao Li, sweetheart."

"Bye-bye," he murmured.

I looked at him and felt a stab of pained confusion. She'd only stirred up Max's feelings. If all she wanted was the letter, I could have met her somewhere or even left it at the front desk . . .

I opened the door and watched her step out over the threshold. She smiled and blushed and—I realized in a rush—tears shone in her eyes.

"Good-bye," I said.

"You're beautiful," she blurted.

"No," I said.

"Thank you," I said.

"You're beautiful," I said.

And then she was gone.

PART TWO

PASSAGE TO INDIA

Chapter 11

I agreed to move our family to India with one explicit condition: I would hire domestic staff guiltlessly and lavishly. I'd outsource shopping, meal planning, cooking, cleaning, and laundry. It was Tom's career that pushed us into India, but I was determined that my work, too, should benefit. I set out to arrange a household where I was free from everything except spending time with my children and writing.

Once again, global economics were on my side. Labor in India was even cheaper than in China. The salary of a full-time worker, generously paid by local standards, made almost zero impact on our household budget. And so, on our very first day in Delhi, I started searching for a nanny.

We'd touched down in the dead of night. My first glimpses of India had been ill-lit vignettes framed in taxi windows: market stalls tarped for night; wild dogs staggering in gutters; bodies dead asleep on pavement. Everything indistinct in the queasy glow of sulfur street-lights and gathering rain; everything falling slowly apart in the monsoon molder. At last the taxi had stopped before a tower of serviced apartments that was very clean, very modern, and annexed to a great gleaming behemoth of a shopping mall. We'd brushed our teeth with bottled water and fallen into a dreamless stupor, all three and a half of us stretched across the king bed: Tom, Max, and heavily pregnant me. Tom's phone alarm had chirped in the morning. He showered and disappeared.

I looked at Max, and Max looked at me. What could he understand of this enterprise—moving countries, shipping goods, carrying a baby in my stomach?

"You want breakfast?"

"Yeah!"

At the buffet I piled his plate with rubbery pancakes, greasy chicken sausages, sliced papaya, and pineapple. The coffee was sour, but I drank a pot all the same, milk curdling in the cup.

Back in our suite I opened the curtains and examined the city by day. Misgiving crept through my gut. The landscape did not match my imagination.

Tom had visited Delhi years earlier. He'd described flocks of green parrots nesting in palm trees, crumbling Mughal tombs, wild sprays of tropical flowers. He'd invited me to fly to India and visit the Taj Mahal, but news broke in Beirut and I hadn't gone. India had lingered between us ever since as a symbol of romance and missed chances.

Now I was greeted by faceless towers and vacant lots. With its bland architecture and listless men and drifts of rubbish, this part of Delhi resembled a hundred other vaguely postapocalyptic towns I'd never hoped to call home.

And there was much to do. Tom had immediately rushed back into full-tilt reporting work, so the project of settling our family fell to me. We had no house, no car, no babysitter, no nothing. No nothing, and everything took forever. Everything involved taxi rides through choked streets to cramped markets where shops could be reached only via precarious stairs. The walkways were crowded and cars loomed close and Max wobbled on his feet, so I'd hoist him onto my hip and stagger upstairs, lugging a swollen belly and a toddler the size of a German shepherd.

I needed a cell phone and a SIM card. I needed a doctor to deliver my baby. I needed to figure out where to buy groceries so I could fix lunch in our tiny kitchen. I needed a power strip. I needed to take the power strip back and exchange it for one that worked. I needed bleach solution to soak our fruits and vegetables. I needed fruits and vegetables. I needed to go back and find out why they hadn't activated the SIM card. I needed passport pictures. I needed to go back and pick up the passport pictures. I needed to go back yet again and pitch a total pregnant lady fit so they'd finally activate the SIM card. I needed mosquito repellant.

In our spare time, Max and I cruised Delhi with a real estate agent. She wore pantsuits and carried clipboards and was optimistic about everything. We toured shining, brand-new apartments near Deer Park and elegant webs of shadowy marble in Jor Bagh and stiff colonial parlors in Golf Links.

The rent was too high; the commute too long; the street too noisy. Tom had announced that he wouldn't live next to a construction site—and now I realized that virtually every block in New Delhi was under construction. We kept looking, and looking more.

––––––

Then Mary came to us.

I started to write "we found Mary"—but that doesn't feel true. Mary cannot languish until found; she must have been the one who did the finding. She is the taker, the chooser—a woman of action and decision, always and ever, amen.

She came to us from a throwaway line on a listserv: "She is a wonderful lady, handles kids and babies extremely well."

I knew the brevity of this ad was probably a bad sign. Most outgoing employers expiate their guilt with reference letters so lavish they qualify as fiction. The women are "amazing," "fabulous," "indispensable"; they are a melding of Mary Poppins and Florence Nightingale, so DON'T MISS YOUR CHANCE to hire them!

This false advertising, of course, only heightens the disillusionment when these saintly figures feed the kids Tootsie Rolls and microwave popcorn for lunch or fill the cabinet with unwashed dishes or give everybody food poisoning.

But I was a beggar, not a chooser—pregnant and exhausted and desperate for childcare. I called and she came.

Other candidates had sniffed and twitched, peering anxiously around the hotel suite as if our temporary home was a harbinger of familial instability.

Not Mary. She sat with her feet firmly planted, rested her hands on generous thighs, and regarded me intelligently from a broad, calm face. Her family roots lay in the borderlands between Bhutan and India. She had studied with the nuns in Darjeeling. She was a widow with two teenage children who had been raised in Assam by her mother-in-law.

I waited for the catch, but it didn't come. Mary had always cared for twins. She'd worked for years in the home of the U.S. consul general. She'd taken courses in first aid and child development. She was fluent in multiple languages. Her police verification had been done, and she'd undergone a background check in order to work on the grounds of the American embassy.

I told her I wasn't sure where we'd be living but named some of the neighborhoods under consideration.

"No problem, Madame."

I explained she'd have to start working for us in the hotel suite, which I understood was unorthodox and awkward.

"No problem, Madame."

"You don't have to call me Madame."

"Okay, Madame."

"No, I mean really—"

"All right, Madame."

"Oh . . ." I was too embarrassed to continue.

For five and a half days a week, she'd get a starting salary of 15,000 rupees a month, or about $235. To her monthly pay we'd add 500 rupees for her phone usage, plus another 2,000 for bus money and lunch—a total of about $40. We'd pay her medical costs, and twice a year we'd give her $50 to buy clothes. For overtime, which she was free to take or leave, she'd earn $1.50 an hour. She'd get a pay raise after six months, and every year thereafter.

Mary didn't quibble, and I wasn't surprised. I'd done my research, and I couldn't find anybody who paid more. I'd heard of full-time domestic workers in Delhi earning as little as $100 a month.

Mary explained, in turn, her only condition: she didn't want to live in the servants' quarters that come attached to many middle-class Delhi apartments. Her husband was a Nigerian man she'd met through church, and it would be uncomfortable—really, it would be impossible—for him to live among the servants of India.

"People are a little bit racist," she explained gently.

I assured her we didn't care where she lived.

She came like that. She came barreling, bellowing, smiling. She forgave us our ignorance.

One Saturday morning, torrential rain pounded the city. Max stood in the window and marveled over the blur of endless silver: "The rain is *on*!" he cried.

Mary phoned. "Rain is too much. I won't be able to reach."

"Mary can't come because of the rain," I told Tom.

"What?"

"That's what she said."

"Call her back," he said. "Let me talk to her."

I handed him the phone. "Mary!" he said. "Listen, you need to come to work today. I don't care how you get here, but you've got to come."

"What did she say?" I demanded disapprovingly as he handed back the phone.

"Nothing. She said okay."

"Are you sure—" I groped for words.

"She can't just miss work every time it rains," Tom interrupted incredulously. "We can't set a precedent like that."

News alerts flashed. Mary's neighborhood had flooded. The subway was closed. Buses couldn't pass. State of emergency.

"Oh God," Tom said. "Why didn't she say how bad it was?"

"You made it sound like you'd fire her if she couldn't get here," I said crossly.

We called to turn her back but couldn't get through. Tom fretted and frowned, pacing guiltily by the windows and dialing Mary's number over and over. I played quietly with Max.

At last, a knock on the door. Mary was soaked to the skin, her pants rolled up to her knees. I braced myself for a fiery denouncement and resignation.

"I'm so sorry," Tom blurted out. "I didn't understand how serious the rains were. I never would have made you come—"

"Okay, sir, okay," she said.

And then she laughed from the bottom of her stomach.

———

When Max napped, everybody took a mandatory break. This forced rest was a remnant of my former mania to preserve silence: I'd repackaged my anti-noise patrols as a generous allotment of "downtime" for all. I'd withdraw into our bedroom to work on my book, and once she was convinced that I really, truly didn't want her to do anything while Max slept, Mary took to curling up on the sofa and slipping into snores.

One afternoon she sprang up and headed for the door. "I'll go for toilet."

"What do you mean?" I leaned sideways and stuck my head into the living room. "Go where?"

"Downstairs, they have a bathroom."

"But we have a bathroom here. Two bathrooms."

She looked confused. "I'm not comfortable."

"Oh!"

I floundered. Either she was warning me that a particularly outlandish assault on our senses was imminent (in which case, by all means, go to the lobby!), or she had been taught that her lowly servant's bottom shouldn't sully our sanctified toilets.

Mired in an unwanted contemplation of Mary's private needs, I regretted saying anything at all.

"Well I mean—" I stammered. "If you're not comfortable, of course—"

"You don't mind?" she interrupted.

"If you use our bathroom? Of course not!"

"All right," she said shyly.

Watching her disappear into the bathroom, I was slapped by sadness. Mary had been treated as an untouchable—banned from the family toilets. Used to the more assertive and plucky *ayis* of Beijing, I was taken aback.

I was new to India. I didn't know yet that domestic staff are routinely forbidden to sit on their bosses' furniture, drink from their cups, or eat from their plates. I didn't understand that, for millions of women across India, domestic work was not a path to upward mobility, but a life sentence. Society deemed them more respectable than sex workers, but only just. Their willingness to work in other people's homes marked them as dirty and undesirable.

I didn't know any of that, but I would learn.

———

A scene from my past life as a reporter materialized down the street: throngs of journalists and network satellite trucks crowded the road. Curious to know which international news event was unfolding at the courthouse by the mall, I texted Tom at work.

"It's the rape case," he replied.

That was all he had to say. The rape of Jyoti Singh was an internationally decried outrage. I'd even known there was a mall involved, but I hadn't realized—and now wished I hadn't learned—that it was the very same mall we now called home. Jyoti Singh was twenty-three years old. She was lured onto a bus and raped with metal rods until her organs were shredded, then dumped for dead on the side of the road. Now the rapists were on trial just down the block. This was one of our first windows onto India.

I sensed there was also something unusual brewing within the hotel, but at first I couldn't put my finger on it. At breakfast I noticed a statistically improbable concentration of babies and gay couples. Most of the couples were white foreigners who did not appear to know one another but were still bound by a camaraderie from which our family was tacitly excluded. They exchanged meaningful looks, stopped to admire the babies, and muttered into one another's ears. Slowly I gleaned the truth from fragments of overheard conversation: a prominent surrogacy clinic stood nearby, and the hotel was popular among couples traveling to India to claim their newborns.

The families were frazzled, jet-lagged, and mired in the multinational bureaucracy required to take the babies home. Some of them had been stuck in limbo for months. And then there was me, staggering under the burden of an unmistakably inhabited womb. As I heaved myself into a chair for breakfast and deflected Max's daily pleas for doughnuts, I was not oblivious to the double takes: *Are you kidding me?* I was simultaneously the embodiment of a physical state that had been denied my fellow guests, and a noisome and not-so-picturesque glimpse into their future as parents. A heavily pregnant mother and a terrible two-year-old among the desperately infertile—just my luck.

But then, after many isolated days, a stranger finally shattered the cone of silence around us.

"Good morning," trumpeted a cheerful American accent.

I looked up. A middle-aged man stood over our table, head tilted with birdlike curiosity, mug steaming in one hand.

"Good morning," I said.

"And good morning to you." He turned to Max.

"Hello," muttered Max.

My new friends were a kindly American professor and his husband, a sweet-natured European doctor who helpfully lectured Max about protein and vitamins. They were trying to take their newborn out of India. The United States had proven complicated, so they were now shooting for Europe, where they'd camp out at a grandmother's home while tackling the American problem.

I didn't know what had inspired them to approach us, and I was too starved for conversation to care. I described the travails of house hunting; they bemoaned the months they'd lived in the hotel. We lingered over breakfasts, bolting one mug of coffee after another.

Within a few weeks, they were gone.

"Racing out" read the hand-scrawled note. "Managed to book flight. Very nice to meet you and Max. Please be in touch."

I was happy for them. They had been truly empathetic, reaching out because they could see, even through their own frustrations, that I was having a tough time. They'd been jovial and kind with Max. They'd been considerate, leaving a note when they could have vanished off to the airport. These were people, I thought, who would make great parents. I was glad they'd found a way to complete their family.

But after all the time I'd spent contemplating motherhood and the erasure of women, I also found the pervasive atmosphere of surrogacy unnerving. The women who carried the babies were nowhere to be seen in the hotel. Their bodies were rented as incubators by rich families from around the planet. The fetuses of wealthy parents took oxygen from their circulatory systems and siphoned nutrients from their blood. The embryos leached calcium to make bones, leaving soft teeth and weakened skeletons. But these women were not mothers; the babies were not theirs—the children were grown for export.

I tried to imagine lacing my hands over my pregnant belly and knowing I had no right to love the creature stirring within. I tried to imagine, but came up dry.

I wasn't condemning or condoning—the reality was simply beyond my imagination. Some women—even most—must pass through the process with perfect pragmatism. We all sell something—why not a womb? The money is good; the money is badly needed.

"I don't like it," Mary said flatly.

I had asked during Max's nap: *Do you know what these families are doing?*

Oh yes, she'd certainly known. Mary knew about surrogacy from the supply side. She knew women who'd carried babies for cash.

"The money is good. But once the baby comes, nobody takes care of these girls," Mary said. "They do it over and over. They get sick. They die young. They give them the money and send them away. I have seen this too many times."

The words came out fast, spilled into air. Then she caught herself. I'd asked her opinion without revealing my own. She'd seen me chatting with the couples downstairs.

"But I don't know," she added quickly.

"I think you do know," I said. "I think you know more than me. But—these guys here—this clinic is very reputable. I think it's probably not as bad as what you've seen."

You're right, but it's not our fault. My friends and I are clean. Of course, you are right, in general, but it has nothing to do with us, specifically.

I'd heard the stories, too: Women kept hostage in dormitories lest they harm the payload in their bellies, forced to display swelling bumps to faraway couples via Skype.

But some women couldn't get pregnant and some couples didn't have a womb between them. Adoption was tricky. The world brimmed with unwanted babies but it was arduous, slow, and expensive to acquire custody of a child. Some Indian families starved girl babies rather than waste food on them, and yet it was both costly and logistically complex to adopt a baby. It was all arranged so poorly, giving everyone so few choices. And I myself had wanted a baby desperately.

Still I wondered: Why was it that, whatever you desired, you could find a poor woman to sell it? You could buy an ass or a vagina or a mouth or a tongue. You could buy a womb, a human greenhouse for unfurled human seed. You could buy hands to change diapers, voices to sing nursery rhymes, backs and arms to carry babies, breasts to flow with milk. You could buy a video of a woman cruelly insulted and then gagged with a penis until she vomits into a dog bowl. Such videos are popular; men watch them. But, of course, men never admit to watching such things. When it comes to culpability, it is always somebody else.

Prevailing culture dictates that we must separate these strands into individual phenomena: sex work, pornography, domestic labor, and surrogacy. But, in one sense, all of those transactions exist along the same continuum—you may buy anything from a woman and discard the rest.

I'm complicit. I do it directly and deliberately. The women I've rented are sweeping the floor outside my office even as I type; I hear the swish of their brooms over the boards.

And so, reader, are you. You may think you aren't, but you probably are. Those clothes and the food you buy cheap, do you know the supply chain, can you trace them back to their raw materials? You can't, and you don't want to. I promise you: Nothing is cheap by accident. You've eaten slavery and worn it against your skin; you've slept in its embrace. I don't mean metaphorical slavery. I mean plain slavery, the kind that was supposed to be abolished long ago.

The other argument is that if a woman is paid, then that's empowerment and shut up about the rest. Who am I to say an illiterate villager shouldn't rent her uterus to rich Americans to earn school fees for her son? Who am I to say a young woman doesn't enjoy getting choked for the cameras? Who am I to judge?

Who am I to feel guilty for renting a mother away from her children? Who am I to feel guilty? Who am I?

I'm not sure anymore because the women won't say my name. Excuse Me. Madame.

There is no quick fix, so you might as well punt. I should think about it later, when my children are grown and I have more time and I won't risk collapsing my family by trying to force my husband to stay home so I can hold a job I don't even want. When at last I have nothing to lose, it will be safe to think honestly.

I traded emails recently with one of the fathers I'd befriended during those early days in New Delhi. He was kind and generous. He offered to send a care package from the United States.

He'd recently turned down the chance to return to India for work. India was a memory he wasn't ready to face.

"I demurred," he wrote. "It was too close to the forced internment. Perhaps some time when it's faded a bit. Perhaps."

Maybe he didn't want to confront the supply chain, either.

Chapter 12

Morning in the hotel room. Mary had taken Max to prowl the mall. I took a few deep breaths, glared at our rumpled bed, and sat down to work. In my mind I slipped out of India and into the chamber that was otherwise sealed, into the forever winter of an invented Moscow, into rooms and streets where my characters had adventures and love affairs and no babies. My eyes drifted to the mirror behind my laptop— I had repurposed a vanity table as a writing desk. Drab gray strands stained my hair; pinprick pupils dotted inhumanly pale eyes; slamming sun and pregnancy hormones had reddened and splotched my skin.

I yanked my eyes back to the screen. I couldn't afford to get derailed by my appearance. I invented a scene, painted backdrops, created conversation. I pounded out two thousand words. They might not be the right words, but they were close. The book was coming together.

It was enough; it was a good day's work. When Max got back I hugged him, touched the bones of his slim shoulders, smelled his hair. We had a routine: after breakfast I sat down for an hour, sometimes an hour and a half, of sacrosanct writing time while Max and Mary trawled the mall.

I was writing, I was working.

I was in despair.

I wasn't going to finish. More scenes remained undrafted than could possibly be written in the remaining weeks before the baby was due. This impossibility was an especially miserable realization since I'd already failed to finish the same book before my first baby was born—and two years had evaporated in between.

At least this time I knew what was coming: sleep deprivation; anxiety and mood swings; diminishment of self; marital readjustment. One year, give or take, hacked off the trajectory of my career.

Again, always and ever, it was a problem of time. Women pay for their families with great hoardings of time. They pay—we pay—with life itself. Show me a working mother who hasn't learned to traffic time. We spend and save; barter and beg and quibble with hours and months; write off a weekend here, a day there.

I was ready for all of that. I wanted the baby so hungrily I'd shorten my life or wreck my body. I was prepared to complete one less book than I might otherwise have published over my lifetime. I wanted the baby, and I would make the trade. No woman needs to convince me that she would give her life for her children, because every mother has already given her life for her children. That is the very first thing that happens.

I had struggled mightily to resurrect the book after Max was born. It had felt, at first, exhausting and foreign—like trying to finish a story somebody else had started. My heart and my brain and my life were shredded, but the words on the screen had not changed. Now I'd go to another hospital and have another baby, and maybe I would change all over again.

For now, I had to swallow another failure, and I had to do so in private, because listening to other people argue that it wasn't a failure or that I shouldn't mind—that was more than I could stand. At the very least, I could keep the truth: I had tried, for the second time, to finish this book. I had tried so damn hard. And I'd failed.

My family had spent my dwindling supply of energetic hours on moving to India. I'd given my time to Tom, so that he could rush off to the office that very first morning and every morning thereafter. I'd given my time to Max, who was scared and unsettled and needed a parent down through the hours. I'd given my time to hunting for apartments, so that we'd have a good place to live by the time the baby came.

My time had been used as capital. It had been invested in the family future to improve our collective position.

Well, fair enough. That's the sort of thing we do in families. I paid slices of time; I paid life; maybe I paid brain cells, or a book or two. I paid and it's gone. My babies are beautiful; my heart is whole; I'm not asking for a refund.

Still it does not escape my attention that I paid in time. There is a lingering expectation that men will pay in money. But when it comes to time, it is almost always the woman who pays. And money is one thing, but time is life, and life is more.

How many ideas, how many discoveries, how much art lost because the woman spent her time somewhere else? How many ideas stillborn, how many inventions undone, how much original thought passed off quietly to a man so that he can take credit—just not to waste, not to miscarry the idea, to pass it, one way or the other, into the world?

I did it, too. I paid my time.

———

Our new apartment was a generous and rambling collection of hardwood floors and long immaculate rooms marching in clean lines toward big, bright windows. We looked out onto a vista of trees splashed by the shadows of birds of prey that circled in the sky overhead.

Down the road to the left ran the back wall of the zoo and the dank forests that grew wild on its edges. Peacocks roamed those groves and monkeys slipped, sometimes, over the wall, and we could hear the bellows of caged beasts, the white tiger who killed a man, the lions and the elephants. Life penned and caught; life flashing in sun and shadow. Life all around us, pressing in.

And our family, we were there, too. We unpacked our boxes. Our hearts and memories were wooden furniture and framed photographs and woven threads handled roughly on docks and now, at last, exploded all over the rooms.

We were there amid all that life, there in all our mess.

One day I sat with Max in the park. The neighborhood children were playing soccer under the stern instruction of their Nigerian coach. The servants' children had no money for lessons, but they clustered along the sidelines to watch. Nobody invited them to play, nor did their faces hold any hope for such an invitation. They passed the time as spectators; the afternoon offered no better entertainment. All the children in that park displayed a firm and fixed idea of their own privileges and limitations.

A rich kid who'd been playing badly noticed the servants' children watching. He tugged the sleeve of a friend, jerked his chin toward the pack of poor kids, and then, together, the two boys rushed toward them, clapping and shouting. The children scattered like ragged crows, skinny and scrambling in their tattered clothes. Having run off the poor children, the two rich kids trotted casually back to practice. The coach said nothing. The mothers watching from the benches didn't blink.

I was shocked. I looked quickly down at Max. His eyes were round and flat and impassive. I wasn't sure whether he'd seen what I'd seen or, if he had, whether he could decode its meaning. And I was scared; I felt a sick wash of doubt about this place we'd come to live.

Our Indian neighbors treated me like a lady of the house. *Madame.* Mine the front gate, mine the park, mine the living rooms where Himalayan tea steamed on silver platters and well-heeled families came and went from Paris and the Andaman Islands.

But that was only half the story of our neighborhood and its residents.

To see the other half, you had to circle around to the backyards. Behind every house stood a servants' quarter, where paint peeled and shared toilets stank and leaked water stagnated, where families packed themselves into single rooms to shiver through the winters and slept through baking summer nights on rooftops in desperate hope of a stray breeze. Children in the servants' quarters amused themselves with broken bricks and died from mumps and got scratched by wild monkeys. Within their drafty rooms the servants and their families dreamed, loathed, accepted—poised, always, to heed a call from the main house.

The neighborhood was like two medieval villages braided into each other: two different sets of roads; two different sets of schools; two different sets of lives.

Chapter 13

She trailed toward us through the traffic. My gut clenched as she came. *Stay away, little girl, please spare me your face.* She loomed in the window and drum-drum-drummed on the glass with one ashen palm, the other hand bunched toward heaven, then toward her mouth, in the universal scooping motion of begging.

Max went silent. I met her crusted eyes with an exaggerated frown. I shook my head. *No.*

She squashed her nose to the glass and stared at Max's plump thighs, the clean plastic cup at his side, his lashes on his cheeks, because he knew, he must have understood, that something shameful was happening.

Every drive through the city traced the same emotional trajectory. Every drive began with promise, with glimpses of gardens and bicycles and children and homemade kites skittering over a smudged sun.

Every drive ended in existential crisis.

Everything changed at the interchange. The red lights were the inevitable moments of psychological crash. At red lights, the beggars waited. Not too many beggars, because the men who managed the street corners were careful not to dilute their profits. They fielded a few beggars, no more, chosen for their capacity to shock. There was only a fleeting moment to shatter the composure of the passengers and send fingers digging into pockets. The beggars' faces were bleached with acid burns; they waved stumps aloft; they lacked an eye or nose. They might be hard-faced mothers who balanced moaning babies on their hips and banged hospital receipts in the window, or children with eyes too old for their bodies.

Tap tap tap.

She saw something in my face. She thought she had an opening.

"No thank you," Max muttered, repeating what I said to the teenagers who peddled dishrags and paperback novels. I did not correct him. I encouraged the fiction that we were being badgered to buy something we didn't need.

I wanted to explain that we couldn't help this child because that would only strengthen the ruthless men who had pimped her into the streets. But he was too young; he couldn't understand.

Jesus Christ, when will this light change?

I never gave the beggars any money. This was agonizing because I wanted, desperately, to give them money. I nearly drowned in shame and self-loathing at those red lights, but I held the line. No money. I had read the reports of NGOs that worked with street children. I understood there was a mafia: a grotesque man around the corner, looking nonchalant. This man was a predator; he maimed and kidnapped and beat. He was the one. He would get the money.

But always the doubt came creeping. Perhaps what I'd read wasn't true. Maybe this particular child could keep the money. And maybe she could see straight through my skin, maybe this small prick of doubt held her fast in the window. She was an expert at reading faces like mine. Maybe she knew something about me I couldn't guess myself.

I may be a fallen Catholic, but my mind will never be free of catechism. Easier for a camel to go through a needle's eye than for a rich man to enter the kingdom of God. Whatsoever you do to the least of my people. First shall be last and last shall be first.

Still I sat with cracking heart and tried to fill my eyes with hard meanness and say no. I forced myself to make ruthless eye contact, and I said no.

When will this light change?

From the front seat, an eruption of sound. Mary was laughing. She laughed and stretched an arm back to nudge Max and pointed at the girl and laughed again. As if it were a performance put on for our benefit, the children not desperate waifs but puckish actors. The laugh was a bomb in the car—an interruption, a shock, a splintering. But I did not contradict her laughter because I had nothing more coherent to offer.

Red to green. Gas. Freedom. Go. Involuntary sigh. Thank God.

The taxi driver punched the gear shift and glared ahead. I wanted to defend myself; to explain that I wasn't stingy or cruel. Max sat withdrawn in unfathomable thoughts. I floundered and scrambled in my mind, contemplating the filthy glorious mysteries of luck, of being born with things, the meaning of money, murder by poverty. It was immoral to have and pointless to give. I could give away everything, and it would be nothing. The money would dry like dew, and we would join the impoverished masses, my children sleeping in dirt and begging from cars, waiting miserably for the hour of a death that would deliver us. And yet if I did nothing I was complicit. My soft life was an obscenity.

As we drove away Mary mused, "I feel pity for these children."

Still her laugh hung in the car.

That was Mary, looking at all the misery in the world and laughing into its face.

———

"Madame," Mary said one day. "You want to buy a lottery ticket?"

The words strung together too fast.

"What do you mean?"

"Our church," she fumbled. "They are raising money for a new church. In Faridabad. They are having lottery."

"Uh-huh?"

"The prize is very nice. You want a ticket?"

"How much do they cost?"

"Madame," she said. "It's one thousand rupees."

"For one ticket?"

"Yes." She gave a forced bleat of laughter.

"That's a lot."

"Yes," she agreed. "Too much. We cannot. But I thought you and Sir—"

"Um." I pictured Mary's husband bragging to church friends that she'd landed a new position with an American family. The pastor pushing tickets into her hands. *Take more, they can afford it!* The image stirred an obscure annoyance.

"The prize is very nice," she pressed.

"What is it? The prize?"

"I don't know," she fake-laughed again. "It's nice, only."

"I have to talk to Tom," I said. "We don't usually donate to religious things."

This was a stall. I didn't need Tom's permission to buy a lottery ticket or anything else. But Mary accepted the explanation as if it were obvious and predictable.

"I'll talk to Tom and let you know," I repeated.

This, I confess, was a tactic I'd started deploying in India against the claustrophobia of shared language. Now that everybody spoke English, I couldn't pretend to understand less than I did. Flustered or frazzled, seeking escape from an awkward conversation or attempting to absolve myself of responsibility, I invariably invoked Tom.

"I'll talk to Tom," I'd say, and later: "Tom said he doesn't want to do it. I'm sorry."

When near strangers work in your home, everybody tends to adopt a role. This is an instinctive and inevitable distancing technique, the only way to carve out some corners of privacy in an otherwise distastefully intimate comingling. As we settled into India, I assigned profiles: bad cop for Tom, good cop for me. Tom escaped to his office, after all, but I was stuck in the house, dependent upon goodwill. Better to hum along, bright and helpless. The more I pretended to defer to Tom, the more he loomed in the household imagination as a benign but unapproachable dictator. I was often pressed to "ask Sir" for schedule changes or salary advances. It was understood that I could not dispense such favors without permission.

I was liked better than Tom, but that turned into a disadvantage. Tom's clothes were ironed, folded perfectly, and arranged in storeroom-tidy stacks beneath dangling lavender sachets in his wardrobe. Mine were wrinkled and wadded haphazardly into overstuffed drawers. If Tom asked for a cup of tea, people scurried. I'd listen to the cups clattering with envy and annoyance—we could ask people for tea? If I wanted a cup of tea, I fixed it for myself.

And I accepted these conditions—an imbalance of my own creation—with pure hypocrisy.

At night, when the staff had left us alone in our shining rooms and Max was sound asleep, I excoriated Tom for his rarefied status. I blamed his tone of voice and carriage for reeking of patriarchal authority. I never copped to creating the character of "Sir." I wasn't even fully conscious of having done so. Instead, I implied—falsely, unjustly—that Tom was a closet chauvinist whose attitudes had been detected and embraced by the like-minded residents of India.

Now Mary wandered off to await the decree of Sir. I turned to my laptop and tried to get back to work, but I was distracted. The lottery tickets stuck in my mind. Once again, the cynical, suspicious tendencies I'd nurtured as a journalist took over. Maybe Mary wasn't a pious widow. Maybe she was a hustler. I decided to check out her story.

A few clicks, and I'd tracked down a handful of parish phone numbers for a Catholic church in Faridabad. After a few disconnected lines and busy signals, I finally got through.

"Hello, my name is Megan Stack and I'm—um—" I stammered to the secretary who answered. Muscle memory had taken over; I'd started to introduce myself as a reporter for the *Los Angeles Times*. I coughed weakly.

"I want to check whether there is a lottery," I continued, realizing how peculiar and pushy I sounded without the journalistic excuse.

"Sorry?"

"A lottery." I spoke very slowly lest the confusion be linguistic. "Is there a lottery?"

Silence.

"Because somebody tried to sell me tickets."

"Tickets?"

"Tickets. To build a church."

"A church?"

"A new church. In Faridabad. New church. This is Faridabad, right?"

"This Faridabad, yes."

"So. Somebody tried to sell me tickets. To a lottery. For a new. Church. I wanted to know. If it's true."

Silence.

"Do you know?"

"I don't know."

"Can you find out?"

"You call back in five minutes."

I called back in five minutes. Again in ten minutes. Again in fifteen minutes. Nobody answered.

I sat on the couch and felt terrible. I'd already gotten fond of Mary, and already she'd started tinkering with my nerves. She interrupted when I tried to explain. She hung up the phone when I was still speaking. She talked too loud, and she never stopped moving. Her pointless hurrying gave me a wild, disoriented feeling. I wanted her to come into the rooms carefully and slowly, to adapt herself to our family, the way we spoke, the way we did things.

Instead she told stories and created situations. She wanted to involve me in her things. She wanted to involve herself in my things. She wanted to make herself useful, to make me useful, to rearrange raw materials.

That night I told Tom about the lottery.

"Sounds weird," he said cheerfully. "Let's not do it."

"Okay."

"Unless you want to," he added. "I'm not the Catholic in the family."

"I don't want to."

"A thousand rupees is pretty steep for a lottery in these parts," he mused.

"That," I agreed, "is what I said."

The next morning I tried to keep my tone light.

"Oh, Mary," I said. "Tom said we shouldn't do the church lottery. I'm sorry."

"Okay, Madame," she said quickly. "No problem."

————

Here is what I knew about Mary at first: She was Bhutanese. Her first husband was dead. Her current husband was a Nigerian migrant who bought human hair from temples and sold it to craftsmen who made wigs and extensions.

She never missed church on Sunday morning. She attended monthly all-night prayer vigils that she believed were the secret to health and luck. She prayed the rosary twice a day. She took Mother Teresa's autobiography off our shelf and curled up to read while Max slept. After a few weeks, she finished with Mother Teresa and picked up a travel book about Bhutan. I watched her pore over the pages.

"Bhutan must be beautiful," I said.

"Yes," she said.

"I've always wanted to go."

"You should go."

"What is it like?"

"It is very nice."

The longer I knew Mary, the less I understood her. She mangled information and botched basic instructions. If I asked her to turn the water heater on, she turned it off. If I told her to feed Max anything but those drumsticks, she'd feed him nothing but those drumsticks. There was some failure of hearing or comprehension or memory—or maybe, I sometimes thought, she just couldn't stop rushing long enough to listen.

It was confusing, because she was also brilliant. She never forgot a face or the location of a home, no matter how long ago she'd visited. She could name, with uncanny accuracy, the location of a broken Hot Wheels car or the castanets from my college flamenco class or any other small object gone missing in our rambling apartment. "In the cabinet next to the sink, beside the potatoes, in a pink bowl," she'd say. And she was right, always right.

She was a glib talker; she could make anything sound good. Non sequiturs, clichés, abstract declarations—they all fell from her mouth sounding like ageless wisdom.

"If everyone is happy, then who will know sadness?"

When she said that, Mary was folding blankets over the sides of Max's bed, propping his stuffed animals against the wall. It was morning, and Mary was telling me a jerky and discontinuous story while she tidied the bedroom. She'd been an orphan. Her brother was gay. Her husband had died in a motorcycle crash.

"This is woman's life," she said.

There was nothing left to straighten. Everything was put away. Mary fiddled with her fingers, shifted her weight, gaze climbing the walls of Max's room.

"What did you do after your husband died?"

"My mother-in-law," she said. "I asked her, 'What should I do?' She said, 'I will take care of the children, you go to work.'"

Mary's mother-in-law had quit her job in the tea fields, taken custody of her grandchildren, and handed Mary over to an "agent" who recruited village girls to work as maids in the city. The mother-in-law had raised the children ever since while Mary earned the money.

"Did you want to come here?" I asked.

"It was okay." Mary laughed uneasily.

"But it wasn't your idea."

"In our culture, the mother-in-law decides."

"Even when your husband is dead?"

"Even now," she said. "If I need to make a decision, I should go to her and ask."

The agent had brought Mary to Delhi by train and deposited her at the home of an Indian family.

"Thank God, they were good to me," Mary said.

At first she never spoke of her early working days except to say, flatly, that men were brutal by nature and that it was simply impossible for a woman to live alone in the Indian capital. It took her two years of work to pay back the agent, she told me. Only then was she free.

"This is life," she said. "This is God's will."

As far as I could understand, Mary's mother-in-law had seized Mary's children and sold Mary into a sort of bondage. But Mary didn't see it that way. The agent had incurred great expense, Mary pointed out. Naturally, she needed to be repaid.

"So if your husband hadn't died—" I didn't know how to finish the sentence. I waved a hand to indicate the child's bedroom, our house, the stretches of New Delhi beyond.

"I would never be here working," she said plainly. "A woman from a good family does not do like that unless something happens. I would be in my village, in my own place.

"This is life."

She kept saying that. *This is life.*

"Mary," I said. "You've been through so much. I honestly can't imagine."

"Yes," she smiled nervously. "If everybody is happy, then who will know sadness?"

When I type these words of Mary's or repeat them out loud, I realize they lack meaning. But when she spoke them, her thick sturdy fingers lost in the work of my home, I heard the prayer of a woman who could not dream of riches or prestige or fairy-tale love. Still she got up every morning and tried.

"Children are children," she said when I pointed out behavioral shortfalls. "They change according to their age.

"It's not easy to become mother," she told me by way of comfort.

Small words stuffed with centuries of human truth.

She smiled to herself, eyes downcast, a universal goddess enjoying a private joke. The children were passing through, we parents were ephemeral figures, but Mary would stay.

———

"Madame," Mary cried one day after taking a hurried call. "My husband is coming! He bought buffalo meat for you!"

Mary always talked in bursts of exclamation.

"What?"

"He is coming on the metro!"

"What? I—"

"You said you wanted red meat!"

"No! I didn't!" The exclamation marks were contagious. "When?"

"The other day you were saying, because you are pregnant—"

Now I remembered: I had complained to Mary that I'd gotten weak and anemic in India, where my diet was vegetarian with a side of chicken. I had confessed that I missed beef—yes, I had! I had not, however, asked her to buy meat for me.

"No, I meant—I didn't mean you should buy some."

"No problem," she said. "He was buying anyway for himself. I told him to get some for you, too."

She looked at me expectantly. I imagined the sweaty hovel where this meat would have been cleaved by some unclean blade; pictured it packed into a plastic bag and carried among shoving and sweating crowds on the metro, and my stomach rolled over. How to get out of this?

"That was really nice—"

"No problem, Madame." She smiled smugly, and I was stabbed by irritation. Mary and her husband couldn't shop for our household. Maybe next time it would be, what, some rusting piece of kitchenware, a stray puppy—

"—but I don't want the meat. I'm sorry."

"Oh . . ."

"I didn't ask you to buy it, and I just can't use it right now."

"Okay." She studied her fingers, laced together as if she were praying, and I had the horrible feeling that she was about to cry.

"Next time, please don't buy me anything unless I really, specifically ask you to." I tried to keep my voice gentle; it caught in my throat.

"No problem," she said.

I shrank away. But I was right, I told myself, I was right!

It was all so embarrassing and petty and yet inescapable; it made me feel right and wrong at the exact same moment.

———

"Madame." Mary had come so quietly I didn't hear a footfall until she was at my elbow. "Anybody is looking for cook? There is a boy in my church—"

"A child?"

"What? No, no. He is grown."

"Like how old?"

"I don't know." She flapped her hand. "Twenty-five, maybe thirty."

"So, a man."

"Yes, Madame. A boy—"

"Mary, uh, we don't usually say 'boy' unless somebody is a child." I sounded priggish, but my head was full of the racial connotations of my homeland. "It's confusing," I added lamely.

"Okay, Madame. So this boy—"

"Man." It just came out.

"Yes, Madame. This boy is sleeping on the floor with people from church. I feel pity for him."

"What does he want to do?"

"Cleaning, cooking. Whatever is there."

"He has experience?"

"Yes, very good experience. He worked a long time for an Italian family but they left India. They loved him so much."

"Okay," I said. "I'll see if anybody is looking."

I gather, from the works of Somerset Maugham and E. M. Forster, that the life of the expatriate colonial was once replete with tennis clubs, daylight gin and tonics, and recreational racism.

Nowadays, the life of the foreign neocolonial has been conquered by the Internet. I haven't played tennis since leaving the United States, and tonic no longer contains quinine—and the racism, while still detectable, has largely been repackaged as progressive-minded critiques of the country at large.

What we do have, we foreigners abroad, are listservs. If you're not on at least one listserv in your city of residence, it's like you're not even there. If you want to buy a used household appliance rather than pay a steep import tax, or recover some of the money you egregiously overpaid for some whimsical baby trifle by selling it on to the next sucker, or find out where to stay with small children on that one island where there might be endangered turtles—you consult a listserv.

Listservs are also the preferred method to advertise domestic staff and fish for applicants. It was easy to dig up a few job leads for Mary's friend, then send his phone number to the families who were hiring.

"I don't know this person," I stipulated. "But he is a friend of our lovely nanny and supposedly he has lots of experience."

The next day Mary came to me glowing.

"Rajesh is going for interviews," she enthused. "He is saying thank you. He is praying for your family."

"Tell him thanks."

"He is saying, 'Your madame is good.' He's so happy."

"Thanks," I repeated. "It's really not a big deal."

The next day Mary came back for more.

"Madame," she said. "Anybody is looking for nanny?"

I helped two more job seekers that week, and even more the next. A couple minutes of my time, a few lines typed. No problem. In exchange, Mary allowed me to bask in the glow of my own benevolence. Half her church was reportedly praying for me.

"She doesn't care about people, not like you," she said one day, describing another employer. "You have a soft heart."

"You've helped a lot of people," she said another day. "You've done a lot of good."

Eagerly I clung to these flatteries. I was still dead-eying the traffic-light beggars to get them away from the car, but at least I was also helping impoverished strangers find work. And then some more strangers, and still more.

Matching workers with job openings didn't cost me anything, and in theory it was a respectable practice. But I began to doubt myself. I couldn't put a finger on the source of my unease, but the entire arrangement had started to smell fishy.

I imagined the mothers of New Delhi chirping over their *masala chai*, comparing notes about this suspicious new American woman who kept chiming in with random candidates for baby nurses and kitchen help.

Oh yes, she emailed me, too!

And you should have seen the woman who came for the interview.

Really?

She was terrible.

What a waste of time!

Maybe that lady—what's her name? Megan something—maybe she's running an agency or something . . . ?

Maybe we should report her to the administrators . . . ?

Mary's phone chimed constantly, and the conversations lengthened. I watched through the window as she followed Max abstractedly through the park, haggling on the phone while he poked in mud puddles.

"I know this sounds crazy," I told Tom that night. "But I almost feel like she's turned it into a business. Like she's taking a cut."

"I had," Tom replied, "exactly the same thought."

"Really?"

"Yeah," he said. "Just the way she always seems so intent about it."

"Yeah."

"Well, tell her to cut it out," he said. "She needs to be paying attention to Max, not dealing on the phone all the time."

The next time Mary came and announced, "Madame—" I cut her off.

"Mary." My tone was unnecessarily curt, strangled by discomfort. "I need to stop helping your friends find jobs. It's getting to be too much."

Her face fell.

"I have a lot of other work to do," I added. "And so do you."

"Okay, Madame," she said, recovering quickly. "No problem."

"Mary?"

"Yes?"

"I feel like you're on the phone a lot when you're with Max."

"No, I never do like that."

"It's okay if you need to take a call, but you shouldn't have long chats when you're watching him."

"I never do that."

"Okay," I said disingenuously. "Good."

Chapter 14

Our household in Delhi was unfinished. We'd barely furnished the flat, half our things were still in boxes, and it would be many months yet before we bought a car. But my pregnancy had reached its end. The new baby would have to join us in all our half-done domesticity.

Tom and I took a taxi south to the hospital before dawn, past the school for the blind and the Oberoi hotel; the Hindu crematorium and the Muslim cemetery; Nehru Stadium and the bands of homeless families stirring to life under overpasses. Street sweepers scraped great clouds of dust over the roads. Trees slumped under the weight of sleeping pigeons. We drove past blackened apartment houses and too-yellow gas stations and onward as thin washes of light watered down the ink of night. "I have loved you for a hundred years," Mohammed Rafi sang on the radio.

The halls of the hospital were calm and dull. We squinted grainy eyes against fluorescent lights. Credit card, signatures, forms. The cleaning crews hadn't yet come sloshing their buckets of disinfectants, and so the odors of the body dominated the hallways.

We were taken to a "birthing suite" to sit in awkward anticipation. I thought of what we had left behind: our apartment, my mother sleeping, and Max, always Max. And now there would be two, and how would that work? Restlessly I roamed the room, squinted out at the lightening sky, inspected the toiletries in the bathroom.

"Emergency C-section is better," I burst out testily.

"Why?"

"No time to think." My stomach was twisted with nerves. "If you have to get cut open, it's easier not to know ahead of time."

It was occurring to me, too late, that having a living creature pried from my sliced womb could not possibly be as painless as I recalled. My first C-section came after two long days and nights of labor that had left my nerve pathways blown out like a speaker system, emitting nothing but dull static and fuzz. After all that labor, the slash across my midsection had felt as insignificant as a paper cut. Only now did I panic at the thought of the knife.

Hunching forward to expose my back for the needle, I tried to calm down by staring into the lush canopy of treetops framed by the window. The anesthesiologist pushed the drugs into my spine. I demanded more drugs. She gave me more drugs, then pinched my toes.

"I can feel it," I said.

She gave me more drugs, and pinched again.

"I can still feel it."

She frowned. "Really?"

"Yes."

It was true. I felt the pinch.

"It's not possible." She nodded at the foot of the bed.

"Wait!" I gasped. "Don't cut!"

"They are already cutting," she smiled.

"Oh."

A curtain obscured my stomach. I was sitting in the audience, waiting for the show to begin—the suggestion of movement, a ripple of cloth, but the illusion is protected. Something bloody was being done to my lower half. Masked beings muttered and murmured. Impersonal tugging and pressures. I wondered whether they sliced first one layer and then the next; whether the body was even like that, formed in layers, or squashed indistinctly together. I wanted to discern the moment the baby was brought up from its bed of blood into the too-bright light of a surgical morning.

I was waiting, most of all, to finally know the baby's gender. Indian law forbids disclosing this detail before birth—too many female fetuses are otherwise aborted. I thought the moment of revelation would be like a movie scene—the howl of a newborn and a yell: "It's a girl!"

Instead there was a bustle of movement, a baby's cry, then silence.

"Can you see the baby?" I asked Tom.

He craned his neck. "I see testicles!"

"Oh!" That's how I got the news.

They laid my son on my chest and I put my arms around him, and he lurched toward my face. His sticky eyes were startled wide, bulging with an entire life unlived. Staring at me, evaluating me, certainty and amazement in his mottled face. We had already chosen his name: Patrick. He stared straight into my eyes as if he already knew exactly who I was and who I had been. This moment stayed like a brand in my memory.

———

That first night back home, once the baby slept, Max came to me.

"You said you would take me to the park," he said softly.

"I know," I said. "I'm sorry."

"I want to go."

"But it's dark now."

"I want to go."

"Okay."

It wasn't an ordinary notion, to go to the park in the dark. But our household normal was nullified; we had shredded our family and reshaped ourselves. Max was still my baby, but now I also had this other baby.

And Max was miserable. I'd left him overnight and returned with a new love who usurped his place in the family structure and demanded all my time. Max watched me with serious sad eyes when I held the baby. He awoke screaming and couldn't remember what he'd been dreaming.

"You have to walk on your feet, though," I told him. "I can't pick you up."

"Okay."

"You have to promise."

"Okay."

I guess I knew that he was lying, just as I'd been lying when I promised the doctor I wouldn't lift heavy weights for six weeks. I suppose we both knew I'd end up carrying him.

I eased myself down the stairs, squeezing the banister and gnashing my teeth. The gash across my midsection blazed with pain.

Outside, the moon hung high in a velvet sky. From the jungled thickets across the way we heard zoo animals low and bellow from unseen cages. Wind tossed the branches and scattered down blossoms.

We moved over the grassy lawn, and Max ran from me, fleeing deeper into shadows, looking for bugs in darkened earth, snapping leaves, sniffing and snuffing at the night. Beckoning me and then running deeper still through lime trees, puckish and taunting, drawing me to him. I called his name. He replied with flat silence.

I thought we might talk—out in the shadows, away from the ears and interruptions of the others. But he was two, and anyway, what could we say? The ruthless maternal betrayal was inarguable. He had been mine and I had been his and now there was another, and no denying it.

So he teased me into the shadows and plunged deeper, testing whether I'd follow. I hadn't brought my phone; I could no longer see the lighted windows of our house. Under the trees, drivers and guards muttered over card games and joints. A suggestion of unseen animals stirring.

"Max," I called. "Sweetie, let's go back."

He didn't answer.

"Max."

Nothing.

"Max, where are you?"

Very faint, very sad: "Here."

I followed his voice until I caught the gleam of his pale small face. He was sitting, girded for a fight, in a grove of fruit trees.

I ached to scoop him to my heart, but every nerve throbbed from walking. I cursed the C-section that had rendered me physically unable to comfort my first baby. Film of tears over the night landscape. My little boy vanishing into shadows. It would never again be just us two.

I sat down and gathered him into my lap. The wail of steam engines cut through the trees.

"Do you hear the trains?" I whispered into his hair.

He nodded.

"There's a big train station nearby," I told him.

"I want to see," he said.

"Okay," I told him. "I'll take you one day."

"Now?"

"No, love. Another day."

I smelled the night coming through the trees, the fresh earth, the rotting leaves, the fallen limes decomposing sweetly into soil. Children called somewhere in the dark. I told myself I would hold him all night long if it made him understand that I loved him now more than ever, that he would never be replaced. But it was late and he was tired and dirty and my breasts ached with milk and we had to go home.

We had to go home.

"Max," I said. "We have to go home."

"No."

"You promised."

"No."

"Please, Max."

"No."

"Stand up right this minute and come." I tried to force my voice to sound strict.

"No."

"Well, I'm going home," I told him. "Stay here if you want."

I staggered upright and waddled away. I stopped and glanced back, hoping he was tiptoeing behind. But he sat motionless, his pale face watching me abandon him in the park.

"Oh, Max."

I couldn't leave him alone or force him to come. I hoisted him against my chest and clasped my hands beneath his bottom and staggered homeward through the darkened park. The seams in my belly strained; I was sure the stitches would pop. He rested his cheek against my shoulder and solemnly accepted his due.

———

One afternoon Max walked right up to the baby, who was burbling on a sofa, and slapped him across the face. It was a deliberate and righteous smack—the kind dealt by a person who feels his honor has been trampled. There was no immediate cause, just the inborn sibling grievances as ancient as Cain and Abel.

The slap rang through the rooms. Patrick erupted in the howls of a barely sentient creature incomprehensibly attacked.

I dropped a spoon with a clatter and came running from the kitchen. Max skittered into hiding. Mary scooped Patrick up and buried his face in her neck.

She chuckled and rubbed his thin back, and I overheard the incantation she murmured into his ear:

"You came for this." She rubbed his shoulder blades. "Life is this, only, *babu*. You came for this."

I rocked to a stop, confused. I wanted to scold Max harshly and then, with great fuss and indignant pomp, gather the victim into my arms—to wordlessly assure the baby that the unprovoked assault was unfair and unacceptable, an aberration that would not stand.

Mary's instincts were exactly the opposite. She was telling the baby that he should expect such unprovoked bursts of pain from a capricious and cruel planet. There was no order, no reason, no protection. The baby should learn to take it lightly, to cheer up, not to cry into the wind. She was comforting him, but there was laughter on the edge of her voice.

This is parenting without privilege, I thought. *This is how you prepare your children when you don't have the illusion that you can protect them.*

I stepped back. I was looking at Mary, looking at India, looking at the world through Mary and India. And I wasn't sure she was wrong.

You came for this. What a thing to say. What a true thing to say. But what an awful thing to say. But what a true thing, still.

Mary caught sight of my frozen face and smiled.

"It is not easy to become mother," she said.

"No," I agreed.

"It will be okay."

The baby's arrival empowered Mary to address me with greater authority. I might be "Madame," but infants were Mary's business.

She'd been too late to influence the early upbringing of Max, but for Patrick she was right on time. I was open to suggestions, too, having been disabused of my rookie certainty that there was one correct method, a single right answer, for the baby.

"You want me to massage him?" Mary asked now. "It will make him sleep well."

"You can try," I agreed, remembering how Max had sobbed during newborn massage. "But if he cries, stop."

"Only the first time, he will cry."

She draped a towel on the sofa, lay Patrick down in a shaft of morning sunlight, and rubbed his tiny limbs with massage oil. He grew quiet, as if considering the merits of this experience. Then he looked as if he were smiling.

"He likes it," I said.

"I will do this every day," Mary said.

This incomprehensible life, I thought. *What business does my child have with a nanny?*

"You will not buy sweets for the neighbors?"

"What?" Mary's voice called me out of musings.

"The guard downstairs is asking."

"The guard wants me to buy him candy?" Somebody taller than three feet expects me to do something for him?

"Indian families do like that."

"Do like what?"

"If you bring home a baby, especially a boy, you pass out sweets. It's good luck, only."

"Where I come from," I huffed, "we bring food to people with new babies. We don't expect them to buy us presents."

Mary laughed nervously.

"Madame," she said by way of changing the subject. "You want me to buy feet?"

"Feet?"

"Yes. Mutton feet."

I looked at her, and she looked back.

"You mean, like, hooves?" I finally said. "Animal feet?"

"Like that. I can make soup."

"A soup of hooves? Of animal feet?"

"I'll make it very nice."

"Uh—thank you. I mean—why would I want that?"

"It will make your milk strong."

"My milk is fine."

"It's too thin. You drink too much water."

"That's not how it works." But I paused. Maybe it really did help. Wasn't there something about gelatin and hooves? But a soup made from sheep hooves—the thought sent acid up the back of my throat.

"Thank you," I said. "But I don't care for feet."

"The baby eats too often," she pressed. "It means your milk is thin. You are always drinking water."

"I'm thirsty. And water is good for milk."

"You are making your milk too thin, believe me," she said. "If you won't eat the broth, then I will make you rice pudding."

"Rice pudding!" Now I was enthusiastic. "Great."

"That will also make the milk strong." Satisfied with this compromise, she hoisted Patrick onto her shoulder, this stout wise woman, this professional hoister of babies, and smacked his diapered rump and crowed: "Six lakh rupees!"

"Why do you keep saying that to him?"

"Oh!" She laughed self-consciously. "We always say that to boys."

"Why?"

"That's how much money they will bring for their families."

"Why?"

"From dowry, Madame."

"But we're not Indian. He's not going to get a dowry."

"It's just something nice to say to boys."

"What do you say to girls?" Mary was India. India was in my house. India was already forming my babies' minds and hearts in ways none of us—not I nor she nor they—would ever fully understand.

"Girls? I don't know." She turned to carry my child away. "Nothing."

Chapter 15

Once we'd settled into the house, I'd hired a housekeeper to cook and clean. That way Mary could concentrate on the children. That ought to be enough, I decided. I mean, you didn't want a *crowd* in the house, right?

Sadly, the housekeeper was a disaster. There is no space to dwell on the depressing particulars here. He was a man, too, and I hate to introduce a narrative thread that would undercut my thesis that men ought to perform more housework. I'll simply say that under his stewardship our house slowly descended into filth, and he couldn't cook very well, and when we finally fired him, a chunk of cash disappeared from what we'd thought was an undiscovered hiding spot.

That was a false start, but I wasn't deterred. I called some more candidates.

One of them was Pooja.

In a show of eagerness, Pooja showed up an hour early and ground her thumb enthusiastically into the doorbell. The napping baby awoke and screamed. I yanked open the door and glowered into her expectant face. Glasses slipped greasily down her nose, and hair dripped onto her shoulders like a shawl tossed over an embarrassing piece of furniture.

"Yes?" I said to the short, nervous-looking person who trailed Pooja inside.

"My husband, ma'am," Pooja said flatly. "Varun."

He grinned at us with sharp teeth.

"Okay." I lingered on each syllable so they'd know I didn't welcome this interloper.

"You're early." I turned to Pooja. "I wasn't expecting you yet."

"Sorry," she said. None of the flutter of the other candidates, who minced and winced to ingratiate. Not: *Sorry, Madame.* Not: *Oh, so sorry.* She shifted her weight and waited, unapologetic and a little bored, for me to say something.

"Have a seat." I tried to warm my tone from "mean" to "brisk."

Pooja glanced at the upholstery as if appraising the difficulty of cleaning the stain of herself from the fabric. Her husband, conspicuously uninvited to sit, retreated haltingly to a sofa against the far wall, all impatience and wounded pride.

I asked Pooja perfunctory questions and scrawled her answers into a notebook. This was just for show. I'd already decided against her.

She handed me her reference letters. I ran an eye over the top sheet and started. I knew the name. "Your old boss was my neighbor in Beijing."

"I worked for her until she moved to China."

I knew then, she'd tell me later. *I knew I would work for you.*

I did not share this belief. The coincidence wasn't enough to erase my distaste. "We'll be in touch," I said. *You're not for us,* I thought.

"Her references are great," Tom said that night. "You should email your friend."

"Think so?"

"Small world," began my email to Beijing. The reply was immediate. "She's a gem . . . You would be lucky to have her . . . I have missed her every day."

This didn't sound anything like the sluggish woman who'd visited our home. Doubtfully, I offered Pooja a weeklong trial. Just until we found somebody suitable, I told myself.

"Once I get a tryout," Pooja told me later, "I always get an offer."

No wonder: Suddenly we were eating creamy potato gratin and hearty butter chicken and melt-in-your-mouth spinach quiche. Pooja scrubbed every room to a shine and amused Max by drawing elaborate elephants and recounting Hindu myths. By the end of the week our house hummed along as never before—a neat, orderly place rich with the smells of cooking.

The coincidences continued. When Mary and Pooja set eyes on each other, they shouted and embraced. They had gone to high school together, it turned out, in a convent school in Darjeeling.

"Maybe the universe is trying to tell us something," I said to Tom. He smiled indulgently.

I offered Pooja the job. She'd earn the same salary as Mary, minus the bus money. She moved into the servants' quarter, and everything became easy. Pooja's rooms were small and grim, but she paid no rent and escaped the expense and risk of commuting while female. She came early in the morning, took a long midday lunch break, and stayed through Max's bedtime—keeping Patrick company in the living room while I lavished stories and good-night cuddles on Max before turning to the baby's last feeding.

Once Pooja took over the cooking, I regressed to adolescent disinterest. I'd shamble into the kitchen and carelessly ask, "What's for dinner?" It was a question that never got old. Pooja gloried in the responsibility—she took careful note of our tastes; surprised us with new dishes; pored over cookbooks.

Pooja puffed wearily when she mopped the floors. She was three-quarters blind, and her grin revealed a tumbledown fence of lopsided teeth. But her handwriting looked like flowers; she knew everything there was to know about Indian cinema and music; she baked the best lasagna I'd ever tasted.

When she held Patrick in her arms he lay rapt, eyes drinking in her smooth cheeks and awkward eyeglasses. She whispered to him in Nepali. She sang to him in Hindi. She turned on the kitchen radio and shimmied to Yo Yo Honey Singh, and Patrick laughed hysterically.

"Babies always love me," she said and shrugged.

As for Patrick, he was so easygoing I found it disconcerting. His day was a shifting round of caretakers, sights, and sensations: oil massages with Mary, feedings with me, and babbling senselessly to Pooja while she cooked. On Christmas Eve, at the tender age of just over two months, he slept twelve hours in a row overnight. He did the same thing the next night, and the night after that, and every night to come. I could have wept with gratitude. In fact, I think I did.

There was a sense of plenty; of life's messy eruption. Pooja's husband found a job nearby. The children thrived, everybody slept, and Tom and I both got our work done. We'd had another baby, but thanks to the extra women we'd hired into the house, there was still enough time for everything. Mary took Max to the park and the zoo and escorted him to playdates. Patrick never tired of hanging around with Pooja.

"If you leave India, please give me warning," Pooja said one day. "Otherwise it's too hard. We get to love the kids, too. You know?"

She was not the first woman I'd hired to care for my children, but she was the first to confess to sentimental entanglement. She was the only one who'd ever talked to me with the linguistic fluency and emotional frankness that made her seem more like a friend than an employee.

Pooja and I were coming up the driveway one winter afternoon. Crows wheeled wildly in the blanched sky, spinning and catching, voices scratching like match tips on phosphorous. Our steps slowed, our eyes fixed on this weird winged dance.

"What are they doing?" I asked.

"There must be a dead crow," she said. "One of their own."

"They're mourning?"

"I have seen them do like that."

We watched for a time.

"Crows do that?" I couldn't quite believe her.

"I've seen it many times," she said.

She taught me that; she taught me more.

Chapter 16

Slowly Pooja dropped crumbs of her story. She was a young widow and single mother from the mountains of Darjeeling. She'd left her son in the village with her elderly father because there was nobody else to raise him. Pooja offered these pieces but never told a coherent story of herself.

Neither did Mary. Their sketchy chronologies did not account for all the time they'd been alive. I assumed jobs had been expunged because they hadn't ended well. Relationships, maybe. Places lived, degradations endured, gambles lost. Other moments were told and retold, repeated until they loomed as crucial turning points that had made this particular version of life inevitable.

Pooja had run away with a man when she was still a teenager. That was the thing she made me understand: that all the events of her life, everything she'd done and seen and been, had flowed from the original, adolescent impulse to take her clothes off with a man. Then she'd had to marry him, and then she'd become a mother. In my earliest understanding of Pooja, the choice to have sexual intercourse had been the only free decision she'd ever made.

"Why did I run off like that?" Pooja diced tomatoes; their sharp sweet smell rose from the board. There was a shrug in her voice. "I'm like that, even now. A little bit crazy. Sometimes I just decide to do something and I do it."

"I understand," I said. "I'm like that, too."

"Yes," she said, laughing. "I have seen."

And so she warned me. And so I warned her back.

———

"I like you," I told Pooja one day. "But if Tom decides he doesn't like you, I can't help."

I waited for this warning to sink in. This was the lesson of Xiao Li: *Nobody who causes this much trouble between you and Tom should stay in the house.*

Pooja nodded like she already knew. She didn't need my help. She was an instinctive genius; she knew how to win people over. After Tom contracted severe food poisoning, Pooja announced he must stop eating "from outside" and began to fix a boxed lunch every morning. Tom, of course, was delighted. There were impassioned summits to negotiate olives in the salad; cheese in the pasta; mustard, mayo, and tomatoes but never, ever onion on the sandwiches.

"I like ol' Pooja," Tom would say.

"Because she spoils you."

"At least somebody does!"

I'd long been unnerved by Tom's cold indifference to the private lives of our domestic staff, but now it occurred to me that I'd misunderstood. I began to think that Tom was eager to show kindness to the people who worked in our house—but first he wanted them to be good at their jobs. This is a fundamental and familiar difference in our characters: I don't expect things to be perfect, and I have a high tolerance for flaws. Tom, on the other hand, glances at things— the restaurant table, the hotel room, the apartment—and immediately decides that something better exists and that he can get it for us. And he does. He inevitably delivers us from "good enough" to "really great" or even "amazing." I'm not always convinced the leap in quality is worth the hassle, but the improvement is real. Only now did I realize that this long-recognized habit was also present in his view of the housekeepers. He had a keen sense of India and China as places brimming with bright and poor people eager for an opportunity. It drove him crazy to see me settle for a subpar worker when he was certain—he just *knew*—there was somebody better out there, just waiting to be found, if only I'd keep looking.

Pooja was the first person he considered worthy of her job, and his goodwill toward her was huge. In his eagerness to help Pooja in any way he could, he became—for the first time since Max's birth—a creator of quotidian domestic events rather than a passerby.

Tom traveled a lot in those days—to meet uranium miners in Jharkand and intelligence officers in Karachi; to meetings in Mumbai and New York. I secretly relished absences that spilled into the weekend, because they gave me an excuse to ask Pooja to work overtime on Sunday.

This was welcome because Sundays were a recurrent disaster. Every seventh day, the cheerful fictions of our domestic life were painfully exposed as a batch of lies. On Sunday Tom discovered that hanging out with tiny children was not a sun-washed field and overflowing picnic basket, but a jumble of physical needs and messy rooms and senseless tears. On Sunday I discovered that my partner didn't know where the diapers were kept and thought it prudent to let crusty dishes fester in the sink because a "maid" would arrive twenty-four hours later.

By the time the sun set on the Sabbath, we were often simmering and hardly speaking. We'd tuck the children into bed with forced smiles, then Tom would tumble across our bed and snore ostentatiously while I drank a beer much too fast and washed the dishes.

No doubt there were deeper emotional yearnings at work. Suppressed worries about family life; religious guilt; nostalgia for youth. The existential dread of the seventh day is a recurring theme in art. But none of that was the real problem. We struggled on Sundays because we weren't used to functioning without a cook, cleaner, or nanny.

The simple replacement of Tom with Pooja turned Sundays into a delight. The house was impeccable. The children were nattily dressed and wholesomely fed and carefully chaperoned. I went with Pooja to restaurants and backyard brunches and birthday parties, where I'd dandle the baby on my knee and sip a glass of wine while Pooja heaped Max's buffet plate and plied apart brawling toddlers on the bouncy castle.

The only one who disapproved was Tom. "Nobody should work seven days a week," he said.

Suddenly we'd switched roles. I was complacent; he was consumed by guilt and doubt.

"She appreciates the overtime money," I argued.

"Just make sure she knows she can say no," Tom said.

"Are you sure you don't mind?" I pressed Pooja.

"It's easy for me," she laughed. "We always work like this."

Tom was mollified, but soon he had a new concern: Pooja's water supply.

Pooja saved plastic bottles, refilled them from our kitchen filter, and packed them into a sturdy tote bag. Every night she'd hoist this sloshing load with one arm and lug home another day's water for cooking and drinking.

Pooja's water situation didn't bother me. I never gave it a thought. Considering the countless Delhi neighborhoods where people survived without any water at all, carrying the bottles across the yard didn't stand out as a severe hardship.

But Tom fretted.

"I feel bad when I see her carrying that water," he complained.

"I guess."

"Couldn't we get the people who deliver our water to take some to Pooja's room?"

"Sure," I said. "We could do that."

Then I forgot. Tom complained again. I forgot again. He reminded me. Now the conversation itself had become an annoyance, so I bought a water dispenser and ordered jugs delivered to Pooja's door. I doubled my tips to the emaciated teenager who now had to lug the barrels of water up the narrow, twisting steps to her rooms, trying not to think about how making things nicer for one person always seemed to make things worse for somebody else.

———

We were visiting the ruins of a Mughal fort near our house when I had a crotch rubbed against my ass. I was standing in line to buy tickets. It was a Sunday afternoon. Max was at my hip, and Tom paced in the grass with Patrick.

The dick was hard, and looking for purchase. I put my hand on the shoulder of my toddler and turned to face the man behind me. I looked into his eyes. He looked back. He was skinny and poor; his wrists poked from his sleeves.

"Back up," I said, and he did. He dropped his eyes to the ground, and his friends laughed and jostled at his elbows, and then it was over. I forgot within five minutes.

That night in bed, the memory slipped across my mind, and I mentioned it to Tom.

"Why didn't you tell me?" he cried. "I can't believe—it's so outrageous. You should have told me!"

"Why?" I said.

"I handled it," I said.

"I should tell you so you can get beaten up in front of our kids?" I said.

He stewed and muttered and smacked at his own face until finally I erupted.

"What does it matter? Don't you know how many times, in how many countries? Why is it important to you? You don't remember I'm a woman? You haven't noticed there are almost no women on the streets of Delhi? Look at the bus stops. Look at the sidewalks. There are no women!"

"Of course, I know," he said. "It's terrible."

But then he looked at me as if that had nothing to do with me. And in a sense he was right, because I was a white foreign woman, but also he was wrong, because there always arrives a moment when you are still a woman, no matter what kind of woman you are. I couldn't believe I was still invisible to my husband in this big, basic way. The failure to see what was in front of him; the failure to imagine the rest.

I'd been shocked at the divergence of our fates after we became parents, but in truth, the gender discrepancy between us had started long before that. I'd experienced sexual harassment in countless cultural forms while Tom wandered unscathed. He inevitably felt compelled to intervene manfully when he happened to be present, but otherwise he was largely oblivious. I seldom called his attention to these experiences because I didn't want them to stick around as memories between us. And we were always so busy, and it was always easier not to think about it, because thinking about it drove me into what felt like an unproductive rage.

But now it all slid through my mind: The years of come-ons from sources and colleagues. The news organizations I'd roped off in my mind as no-gos because I'd sexually rejected some man who'd since become powerful, and didn't want to risk getting undercut and black-balled. The times I thought I was about to get raped. All the things that had been said to me, or said about other women in front of me, to be sure I didn't misunderstand my position as an amusing but ulti-mately inferior presence. We were welcome as long as we were young and beddable, and then we were supposed to do what self-respecting women did: disappear into a household somewhere. Tom had faced none of that. Tom had been free to move through his career; there had been so little for him to navigate. And I'd never explained it to him. I'd assumed he just knew, because I thought it was obvious. I'd been treated like an accessory. I'd been groped and pawed and cor-nered. I'd let sly remarks slide off my back. It was all in the game, and I was so eager to play.

But now he looked at me blankly, as if I were not part of it, and it occurred to me that he had no idea. Did he really think his wife had been clever enough to be a woman in the world without being a woman in the world?

There was so much to say I couldn't stand to start.

———

When the boys napped and the air in the house stood thick with after-noon stupor, Pooja and Mary sprawled on the floor under the whip of ceiling fans. Together they fiddled with hair and examined fingernails and whispered in Nepali. Together they fell into gape-mouthed sleep. They rose together, and together they worked: Mary mopped floors and washed clothes while Pooja cooked. When Pooja shopped for fresh vegetables and meat, Mary carried Patrick along for the ride. "Just for an outing, Madame, some air."

"Bahini," they said. *Sister.* Shouts of *"Bahini!"* between rooms and down halls. Mary and Pooja whispering their secrets, laughing at jokes they refused to translate, crying together. I turned my rooms over to them, and they created a kingdom of women and children. I passed through on my way to my desk, my computer, my language, and my imaginary worlds. The house was full of mothers. The more they took over, the more I could withdraw into work.

They made it all so easy. In the haze of memory, it looks perfect. I know I was working hard then and beating myself up for not working hard enough, and that every day I tried to split myself between two babies. I was struggling. I cried sometimes. There were mornings when I doubled over in the shower with anxiety. But when I remember those days now, I think they were perfect.

———

A friend wrote me in a panic. She was pregnant. She'd gone to a cremation. It was a colleague's brother; she'd felt obligated. But people had chastised her for exposing her unborn child to the funeral pyre. In India, pregnant women are not supposed to attend cremations. The soul of the dead is burned free and, it is said, may find its way to the fetus and leave its mark.

"Am I ridiculous for feeling weird?" she asked.

I happen to believe that feeling weird is a sign of vitality. The world is a weird place full of weird portents; who can pretend otherwise? I myself have felt weird about linoleum patterns and paper factories and thousands upon thousands of minor objects and cameo personalities.

So, of course, I replied: "NO!"

"I'll ask Pooja," I added. "She's so smart about things like this."

Pooja had become my trusted reference for all questions of history, culture, and health.

"It's okay," she said immediately. "The same thing happened to me."

"Really?"

"My husband died when I was pregnant," she reminded me. "I was scared to go to the funeral, but I had no choice.

"But"—she shrugged—"nothing happened."

My friend should sprinkle holy water around the rooms of her house and on any clothes worn to the crematorium, she added.

"What kind of holy water?"

"Any holy water," Pooja said.

I knew of precisely one kind of holy water, and surely Pooja didn't mean fonts by the church door. Or maybe she did.

"From a church? A temple?"

"Like that," Pooja agreed.

"Which one?"

"Any one," Pooja said impatiently. "Just so long as it's holy."

"Where do I get it?"

"Anywhere."

Mary was nodding along, as if to say, "Obviously." I still didn't understand, but I stopped talking.

————

"Madame." Everything that Mary ever brought, every cataclysm or joyous eruption, began with these two syllables. "You have anything tonight?" She watched me, face pursed for discussion.

"What do you mean?"

"You're going somewhere?"

"No."

"I want to go little early."

"Okay." That sounded too indifferent. "How come?"

"I'll go look for rooms," she said. "Our landlord said we have to move out."

"Why?"

"I don't know."

"I'm so sorry." I was panicked, pulse picking up in my throat, imagining Mary spat forth into the city's bellow and smog and crowds of cruel strangers.

"It's okay."

"But what will you do?"

"It will be all right," she said easily.

Mary never got fazed. She had a level of equanimity so total it was like a superpower. It's not easy to describe without sounding trivial: Mary had mastered an all-embracing calm that carried her—and sometimes carried me—through one predicament after the next.

She canvassed friends for rumors of affordable places, and a few days later, she and her husband moved into a flat. Mary was pleased by the new digs: a proper apartment with a separate bedroom and roof terrace. I overheard her calling church friends to tip them off to the identical flat that stood vacant next door.

There was one drawback: The apartment was out by the airport, clear on the other end of the vehicle-choked Indian capital. To reach our house, Mary would ride multiple buses and waste hours every day in standstill traffic.

"Is she going to keep working for you?" friends asked incredulously.

"I think so," I said uneasily. "She hasn't said anything." These questions made me wonder whether I should have involved myself by helping her find a closer room or offering her a rent subsidy.

"That's a terrible commute," everybody said.

"You should be ready for her to quit," they warned.

"I don't think she'll quit," I said tentatively.

I was right. She didn't quit. And then they said, "She must really love your family."

But I didn't think that was true, either. With Mary, it never felt like love. We were her duty, nothing more but also nothing less.

———

"Madame."

Now what?

"You will travel somewhere?" Mary had cornered me again.

"Um." My thoughts flopped helplessly. "Why?"

"I want to fix my passport."

Then we loudly talked our way through a forest of interruption and confusion as I struggled to identify what she wanted. Gradually I understood that Mary urgently wanted a passport. Her husband's visa couldn't be renewed again, and therefore he'd have to leave India. Mary wanted a passport to go to Nigeria with her husband so that they could get married.

"Wait." I cut her off. "I thought you were already married. To your husband."

"I just say like that," Mary explained. She used the same phrase when Max balked at going to a friend's house. *He's just saying like that. Once he goes he will enjoy.*

"Say like what?"

"I say he is my husband."

"But you're not married."

"No."

"Okay."

Mary's boyfriend wanted to get married in Nigeria, she explained, under the gaze of his family. He wanted everybody there—

"The problem is," I interrupted, "we usually travel over weekends or holidays, and then the government offices are closed."

I was still thinking of the problem as she'd presented it: a question of family vacation. I now realize—starkly, cringingly—that Mary suggested getting her passport while we traveled only because she was too shy to suggest inconveniencing our family by taking time away from her usual working hours.

Recalling this incident now, I'm frankly ashamed that I didn't immediately offer her a day off. I can't understand why I didn't. No, that's not true. I remember why.

By this time, I'd gotten used to treating my own time as the cheapest in the family. If a child tossed with fever, I was at the bedside. Tom had to show up at his office, but there was no reason I had to draft the next scene on Tuesday instead of Wednesday. In theory, I could even take a nap. In theory, I could even do nothing. In practice, between the children and my own ceaseless scramble to scrape another hour of writing from every single day, I never, ever took a nap. But this daily hustle did nothing to change the household calculus: My work could get shoved, and so it did—always, and for everything. Every outgrown pair of shoes, trip to the dentist, or preschool obligation—any crisis or errand affecting anybody in the family— inevitably devoured another chunk of writing time. I accepted my status as lowest household priority, below the helpless children and the rigors of Tom's formal employment, but there were side effects: all this enforced selflessness made me much more selfish. If Mary had plainly asked for time off, I wouldn't have said no. But because she'd shyly soft-pedaled—certainly nobody had ever taught Mary how to negotiate—I allowed myself to believe it wasn't very important.

"Is it urgent?" I asked.

"No, Madame," she said casually.

"Anyway, yes, you should get your passport," I said cheerfully, heading out of the room. "We'll find a time. Don't worry."

———

Mary was full of stories that got into my imagination and stuck. They were tales of innocent girls from faraway lands and the ruthless men who stalked the deranged streets of a nocturnal city. Awful stories; senseless stories; stories that fell apart on examination. But if you allow that truth can exist even where fact is absent, then you could read from these fantastic tales some truths about the city—and some truths about Mary.

She told me about a nanny who cried every day because her husband beat her mercilessly. Sold by her parents into bonded labor, she'd spent her childhood working for cruel bosses. "They used to beat hell out of her," Mary would say. Now this unfortunate lady had failed to get pregnant, so her husband had the right, by communal custom, to demand one of her sisters for sex and progeny.

More characters:

The corrupt landlord who killed himself after demonetization because his ill-gotten cash had been rendered useless.

The teenage maid from Assam who was beaten to death with a cricket bat because she didn't speak Hindi and couldn't understand what her boss wanted for dinner.

The white backpacker junkies who lay like trash in the gutters where Mary lived, kicked and raped and pissed upon by passing men.

The dowdy middle-aged foreign woman chased into an empty garage and gang-raped while Mary's neighborhood thrummed on impassively. Mary had tried to intervene. She'd run to a group of cops and begged them to save the woman, but they shrugged.

"What did she come here for?" the police snapped as they brushed Mary aside.

That line stuck with me for years. With typical uncanny precision, Mary had conjured the classic image of a white woman getting raped by dark men. The idea that has, above all others, justified white outrages of murder, colonialism, slavery. It hit me like a warning and a plea and even as subliminal propaganda. I was the outsider, I knew, but then so was Mary. *What did she come here for?* What did the police mean, if indeed they had said that? And if Mary was embellishing, what did she mean? I puzzled over *here,* because *here* was a place where outsiders could expect no mercy. *Here* could be the street, the impoverished neighborhood, New Delhi, or the entire country of India.

What did she come here for? Tom and I had journeyed here from elsewhere because it was interesting and we had something to gain. We were accidental migrants; we could change course at any time. Mary and Pooja had come here desperate for money. All the world was moving, migrating, seeking, fleeing. The longer I lived on the other side of the planet from my own home, the more this question struck me as profound and unanswerable.

What did she come here for?

Mary had already told me the answer.

What did she come here for?

Mary's voice asked, and Mary's voice replied.

You came for this.

Chapter 17

Mary waited for me that night. Instead of bustling out the door once Patrick went to bed, she sat strangely motionless on the couch. Crescent stains of fatigue hung below her eyes. Birds gathered in the trees outside and screamed with the hysteria of dusk.

"All night we were awake." Mary rubbed at her hairline. "That place is full of spirits."

"What do you mean?"

"My husband has high fever. His head is paining. Demons are bothering him too much."

"Oh." I considered. "Your apartment is haunted?"

"Yes."

"What will you do?"

"All night we prayed. We said rosaries, we put holy water. We prayed for that demon to leave us in peace, but that demon is very strong."

"Wow."

Max sat between us, head bent over a picture book. I studied the back of his neck.

"Maybe your husband should go to a doctor," I finally said.

"He will go," she said. "His fever is too much."

"If you need anything, you can call me," I said.

"Thank you."

I knew she wouldn't call. She never called. She relied on friends from church. Sometimes I had the strange idea that Mary sensed my desire to be useful and withheld her problems out of some subversive impulse. She had to work long days in my rooms, fine, but she wouldn't let me congratulate myself as her benefactor.

By naptime the next day, she sprawled on the sofa with a dripping towel slung across her eyes. I started to point out she was getting the furniture wet, but something held me. I looked closer.

"Are you all right?"

She lurched upright. "I'm not feeling well," she muttered.

Patrick's bellow came through the monitor. I carried him back into the living room, sat down on the floor, and watched Mary blink around. She reached down and pulled Patrick absentmindedly into her lap. Usually the color of a pink rose fading to brown, her skin was ash and mustard. Her eyes had fallen deeper into their sockets. Her face looked almost reptilian in its lifelessness.

I started to reach for her forehead, then stopped myself.

"May I touch your head?" I felt foolish.

"Yes."

Heat boiled beneath her skin.

"You have a fever," I told her. "A high one."

I took Patrick back and nestled his head under my chin.

"Those spirits—"

"Mary!" I interrupted. She had been telling me stories again, pulling me into her lurid swirl of superstition and ghosts. But now I snapped to myself and saw the plain facts.

"Did your husband go to the doctor?"

"Yes, Madame."

"And?"

"He has typhoid, Madame."

"Mary!"

"Typhoid, you know? They did a test—"

"Mary!" I cried again. "Why are you here?"

"I don't know—"

"But—how could you—the kids are here, Mary," I sputtered, clambering unsteadily to my feet and backing away with Patrick in my arms. "If your husband has typhoid, you probably have typhoid, too. And you might give it to the kids."

"Oh," she said slowly.

I wanted to kick her out forever. I wanted to put her to bed and nurse her to health. *Moron,* I thought in outrage. *If my kids—*

But she was sick; she was so sick.

I turned around and walked away. I handed Patrick to Pooja in the kitchen. "Mary can't be near him," I said grimly. Then I shut myself into the office and found Tom online.

My hands trembled on the keys. Mary might as well have opened her purse and announced she'd carried a cobra into the living room. She was supposed to take care of the children. Her presence in our house rested on the assumption that she could anticipate and avoid danger.

"Mary JUST told me her husband has typhoid," I began. "I Googled typhoid and the first thing to leap off the page was HIGHLY CONTAGIOUS."

Three excruciating, unpardonable minutes passed. Then Tom weighed in: "What the fuck?"

I glared at the screen. This was not an acceptable level of engagement. I let my silence draw him out.

"Is her husband over it now," he finally added, "or is he still sick?"

"Still sick."

"Am assuming you already sent her home?"

"No."

Tom has always provoked in me an inconvenient impulse to honesty. This was clearly the wrong answer. But that was the point of involving Tom: He could slice through the clamorous circus of our household and arrive at the only logical next step. It was like consulting with myself, minus the background noise.

And, too, it was implicit between us that my decisions were often clouded—or at least made uncharacteristically sluggish—by my desperation for writing time. In this case, for example, I simply did not want to accept that Mary might have contracted a terrible disease that could keep her out of the house for an untold stretch of weeks. Her absence translated into my own lost work.

I got off the computer. I didn't wait for Tom's recrimination. Whatever he was going to say, he was right. I was compromised by my own desire to avoid household disruption.

"Do you feel well enough to take an auto home?" I asked Mary.

"Yes, Madame," she said unconvincingly.

"You need to see a doctor. Do you have a doctor?"

"There is a clinic in Munirka."

"Go today," I told her. "But Mary—you cannot come back here until you are completely well. Do you understand?"

"Yes, Madame."

———

I didn't even try to work the next day. After breakfast I took Max to the park. I liked the park, with its beds of hollyhocks and jasmine shaded by jamun and lime trees. But I disliked going there with Max, who was stubbornly indifferent to the flower beds and picturesque nooks and was drawn, inevitably, to the scabbiest edges—dried patches of bare earth near the trash cans, punctuated by rat holes where, we'd been warned, venomous snakes liked to hunt.

"Don't you want to go over there?" I asked the top of his head.

"No." He clawed at the dirt with his fingernails.

The phone rang. It was Mary.

"Did you get the results?" I demanded.

"She said I have typhoid."

"Oh no."

"Yes." Mary hesitated.

"Okay," I sighed. "Well, get some rest. Do you need anything?"

"No, Madame." She sounded small and weak and very far away.

"Call me if you need something. Okay? And don't come back until we've agreed it's okay," I couldn't resist adding. "Okay?"

"Okay."

Pacing in the grass, I called the boys' pediatrician. This doctor had practiced in the United States before returning to India to set up a children's clinic on the ground floor of his family home. He was an old-fashioned family doctor who did everything from weigh-ins to vaccinations himself and responded to panicked text messages in the dead of night. He was kindly and tactful, with a gnomish face and a sly sense of humor, and my children loved him.

Now, as I waited for the doctor to answer, I absentmindedly watched Max poke his fingers in the mud. This scene would have driven Tom wild with anxiety, and so, as usual, I felt I was doing something slipshod behind my husband's back.

I knew what Tom would say: The dirt likely contained animal feces and parasitic worms. Max was apt to poke his fingers into a nostril or mouth. And, no, I hadn't carried any hand sanitizer.

It's not that I was fearless—just the opposite. I feared the bands of wild dogs who lolled in the grass. I feared the knots of loitering men who played cards. I feared the speeding cars of my reckless neighbors. I feared the deadly diseases transmitted by a single bite from the wrong mosquito. I feared the cobra that had been spotted in that very park. I had so many fears that I had no fear at all—I felt we were surrounded by so many dangers I could not afford to indulge my fear of any of them.

That's because, most of all, I feared raising neurotic children. I imagined shrinking boys who wouldn't play in the mud without fussing over sanitation. Sickness could be cured, but if my kids were harangued until they shrank from the world, there would be no treatment.

I'd tried to explain this to Tom, who'd replied with cutting remarks. It was, however, a satisfying conversation to have with the pediatrician, who'd chuckle knowingly and tell me I was right. All of these thoughts trickled through my mind as I waited for him to answer.

"The nanny has typhoid," I blurted when I heard the doctor's voice. "She just told me."

"She has a fever?"

"She has typhoid."

"How do you know she has typhoid?"

"She went to a doctor."

"What doctor?"

"Well—I don't know," I said impatiently. "What difference does it make?"

"It makes a big difference. False diagnosis of typhoid is very common. These people go to some cheap clinic, and the first thing they get told is they have typhoid."

"They did a test."

"A blood test?"

"Yes."

"Which test?"

"I didn't examine her medical records."

"Well, you need to," the doctor said in his relentlessly reasonable voice. "I don't trust this diagnosis."

"So what should I do?"

"Wash your hands a lot. Wash everybody's hands."

I waited for more. No more came.

"That's it?"

"Anyway, she shouldn't be in your house if she has a fever."

"Right," I said. "She's not."

"So you wait. Wash hands. Watch the children for any signs of illness."

"When can she come back to work?"

"She has to be completely clear of fever."

"I can't believe this," I groaned.

"I can," he said. "Next time, take her to the doctor yourself."

"I didn't know any of this. I'm not used to—" I groped to finish this sentence. Nannies? Motherhood? India? "Typhoid," I finally choked.

"Look, I could tell you so many stories. There is no concept of health or medicine or even hygiene. You can't underestimate the ignorance of these people. There is a reason they are our maids and gardeners."

I ignored this last comment, which I considered unworthy of our doctor.

"So?"

"Just wait," he said. "There's nothing else you can do."

————

Mary stayed home. I tried not to think of her misery—she and her husband turning with fever, long days in the dead air of a stultifying flat by the airport, the ceaseless roar of the lucky ones cutting tracks through the clouds overhead, steel birds on the skies of delirium.

I didn't lose as much writing time as I'd expected. Pooja kept the house clean and the meals fresh, and still found time to help mind the kids. We washed our hands constantly. She didn't get sick, and neither did I, and, most important, neither did the children.

We never found out whether it was typhoid, but Mary recovered and came back to work to announce that prayer had vanquished the demons.

Soon the entire incident melted away into the mists of our household. Nothing ever stayed the same; everything was always changing. Threats reared up, only to recede. Sometimes I sensed that our family was about to slide off the edge of stability into something truly apocalyptic. I dreamed nightmares; stood completely still while panic crawled over my skin; woke up full of dread. But somehow each day rolled into darkness and morning always came. This typhoid scare went away, too. Another crisis would soon take its place.

I knock on wood as I write; I knocked on wood then. I knock on wood every day. I avail myself of every rite of the religion I've abandoned: I cross myself. I sleep with a rosary under my pillow. I keep a Bible in the boys' room. I sprinkle the rooms with holy water from Mary's church. I write formal entreaties to the djinns of Delhi and shove them into the cracks of the caves where the spirits are said to dwell. I was born superstitious long before children and India, but now I am hopelessly ritualistic. It's the stabbing gut fear of motherhood. It's living in a place crowded with overlapping religions and tableaus of human desperation. I knock on wood, I fill my wallet with four-leaf clovers, I wish on stars and numeric coincidences. I fast and I bargain and I pray.

It may not help, but it doesn't hurt.

Chapter 18

By daylight, in our rooms, we all swung along the arcs of our assigned orbits. I am sure Mary, Pooja, and Tom each sometimes found their roles stultifying. I know I did. Still we got up and performed our duties; they gave our days a frame and a meaning.

But every sun reaches its peak and then plunges to earth, and when night came we mercifully split from one another. I slipped into the wildness of sleep, into the private space of my bed with my husband, the arguments we had, the love we found. The children tucked away in the glow of night-lights, everybody wrapped in dreams.

And Pooja and Mary broke forth into the world, to deal or dream or drink, to resume living as the people they had always been, their unchangeable selves, the people I could not know. All of us played our parts in the light; reserved our honesty for the darker hours.

The worst things happened at night, and the best things. All the truth came at night.

———

I slammed out of sleep that morning, lurched awake. What woke me, why? Darkness stood thick in the rooms. I took my phone in hand to check the time—five a.m.—and read the text message from Pooja with the afterclingings of dream still draped like cobwebs over my eyes.

2:30 am.

Mam I have to go back to Darjeeling. Please send my
salary to my sister's bank acct. I need it desperately. I'm
sorry mam try to understand.

Now I was vertical. Back to Darjeeling, in the middle of the night,
with no warning? It wasn't right; it didn't make sense. Something had
happened. What could have happened?

We'd just been together. She'd stayed late the night before, playing with Patrick while I put Max to bed. Then she'd wrapped herself in a bulky sweater and headed home. She didn't have far to go:
windows and walls split the space, but she slept about fifteen yards
from us.

I sat in the dark and tried to understand. The sudden disappearance would have been improbable at any time, but to leave now, with
monthly payday coming? No, even if she hated us, she wouldn't go
now. There must be some emergency, somebody sick, but why didn't
she say?

I dialed her number; her phone was switched off. I tried her sister
and then her husband; nobody answered. I sent text messages. *I'm
worried. Have Pooja call me, please.*

"Tom," I hissed.

"Huh!" He jerked out of sleep.

"Something's wrong. Pooja's gone."

"What do you mean?"

"I don't know. She sent me a text in the middle of the night—"

"Something happened last night," he murmured, eyes still closed.
"I heard something—"

"What?"

"People were shouting. A woman was screaming." He propped himself up on an elbow, frowning to remember. "The dogs were barking."

Fear spilled fast and liquid through my belly.

"Did it sound like Pooja?"

"No. I don't know."

"Why didn't you do something?"

"It didn't even cross my mind that it would be Pooja."

"I'm scared," I said. "I'm going to her room to check."

I tugged a cardigan over my pajamas, turned on my phone flashlight, and tiptoed downstairs. The dying night stank of trash fires and cold diesel steam. I turned away from the iron spikes of the front gate. I was not seeking my usual exit, toward the park and the main road. This time I headed in the other direction, around the back of the driveway, dodging moldering stacks of abandoned construction materials and a squat toilet, dragging open the rusting gate to the brick-paved alley. I had almost reached the cramped dormitory of the servants' quarter when I realized I wasn't even sure which door was hers. *I should know,* I thought. *Why don't I ever come back here?* I was shivering in the alley, trying to remember, when I noticed a mess of broken dishes. Smashed teacups; a salt shaker; a cheap little plate painted with candy-colored apples, all heaved down from the window above. The small physical bits of Pooja's life, scraped together through years of work in other people's homes, dashed now on the bricks. Darkness held fast, and the silence was terrible. I listened to the emptiness of a sleeping street and understood that Pooja had gone.

I wanted to see her rooms anyway. I was drifting into investigative mode, half afraid I'd find blood, a body, God knows. I couldn't be sure she'd sent that text message. Maybe somebody had taken her phone, maybe the text was meant to distract and mislead, to buy time for escape . . .

A battered mutt sprawled over the dirty stairway to her room. Scars and stains covered the dog's hide; stinking and snoring, he lorded over the stairs like the hound of Hades. I knew the residents of the quarter had fattened him on food scraps and trained him to attack strangers. This dog was their security guard against the night. Still I tried to pass. As I wedged a foot over his haunches, a chesty rumble erupted. I froze. He growled again and snapped his teeth. I backed away, spun, and ran.

Back in the bedroom, I turned to Tom and named the fear that had been gathering itself since I'd first read the text from Pooja.

"What if he killed her?"

———

The absence of Pooja filled the house as we moved through the routines of daybreak. Diapers, bowls of fruit, coffee, showers. I watched the clock, waiting for Mary to cross the city by bus. Everything was now contingent upon Mary. She'd know something, or she'd suggest a course of action. She was the only remaining guide who could lead me back to Pooja.

I told her about the text message, the screams, and the smashed crockery. I wanted to call the police, I said, but Tom was against it. Notoriously corrupt and abusive, Indian police are never summoned casually.

"Let me see," Mary said firmly. "I'll go and check."

She came back important with news.

"The neighbors say there was a big fight," Mary reported. "I moved all her things upstairs. Everything was lying in the street. They were smashing everything, throwing things out the window."

"What else did they say?"

"A very bad fight," Mary repeated impatiently. "She and Varun were fighting."

"Is anybody there now?"

"In Pooja's room?"

"Yes."

"Nobody is there."

"You opened the door, or you knocked?"

"The door was open. They didn't lock it."

"I'm afraid she might be dead."

"No," Mary said unconvincingly. "We will find her."

"Did you call her?"

"Her phone is off."

Tom went off to his office, Max went to school, and Mary took Patrick to the park. I paced, tried to write, gave up, and waited. The day passed slowly. I ordered pizza for lunch—an exaggerated reaction to the missing cook.

In the afternoon, Mary came to me in the kitchen.

"Madame," she announced. "I talked to Pooja."

"What?" A rush of relief—Pooja was alive! "Where is she?"

"At her sister's."

"She's all right?"

"Yes."

"Why didn't she call me?"

"She will call you," Mary said. "I told her," she added imperiously. Mary had won this round, that much was understood.

Instead of waiting, I called Pooja.

"I thought you were dead," I said when she answered.

"It's not like that."

Pooja had fled, but not all the way to Darjeeling. She was exhausted and sore and it was too much to accomplish in the middle of the night—to buy a ticket and cross India by rail, broke and alone. Instead she took a motorcycle rickshaw to Delhi's outskirts, where her sister worked as a cook for another foreign family. There she stopped. Afraid to come back to our place, but hesitant to leave Delhi, she hung in limbo, a guest in yet another staff quarter.

———

A few days later Pooja came back to talk. We sat in the living room beneath the high clean ceiling and crystal chandelier, before the wide, tall window letting onto thick clots of green leaves. A shudder of March heat stole into the room. It was the first time we'd sat formally together since her job interview. It felt serious and unnatural.

We all looked at each other: me and Tom, whose presence added moment to the meeting, and Pooja and her sister, brought along for moral support.

Pooja perched awkwardly on the edge of an armchair. Varun had uprooted fistfuls of her hair and blackened her eye. Tears caught at the bottom of her glasses and leaked down her bruised face. Her cheeks shone like seashells, soaked and shellacked in days of salt water.

She told us how it started: Varun suspected Pooja of sleeping with the water deliveryman. He couldn't fathom her explanation for the deliveries: Why would her boss send water to her door, why should we care? He was furious that Pooja let a strange man into their rooms while he was off working.

"He said, 'You're sleeping with that water guy. You're calling him when I'm away,'" Pooja said.

I was so amazed by the improbability of this suspicion that I could hardly listen to Pooja talk. I wasn't even sure the person who brought the water had reached the age of legal manhood—he was a skinny slip of a teenager in scuffed sandals and grubby clothes. His body odor made Pooja and Mary titter and groan behind his back. My imagination couldn't conjure the image of him and Pooja in a passionate embrace.

"I tried to tell him, 'They won't deliver the water at night.' But he just got angrier. He called me horrible names. Accused me of everything. Then I got mad and started to shout back. Then he beat me."

"He's beating her all the time." Her sister leaned across, a barricade of flesh between us and Pooja. "Tell them," she prodded Pooja.

"He does like that," Pooja agreed weakly.

"We want you to come back," I said. "But we're trying to figure out whether it's safe. And even whether you want to come back."

"How can I face the neighbors?" Pooja said. "Everybody saw me. They just stared at me. Nobody helped."

The memory brought fresh sheets of tears.

"This shame is for them," Tom intoned sternly. "The shame belongs to the people who stood by while you were beaten."

This was a voice he assumed on assignment, a slow, menacing tone suited to unpredictable militiamen or intransigent hotel clerks. These declarations wouldn't help Pooja when she overheard muttered taunts from packs of drivers and security guards; when women avoided her eyes; when she sat embarrassed in her dingy room. I knew that. Pooja knew that.

"Thank you, sir," she said.

I was irritated by everybody: by Tom's pronouncements and Pooja's fixation on the gossiping neighbors and by myself, most of all, for having nothing to say. I hated the banality of it all—the complaints and inconvenience and wasted time that thrived on the assault like scum on stagnant water. My irritation grew, I knew, from smothered despair. Pooja had been hurt. Maybe she would be hurt again. We could make gestures, but we couldn't protect her. Maybe she would be murdered; maybe everybody who worked for us would come to ruin; maybe we would go to hell for sitting as spectators to this misery. I'd been all around the world, and I've never yet found a place where women aren't hit and exploited and hated. Men needed us, but God, they hated us, too. Deeply, chronically hated us.

Pooja had given us all the bounties of her sardonic, generous mind and spirit—but we had to take the rest of her, too. And I wasn't sure I could stomach it. The fragile membrane that had separated the harrowing existence of the vulnerable women we employed from our quiet domestic life had finally burst. This was my house, but I couldn't control it. The seamy disputes and bottomless despair I had subconsciously hoped Pooja and Mary and Xiao Li would drop at the threshold when they kicked off their street shoes—all of that had now exploded into our living room. It was in the bruises, in the way Pooja slumped while I held myself erect, trying to exist both inside the room and above, lingering back in a place where such things didn't happen—at least not close enough that I had to get involved.

I was annoyed, too, by Pooja's sister, who leaned into the conversation with the haughty, round-eyed air of a blameless bit player in a royal scandal. She'd catch my eye and hold it without any particular expression. When Pooja spoke, her sister followed along like a stage mother who's memorized the script. She kept interrupting.

"He said he would kill her," the sister interrupted now. "Tell them," she prodded Pooja.

"He always says like that," Pooja said slowly. "But this time I feel scared. I feel he may do anything. Because he didn't really expect me to leave him."

Tom and I looked at each other.

"Do you think it's a good idea for you to stay in your quarter alone?"

"I don't know. I'm afraid he'll come back."

"Can he get in? The dog—"

"He feeds the dog," she said. "That dog is a friend of his."

"But the guard—"

"The guard will never mind."

"In the end," I said, "you have to decide."

"And," added Tom, "you really need to think."

Then we explained our conditions. Pooja could come back to work, but only if she got rid of Varun. He would be forever banned from our house, including the quarter.

She had time to decide. We agreed that she'd hide out for a few weeks at the high-security apartment complex where her sister worked. We'd tell everybody she'd gone back to Darjeeling. Pooja must tell nobody about this plan. Not even Mary; especially not Mary. Everybody had to think that Pooja had gone to her village—and to repeat this story, over and over, to Varun.

We all wandered down to the park, where Mary had taken the boys. "Pooja is leaving," I told Mary.

"For good?"

"Yes."

"Oh." She paused. "Why?"

"It's not safe for her to stay."

"Nothing will happen," she exclaimed. "Don't worry! She will settle down."

"It's what she wants." I ignored the implication that the beating was a behavioral eruption on Pooja's part. "And we think it's better, too."

Pooja walked over, her sister trailing, through the grass and past the jasmine hedge. Pooja and Mary spoke quietly in Nepali. Mary threw her arms around Pooja's neck, and as their chests parted a jagged cry ripped from Mary's throat. Just one cry, and then silence. She snuffled back snot and turned her face to the children. I wanted to pull Mary aside and whisper the truth, but I stopped myself. Her cry hung in my ears, and guilt ate my windpipe like heartburn, but I stayed quiet.

Mary was still Mary. I trusted her with my kids, but I didn't trust her to keep her mouth shut.

Pooja and her sister walked off slowly through the afternoon light, moving toward the market and the city beyond.

———

Mary called Varun to deliver our ultimatum: he should gather his belongings and get off the premises immediately. The drivers and guards were informed that Varun was persona non grata. True, these men were his friends, but at least now they couldn't claim they hadn't known.

"Do we really have the right to tamper in her private life?" I asked Tom that night. "I don't like it."

"Her private life is part of our private life," he said. "We can't have our kids around domestic abuse."

The children had been oddly untouched by this crisis so far. They carved their own paths through the house, perfectly present but somehow oblivious to the machinations and compromises of the adults. But their ignorance was fragile.

"True," I said.

Sometimes when Tom and I stretched side by side in bed, having a conversation like this, I'd mentally slip out of my skin to eavesdrop on a couple discussing their servants. It was a disgusting sensation, and I was filled, each time, with a yawning despair. In order to liberate ourselves from the chores, to continue the work we believed was crucial, we had converted our home into a job site. I was a manager—not of a bureau or a newsroom, but of a claustrophobic domestic universe. We held a dismaying amount of power over vulnerable people, and that meant grappling with the ethics, finances, schedules, and personalities. Every time we talked like this—which was often—I disliked Tom and disliked myself and felt a queasy certainty that Tom, too, must share this disgust. For me to be this person with Tom, for Tom to be this person with me, degraded our love affair and sullied our family. And yet it never stopped; every crisis resolved was soon replaced by another.

The next day our landlord's driver stopped me in the street.

"Big problem," he growled, gesturing angrily back toward Pooja's room. "Shouting. Throwing. Very bad."

Back upstairs, Mary reproached me for whipping up unnecessary drama around a mundane domestic dispute. As far as Mary was concerned, Pooja was behaving with hysterical self-destruction—and I was egging her on.

"This is family life." She kept saying that.

Pooja's husband had pushed her down the stairs and dragged her into the street by her hair.

This is family life.

"I tried to tell Pooja, 'You've been with him ten years, and he never killed you,'" Mary said. "He's not the type."

"You don't know that," I said.

"Don't worry," Mary said. "Pooja will calm down and say sorry."

"Sorry to whom?"

"To Varun," Mary replied. "She should be careful. Varun takes good care of her. She won't find another man so easily."

Soon the story spread among our neighbors. I was pulled aside by well-meaning matrons determined to warn the ignorant foreigner about predictable traps. Husbands shouldn't be allowed in the quarters, they tsked.

"Always some trouble," they said knowingly.

People from northern India always drank too much, they added.

"You don't know these people like we do."

———

"Maybe it's a mistake to let Pooja stay," Tom said one night.

"What are you talking about?"

"What if this guy shows up and kills her? That kind of thing happens all the time here."

"So"—I fought to keep my voice smooth—"besides getting beaten up, you think she should be fired for getting beaten up?"

"No, I guess not," he said slowly. "Well, of course not."

We tried to find a solution. Tom suggested Pooja could sleep on a spare bed in the children's playroom, but I didn't think any of us—including Pooja—would be willing to give up that much privacy.

"Maybe it'll be better in the long run," Tom sighed, "if she decides not to come back."

———

Mary still believed I was ruining Pooja's life—or helping Pooja ruin her own life—and she was desperate to salvage the situation. She grew so distressed she even broke the unwritten code regulating the distribution of personal information among employers and employees. She told me one of Pooja's secrets.

Varun was not really Pooja's husband, Mary said. In fact, he already had a wife and child.

"Pooja didn't want you to know," she said guiltily.

I couldn't see how this made any difference to our current predicament. But to Mary, this information was key in grasping the danger that Pooja faced. Not only had she kicked out a perfectly good man— *she had kicked out a man who had someplace else to go.* If Pooja didn't want him, there was another woman who'd take him back.

"Pooja doesn't understand," Mary fretted. "It's not easy to be a woman alone."

But all was not lost, Mary assured me. Varun had been haunting the surrounding streets and market, asking the drivers and guards about Pooja. He was hunting for her.

"He doesn't believe she went back to Darjeeling," Mary said.

My stomach was in knots; I chewed my knuckles. If our deception didn't work, Pooja would have to leave our house. It was a parting I couldn't stand to imagine.

"Nothing bad is happening," Tom told me in bafflement. "Everything is going to be fine either way."

Still I woke every dawn with dread in my gut.

Chapter 19

Pooja came back to work, but it was all wrong.

On those long afternoons of early summer, when our rooms steamed and thickened in the syrup of slanting sun, Pooja's sadness hung like laundry that wouldn't dry. She and Mary no longer hollered to each other down the halls. They walked soberly; their voices were flat; they whispered in corners. Pooja cried a lot.

I talked to Pooja about the things of the house. The foods she might cook; the reorganizations she might undertake; the repairmen she should call. "Yes, ma'am," she said absentmindedly. I pushed her toward Patrick. She cuddled and sang, but when she turned from him, her face slumped back to listlessness.

"Are you all right?" Obviously, she was not.

"Yes, ma'am."

I didn't want to poke at Pooja's raw wound, so Mary became my surrogate. When Pooja set off to the market, I'd corner Mary and press for information. Was Pooja all right? Was Pooja going to be all right? What did she want, what was happening, what could we do?

"Pooja isn't strong," Mary reported.

"What does she say?"

"Pooja doesn't know what-all happens to a woman by herself," Mary said. "Her sister gives her bad ideas. I told her, 'Your sister is young. She isn't a mother. Think of your son.' But Pooja doesn't listen."

"He hit her."

"Married life is like this." She shrugged. "Now she is alone."

I didn't insult Mary by pointing out that my husband had never hit me. To pretend that we chose from the same options; got judged by the same criteria; that I wasn't swaddled in layers of dense and obvious advantage—I couldn't do that.

"Mary," I finally snapped. "Varun can't live here anymore. Tom said so. If he comes back, she'll lose her job."

"Oh." Invoking Tom, the patriarch, always made her go quiet.

Mary plainly relished the roles Pooja's predicament offered to her. She was my trusted informant, and Pooja's life adviser. She was serene and all-knowing. Her circumstances were stable and respectable by comparison, and her insight anxiously sought.

"I told Pooja, 'Have faith. God is there,'" Mary said. "But Pooja says, 'I'm not like you. I don't have a strong heart like you.'"

Mary even tried to take Pooja to church, but here she was overplaying her hand. Pooja was heartbroken, but she wasn't about to turn to Jesus.

One day Mary burst in with news.

"Varun went back to his wife." Defiant and accusatory, she threw this at my feet. Her head stretched and trembled with the enormity of her ignored warnings; her eyes roamed my face. She wanted to know whether I would finally own up to what I'd done.

I turned away.

Pooja was disappearing into silence. She stopped eating, and the weight fell from her bones. Her shoulders hunched sharp beneath her clothes.

"Are you all right?"

"I'm all right."

Now that the worst possible outcome was a fait accompli, Mary turned philosophical.

"I told Pooja, 'That woman must have cried a lot when you took Varun from her,'" Mary reported. "'Now it's your turn to cry.'"

I frowned at Mary. "That's not a very nice thing to say to her."

"Pooja should understand how life works."

One day I passed Pooja on my way to the bathroom. She was coming out; the flush of the toilet roared behind her.

"Disgusting," she muttered.

"Excuse me?" I swung around, stopping her steps.

"Sorry, ma'am. I said, 'disgusting.'" Her face was empty. "I have my period, and it's just—gross."

"Oh," I said. "Well, it's just—" We were both on the early edge of middle age. Pooja didn't need my right-thinking Western warnings against stigmatizing menstruation. But I was surprised. Pooja was matter-of-fact about bodily functions, changing Patrick's diapers without a wince.

I continued on my way, vaguely demoralized by what I interpreted as an eruption of self-loathing.

The days went on, and Pooja sleepwalked through cooking and cleaning and babysitting.

"She'll get over it," Tom said.

"I hope so."

———

It was just one thing, in the end. A domestic dispute. A fight in the night. The bruises healed. The neighborhood gossips scented a fresher scandal and drifted away. Time swallowed us along. The beating was over—except that it wouldn't go away.

We couldn't sweep up that night or disinfect it or rinse it down the sink. That was the beginning and the end; the start of the great unspooling. We had woken up to find Pooja vanished, but we had assumed her disappearance was reversible. We had tracked her down and brought her back, but she wasn't the same and it wasn't right. We had started to lose Pooja, piece by piece.

On the weekends Pooja drowned her sorrows. She slept at her sister's place, or her sister spent the night in our quarter. They dressed up and hit the town.

We'd wake to squeals as they raged home in the small hours before dawn. They'd blast corny dance music and scream like teenagers at a pop concert. I tossed and sighed in bed. I understood that Pooja had spent her true adolescence getting knocked up and widowed, that everything had gotten very serious very fast, and that now, at last, she was enjoying a delayed youth. Warped because she was old for these antics. Dicey because New Delhi is not the place to get drunk and stumble through the streets. Pathetic because it all seemed desperately imitative rather than free and fun. But it was her right.

Pooja, please turn down the music. We can't sleep. I texted her around four one Sunday morning.

The music immediately stopped, but come Monday Pooja feigned ignorance—what music?

She was changing. Her face was harder. She bought trendy eyeglasses and a new phone. She and her sister combed the Tibetan market for miniskirts that choked their thighs, leather vests too small for their breasts, lipsticks in garish shades of orange and magenta. Pooja chopped her hair to her chin and dyed it red.

"Some men were bothering us on the metro," Pooja told me one day. "My sister, you know, she was just screaming at them, 'You never saw a girl in a short skirt before?'"

"What did they do?"

"They were shouting back, but it was okay."

"Pooja," I said, "you should be careful."

"Yes, ma'am."

"People are crazy."

"I know, ma'am."

"I'm worried about this stupid partying," I complained to Tom. "I don't like it."

"Pooja has gone through a tough time," he reminded me. "And she has a right to do whatever she wants on her days off."

"You're right," I sighed enormously. "You're right."

———

Monday morning. No Pooja. I cooked breakfast for Max and fed Patrick and still there was no Pooja.

After many rings, she answered her phone.

"Pooja."

"Yes," she croaked.

"Where are you?"

"What?"

"Where are you?"

"Sorry, ma'am, sorry, sorry."

She hung up. I called her back.

"Where are you?"

"I'm just coming." I heard crashing sounds.

"Are you at home?"

"Yes, ma'am."

A few minutes later the key rasped in the lock and Pooja staggered through the door.

"Sorry, ma'am," she gasped. "I forgot it was Monday."

"What do you mean, you forgot it was Monday?" I was barefoot, holding Patrick, needing more coffee.

"Sorry," she said again.

Patrick and I both regarded Pooja skeptically. Sooty streaks of eye makeup smeared down her cheeks. From the piscine gape of her mouth fogged the stench of rotgut alcohol. She lurched toward the kitchen, toppling into a wall and pushing herself upright again as she passed.

I didn't say anything. I just watched. I figured she'd glance into a mirror and realize she hadn't washed her face. That, or she'd chop off a finger slicing apples.

Mary arrived and herded the children into the playroom. I found Pooja in the kitchen, very slowly washing breakfast dishes.

"Do you want to go back home?"

"No, ma'am," she muttered. "I'm okay."

"Okay," I said. "But you can't take Patrick to the park this morning."

Her head snapped up; her mouth worked emptily.

"Why?"

"You're drunk."

"No."

"I can smell it from across the room."

"I went out last night but—"

"You can't walk a straight line."

"I didn't—"

"Stop it."

"Fine."

"You didn't even wash your face!" This, for some reason, struck me as the most glaring insult. "You can stay and cook and clean, but you cannot watch the kids today."

I waited until Max was at school and Mary was pushing the stroller under the trees, then followed an ostentatious volley of slamming and banging down the hall to the boys' bedroom. I found Pooja stalking in circles over the bright rubber floor mats, clattering toys and shoving drawers.

"What are you doing?"

"I won't work here anymore," Pooja choked.

"What are you talking about?"

"If you don't trust me with Patrick, I won't work here."

"I didn't say I don't trust you. I said you can't babysit when you're drunk."

"I would *never* hurt Patrick." Now she was sobbing, and I was losing patience. Bad enough she'd come to work drunk, she was determined to have a scene.

"Pull yourself together," I snapped. "What is going on with you?"

She didn't answer. I watched her huff and sob for a minute, and then I lost my temper all at once.

"Go if you want, but if you walk out that door don't bother coming back!" The words were falling out of my mouth unplanned. "You think I don't know how much you're drinking? You think you're being discreet? You think I'm a fucking idiot?"

She started to say something.

"Let me finish," I roared. "You have your private life. You have your own time. But don't bring it into this house. Don't let me see it."

"But you drink—" she said.

"I drink, but not when I'm working. And I don't get *drunk*! It's not appropriate. The next time I see you drunk, you're fired."

She stared at me, speechless, heaving. Looking at her wrecked face I felt another surge of anger.

"Did you even look in the mirror?" I demanded meanly. "You've got mascara down to your mouth, and you smell like old beer."

The shame that washed across her soggy face stuck the words in my throat. We stood there staring at each other, breathing ragged, rage spent.

"Pooja." I touched her arm awkwardly, then pulled my hand back. "Listen. I know you are going through a bad time. But you cannot come in here drunk. Never. Do you understand me?"

"All right."

———

I was writing. Lost in imagination, lost in language, I had no attention for the world around me.

The boys had gone with Mary and Pooja to a neighborhood birthday party. In those days there was always a party somewhere. Ever since I'd turned Max's afternoons over to the nanny-supervised play group circuit, his social life was more varied and incessant than mine had ever been. With his entourage of baby brother and two nannies, he partied his way through a knee-high version of Gatsby's rolling bacchanals, skipping from one house to the next with brief breaks for sleep, food, and school. Splash pools, sprinklers, pizza-making parties, trampolines, pet puppies. Garden classes in painting, pottery, soccer, and tae kwon do.

For me and the kids, this arrangement was brilliant. The stretch of afternoon between nap and dinner was a miraculous window of writing time. An entire room of time, really, inviolate in the architecture of the day. The kids would wake from their naps, then a brief scramble of cuddles and helping with shoes and making sure water cups were full and kissing their hair—and then they'd rush off into the day, leaving me blissfully alone with my manuscript in a clean and empty house.

I was writing with perfect concentration that day—and so I noticed too late the swell of darkness. These weren't the bruised clouds of a rainstorm, but something more total, like a fader switch cranking to black over the city. The air in my office congealed into lightlessness. Then I was on my feet and moving through the house. Outside, trees tossed and dogs howled. The wind came up fast and strong, and everything loose went sailing. The neighborhood erupted in slamming shutters and splintering wood and flying tools. Branches shredded clean off trees; trees yanked straight out of the dirt; trash washed against the sides of houses and stuck there suspended by wind. One minute it wasn't, the next it was.

Hurricane, I thought. It was the only phenomenon I'd ever seen that looked like this. It didn't make any sense, because Delhi is land-locked, but the similarity was too perfect to ignore.

I called Mary, called Pooja, Mary, Pooja, Mary, Pooja. *The number you are calling cannot be reached . . .*

Then my own phone rang, and I pulled it to my face. But it was just another mother whose children were also at the party.

"I can't get through." Her voice was shaking. "And the roof of our shed just blew off."

"I'm walking over." I was already looking for my shoes.

"I don't think it's safe," she said.

I couldn't think about that. The reality had slammed against me in stark detail: I had let my children not only out of my sight, but out of my protection. I usually kept tabs by phone, but now that crucial link was cut. I could not give instructions. I had to depend, blindly, on the judgment of Mary and Pooja.

And I felt, suddenly, that I didn't trust them. Not for something like this. They might panic and try to walk home through the storm. They might get into a car. With a natural disaster raging and communications stripped away, I realized the shallowness of my faith in these women, and I was scared.

Pointlessly, I grabbed an umbrella as I ran out the door. I imagined we'd hunker down at the neighbor's house until the wind died, and then it would rain. I still thought it was a hurricane—I didn't understand that it was a dust storm, also known as a black blizzard.

Outside the wind screamed and grabbed. All around me dust and trash flew. I tucked my chin and stared down to protect my eyes from blowing dirt. Thunder groaned and bellowed overhead.

On the brick alleyway by the market, the sidewalk tailor struggled to tarp down his sewing machine. Max called this tailor *"cut-cut wallah"* in homage to his enormous silver scissors and hung around watching him stitch curtains and hem trousers. Now I handed the tailor my umbrella. It was knocking me off balance, and I thought maybe he could use it. He took the umbrella. We said nothing.

I fought gales all the way across the neighborhood. The swampy completeness of the dark was terrible. It was hot and weird, an abstract painting of a tropical disaster among derelict homes.

But when at last I reached the party, everything was incongruously fine. The children rolled and shrieked through cool, yellow-lit rooms, trailing their tattered princess dresses and clattering wagons. The nannies sipped laconically on sugared tea. All the trappings of the party lay scattered—platters of cookies and cupcakes; bowls of chips; discarded games. The children chattered and squabbled with exaggerated energy. The storm had heightened the sense of rarity and excitement.

Max raised delighted eyes to me—*Mommy is here!* But then he turned and skittered into the writhing forest of children. Patrick squirmed back toward Pooja when I tried to pick him up.

Mary laughed.

"They don't want to go home!"

It was true. They weren't scared, and, in fact, they didn't particularly want to see me since I represented the end of fun. Mary and Pooja had constructed this small pocket of safety on the edge of cataclysm. I shouldn't have been surprised—their entire existence was, essentially, doing just that.

At least nine people died in that storm. Walls collapsed; power lines caught fire; uprooted trees blocked the roads. But the odds of survival are always stronger than they look from a distance. We went home and drew baths for the boys.

The next day Mary reproached me.

"That *cut-cut wallah,* he was waiting for you," she said.

"What?"

"You gave him your umbrella to hold and never came back."

"No!" I said. "I just gave it to him . . ."

"He wanted to get out of the storm," Mary said. "But he kept waiting for you."

"I just wanted to give it to him," I protested. "I didn't mean for him to guard it!"

"He said, 'How could I leave, somebody will take this umbrella?'"

"Oh God," I groaned.

I've been giving that *cut-cut wallah* money every Diwali since. We have money, we make a mess, and then we buy our way forward. Not because it makes things all right, but because it is better than nothing.

Chapter 20

Tom was worried, again, about Pooja. The summer heat was especially brutal that year, and he was fretting over her rooms.

"How can she stand the heat back there?"

"Well," I said tentatively, "there's a ceiling fan."

"Why don't we buy her an air conditioner?" he asked. "How much could it cost?"

"I'll find out." This dialogue was shameful: Once the dogged defender of domestic workers, I was now the cruel skinflint who expected our housekeeper to suffer 120-degree heat with a skittish ceiling fan.

By the end of the week, I'd gotten a window unit installed in Pooja's room. Once it was done, I couldn't believe it had taken us so long. The heat of a Delhi summer is exhausting and disorienting; a physical condition so extreme it qualifies as an existential state. And yet we had housed a full-time worker without this basic gesture of decency.

At times like this, our life in Delhi gave me the weird sensation that I was an unwitting subject in a psychosocial study. *How long before this seemingly decent American family realizes the maid is about to die from heatstroke?* I thought of people who abused the "inmates" when assigned to role-play as prison guards in the Stanford experiment. I remembered that normal people tortured other people by electric shock in the Milgram experiment. *See how observing the behavior of others has normalized the dehumanization of domestic workers?*

And yet nobody—not even Pooja—seemed to think she was entitled to the air conditioner. Mary gossiped about the machine as if it were a spectacular chunk of jewelry. Pooja thanked us somberly. Fed by this response, we allowed ourselves the self-satisfaction of charity.

It didn't last. Soon we heard from our landlord, a gruff Punjabi businessman who lived on the ground floor. He emailed Tom, who forwarded the note to the undersecretary for household and personnel detritus—i.e., me.

"It has been brought to my attention," the landlord wrote, "that you have fitted an AC for your maid in the staff quarter."

This wouldn't do, he said. The electrical wiring couldn't handle an air-conditioning unit.

"The load of AC can result in short circuit and fire," he wrote. "Please get the AC removed immediately as the major accident occur."

That sounded right. Given the shoddiness of the servants' quarter, I could easily believe that the wires were dangerously slapdash.

"Now I'm worried about fire," I told Tom that night. "And I don't know if that air-conditioning shop will do a return—"

"It's bullshit." Tom cut me off.

"How do you know?"

"Because—I'm positive."

"So what do you suggest?"

"Ignore him."

"I don't think we can."

"He's not going to do anything. You'll see."

Doubtful, I told Pooja about the landlord's email.

"It's not true!" she cried. "He just doesn't want me to have air-conditioning because now his driver is also asking."

As the mercury climbed and the air conditioner clattered to life, I waited for the next salvo from the landlord. None came.

I considered removing the air conditioner, anyway, just in case the fire risk was real. But then I imagined Pooja wilting into heatstroke. It was another unwinnable predicament that made all our choices seem terrible. There we lived in a jerry-rigged maze of tangled electrical wires and faulty plumbing and rabid dogs, in a colony without a fire department, congratulating ourselves for giving the boys a fabulously enriching experience.

The neighbors didn't like the air conditioner, either. The lady next door sent a guard to complain. *Tell your maid her air conditioner is disturbing my sleep.*

This, too, we ignored. This neighbor had once cooed over Max and promised to invite us to her son's wedding. Once the air conditioner arrived, we were dead to her.

As we prepared for our summer pilgrimage to America, I felt we were leaving Pooja alone. Too alone. Precariously alone.

We offered to buy her a ticket back to Darjeeling, but she insisted she'd rather stay in Delhi and rest during monsoon. I didn't like it. I believed almost anything could happen before we got back: looters could empty our house, Pooja could vanish again, an earthquake could flatten the neighborhood. I always had that feeling in India— that things move too fast and loose, crowds of people and a tangle of tongues and faiths and everybody living on a web of fault lines, so that if you turn your back on something, you must be prepared to lose it forever.

Pooja was still in the wind, somehow, flying like those uprooted trees in the black blizzard. She hadn't crashed yet, but I could feel it coming.

———

Back in America we swam in the Atlantic and waded in creeks and slurped ice-cream cones at picnic tables. I never stopped moving. I never stopped eating. Somebody handed me a beer. The waves crashed; the boys grew brown and strong; I pulled fresh air into my lungs. My hours were packed with small children and their steady slur of physical needs. Scrubbing baby food from high-chair trays, the stink of sponges in the morning, brooms, crumbs, diapers, shopping. *Would you mind please keeping an eye on him while I just quickly . . . ?* My mother, Tom's mother, my sister-in-law: speaking to everybody like they worked for me. Worrying I didn't know anymore how to talk otherwise to women in a house. I said *please* and *thank you* and *would you mind,* I smiled, but I was assigning tasks.

I imagined myself into the life of America. There was no nanny to lead the boys away, and so they were with me always. Space never opened around my body. Silence never reached my ears. No minute came for thought. The days were messy, frazzled, and unmanageable, but still I was happy. I liked the long days with the kids. I liked the logistical ease of America. There were public libraries and clean toilets all over the place. Whatever you needed to buy, there was a vast bright store with a big flat parking lot outside. The tap water didn't make you sick. The air was so clean I imagined it was full of vitamins. Formidable household appliances of the sturdiest materials roared on fat streams of American electricity. The power never failed. The roadways were organized although needlessly aggressive. Organized although needlessly aggressive, in fact, was a good way to describe American life.

I jogged empty streets before dawn, the sleeping houses strung like night-blooming orchids along the vine of the road, their treacly perfumes leaking into the fading night. The intoxicating stink of fabric softeners and hand soaps and air fresheners, obscene against the green breath of trees at night. But it was all so easy, and it made you sick so slowly, so imperceptibly. You didn't eat a bad lettuce leaf and puke your guts out; you stewed in a soup of laboratory experiments and plastics and bleach until you had peanut allergies and cancers and superbugs.

I thought about intergenerational living. It didn't make sense that our mothers lived alone while we scraped around for strangers to watch our children. Maybe we'd been duped. Maybe we Americans were chum for the global economy, deluded by advertising, getting isolated and crazy so that we'd buy more stuff. Was that possible? In this configuration—each one in his own home—we all spent more money. We needed a washing machine for each house. We needed a car for each house. We needed a house for each house! We got scared, so we needed alarms and guns. We got lonely, so we needed drugs and liquor. We were excellent consumers; the best in the world. We consumed products until we couldn't store them, and then we consumed containers to hold what we couldn't store. We consumed food until our fat began to sicken us, and then we consumed drugs and surgeries to right the diseases of our consumption. We consumed so enthusiastically it was killing us.

All of this bleakness, but America was still my only place. The American night crackled, full of ghosts and brand-new possibility and ancient, wicked things. It moved my blood, the sense of the great darkened land stretching west. I want to buy a pack of cigarettes and drive out into it, to drive until dawn, drinking gas-station coffee and listening to American radio all the way.

Maybe I'm spoiled because I have nannies and cooks. Maybe you're spoiled because you have parking lots and public schools and your kids can drink the bathwater. Maybe we're all spoiled in some way or the other, even if it's only by freedom or fresh air.

But everything has its underbelly.

———

Back in Delhi the house smelled like tight hot afternoons and dust. The garbage collector who hauled our trash had died while we were gone. He was just a teenager, the younger partner of the father-son team who went door to door, gathering the neighborhood's trash.

"How did he die?" I asked.

"The heat," Pooja said simply.

He was a scrawny kid who lurked in his father's shadow. They wore rags, their too-short pants held up with faded rope. The son was peripheral. His father was the one I always noticed. His hair was greasy, unevenly chopped, streaks of coal and steel over a sun-charred face. Even before his son died, his eyes boiled with such a potent distillation of anger and pain it was destabilizing to meet them.

They charged us a few dollars a month to collect our garbage every morning. Up and down through the neighborhood they trudged, pushing their rusted, busted cart with its stinking load of rubbish. When I waved they always waved back.

The pair were loathed and ridiculed. They were Muslim, and they handled trash. It is hard to conceive of more disgusting figures in the eyes of our neighborhood, where I'd heard bigoted remarks about

Muslims tossed off thoughtlessly. On top of their religion, the garbage collectors were unreliable. They didn't keep a consistent schedule; sometimes they didn't show up at all. Even softhearted Mary had chewed them out for erratic performance.

The day the garbage collector died, it was so hot the pavement was melting. They were working, walking back and forth in the sun, and they didn't drink enough water. The son collapsed and groaned.

The security guards and drivers, clustered in plastic folding chairs at the gates, looked at him and laughed. At least, that's what Pooja told us: They didn't help him, and then he was dead.

They thought he was drunk. That was the neighborhood explanation. They thought he was joking. As if these tragically unloved figures might suddenly be cutting up, lying down on the excruciating pavement and groaning for a chuckle. And what joke could that be, what possible punch line?

One morning Mary knocked on my office door. The garbage collector was waiting outside.

"He is asking some money to bury his son."

"I'm coming." I sat there feeling like I'd been kicked in the belly.

"The garbage man is asking for money to bury his son," I texted Tom.

I wanted to involve him in the awfulness of this visit. I wanted to implicate him, not only in the crime of assigning a cash compensation to the petty horror of our implacable street, but in the underlying sin of our life in this filthy-rich neighborhood of people who sat around and watched a young man's needless death. I had found myself contemplating all the evil of humanity, and I didn't want to face it alone.

"Jesus," he replied. "Give him five hundred rupees."

"Okay." This was two months' pay; the equivalent of seven U.S. dollars.

"Don't you think?"

"I think he'll be glad to have it."

I took the money from my wallet. I was tempted to give it to Mary to pass along. I didn't want to see the father's face. I shrank from his grief. But I forced myself to go to the door and open it and hold out this offering for the man to accept. I forced myself to look into his eyes. His face was worse than I remembered. It was a face that belonged among cages and torture and the bottoms of dark wells.

"I'm sorry," I said. It was inadequate. Everything was inadequate.

I closed the door and went back to work.

Chapter 21

I finally typed the last lines of the first draft of my novel. It was the middle of the night. Everybody was asleep. A lizard scrabbled over the wall, hunting for bugs.

I looked at the blackened windows and remembered lost seasons in Moscow, and that one perfect summer in Beijing when I'd begun this book, veins bloated with confidence, throwing dice and winning every roll. I thought the novel was something to finish fast, the next idea in a long parade of ideas.

And then the babies came, and I realized I was also destined to bleed and fall short and watch from shadows while other people won their crowns. My ambition could find no object except for these hundreds of thousands of words that I showed to nobody. I spun daydreams. I cuddled my children. I listened to music. *Baby, sweet baby if it's all the same, take the glory any day over the fame.* I instructed myself to enjoy the fruits of my labor. I pined and cried and understood failure and accepted obscurity and lost patience and found it again. All those words. All those days. The sentences abandoned halfway through because a child screamed. The scenes that came as fingerprints of themselves from a dead weary brain. All of that.

But at least I'd kept writing. I hadn't written perfectly, but written I had. I took something out of myself. I made a piece of work. Now I wanted to burst from my house and pace the darkened streets; wake up Tom; phone people I hadn't seen in years.

I'm done.

I wasn't done. Only a draft was done. A draft is nothing. A first draft means you've bought the stone. You haven't carved anything; there is no sculpture. You've produced a block, nothing more. For a few days, though, you can thrill to its existence. This first creation is more godlike than anything that will come after. Chipping, adding, polishing, perfecting—this is the same familiar human enterprise, the improvement and reduction of something extant. When you create a draft, you bring material from nothingness.

I imagined writing the acknowledgments for the novel. I would thank Tom, of course. Tom first, Tom always. I tried to imagine what I would say: "You definitely could have been more supportive, but on the other hand, you didn't divorce me."

———

Goa in monsoon season. Sun buried behind opaline sky. Cracked sea of metal, veined with silver and bronze. Pale sand gone to crumbled moss under the passage of feet, studded with tiny seashells.

The boys held white crabs in their hands, they chased fish into open water, but red flags snapped on the beach, and lifeguards called them back to shore, every time back again.

I stood in shallows and felt the water tug at my feet, watched everything slide weightless in the drag of undertow, crouched down until my face almost broke the singing shushing skin of the water, snatching at shells and pebbles as it rushed to the deep. Breathe the salt, breathe the terror of the tug toward open sea, toward something vast and unknowable, an ocean that cannot be fathomed. We dabbled on its edges, over and over we brought our children to plod and plash.

"We have beach boys," Tom said, all quiet happiness. "They love the beach so much."

"Yes." *That's because this is where we bring them. We could have chosen mountains, we could have chosen forests or desert. They love what we present to them.*

They dipped themselves into the edges, tasted the salt, and marveled at the small pieces of life they could steal from the shallows. They wondered over tidal pools. They feared the waves.

Watching how the water turned and scraped, I felt vertigo. I didn't want my babies to be dragged out to sea, out to see. I didn't want the world to carry them out of my reach. But this is my duty, now, to watch them test the depths and quietly accustom myself.

Tom was telling Max something, explaining, bent low. Max ran to me and said: "Mommy, the moon is pulling on the sand."

"The moon is pulling on the sea, sweetheart, on the water."

"No, it's about the sand. Daddy told me. It's why the beach is different every day. The moon is pulling the sand."

And I stayed silent; I turned my face to the horizon. He could find out in his own time. I didn't care enough to interrupt our reveries with facts. Anyway, I was the only woman in our family; what would they know about waters and tides and bloods? These truths are fluid, and men aren't involved.

Men were coming now, incongruous figures in uniform moving over the sand. Workers from one of the hotels, waiters or porters or front desk staff in matching black trousers and white shirts with collars. They came staggering and skipping down the beach, bearing on their shoulders a statue of the elephant god Ganesh. They neared the water's edge and then stopped and prayed. Then four of them picked up the clay statue and waded with it into the water. The rough sea slapped and curled. Over and over the waves pushed them back to shore, and the men fought their way forward again. Their trouser legs were soaked; the salts of sea and sweat slicked together on their faces. Always, everywhere, water is sanctified. This presentation of Ganesh to the sea represents the divine melting of matter into the absolute. Ganesh will return perpetually to Kailash. Ganesh was created from the dust of his mother's skin. Her husband chopped off the child's head, and only when he saw his wife wrecking the world in the rage of mothers did he adjust his thinking. *Never mind, I didn't understand, you are my son, too.*

The hotel workers could not force their offering into the mouth of the sea. The absolute did not accept their clay. Finally they turned and walked back up the sands. Sometimes the act of offering has to be enough. Their part, at least, was pure. The next day Tom and Max would discover the statue washed up on the beach, mud skin melted to reveal the straw skeleton beneath.

A fisherman hauled his net up onto the sands, combing its strings with calloused fingers. His catch was paltry: a jellyfish and a single white fish that gasped on the sand, gills shuddering in and out. The boys leaned over for a closer look. I let them look. Why shouldn't they look? They didn't know what death was, and even if they did—well, even if they did. Still there was some impulse—don't let them look. And its echo—make them see. In the end I stayed neutral. They didn't ask, and I didn't volunteer. The fish had no hope; it was dying on grained earth, drowning in air. My boys are animals, could they sense its plight? Finally Patrick, the baby, set down a starfish by the fish's head. He had been carrying this starfish for half an hour; he wouldn't let anybody touch it. Now he offered it to the dying fish as if he'd been saving it always just for this. Then they lost interest and drifted down the shore. When the fisherman finally carried away his catch, I pointed out his retreat to the boys so they wouldn't cry. "Say, 'Bye-bye, fish,'" I coaxed them.

"Bye-bye, fish," they repeated.

We gave them what of India we could reach. They grew up with things we never had. With passports and airports and embassies and hotels; with being foreigners, the only white face in a room. They heard their parents say "home," and they were confused to realize we meant a place they hardly knew on the other side of the planet.

My boys are alien to my past self. I was the child of a few rooms, a patch of woods, a handful of adults. Predictable, dull, and contained. I starved for the world; I nearly died looking for an escape. They are children of the world. The world is all they have. They don't have a hometown. They don't expect things to be comfortable. They don't expect places to smell good. They don't expect people to look like them or to speak their language. They don't complain. I don't know how they are being marked by this life or what it portends for them. I guess and I hope. I hope it helps more than it hurts.

Chapter 22

One little-discussed problem with hiring domestic help: it is difficult to maintain the professional equanimity of a boss in your own home, at all hours of the day, with privacy stripped away and your every snack and sniffle on display.

Imagine: You didn't sleep; you had a quarrel; the baby is crying; you've burned the last egg. *Goddamn it.* But don't forget, you are the boss. You are in a condition of intimate emotional disarray, but you're also in the midst of a professional situation, and it's all happening in your kitchen. Your employees watch you stalk around in your bathrobe. In this sense, they have the private knowledge of family members.

But you can't snap at employees the way you might snap at a family member. They are vulnerable to your whims. And, unlike a family, they don't love you. Why should they? Sometimes I saw myself through the eyes of the women who worked in my house and felt they couldn't possibly like me, let alone love.

In some ways, I was a bad boss. I couldn't have predicted the corrosive potency of the emotions that rushed through my nerves when my kids were involved. The house was there, all around us, no escape. And I'm a flawed human. More than once, I lost my temper. In the hangovers that followed these rare eruptions I experienced a paralyzing self-loathing. I hid in the bathroom and cried. I reminded myself that these arguments were unfair. In fact, they were not arguments, because an argument implies equality of status. When one person has power, it's not a fight, but something closer to abuse. I was free to say whatever I wanted, while the women in my employ—for a thousand reasons—were muzzled.

Then I'd apologize, only to worry that I shouldn't have apologized, that the entire thing had shown my weakness.

It wasn't only that I lost my temper a few times. There were other behaviors—subtler and more frequent—that made me a bad boss.

Here's one: I stalked Pooja on Facebook.

———

It started as procrastination and idle curiosity. I pecked her name into Google and clicked through to her Facebook page. Who knew Pooja had Facebook? She hadn't configured her account for privacy, so I could see everything she posted. A little more snooping led me to Pooja's sister, who also posted a trove of Pooja pictures. I didn't send them friend requests or tell Pooja I was watching her online. I didn't want her to censor herself.

That's because, in truth, I was mesmerized. In our house Pooja was steady, calm—even nerdy. Her quiet intelligence and careful bearing were the ship railings that kept us all on deck.

The Pooja of Facebook was frivolous and wild, a volatile woman who stayed up late squinting reddened eyes and hoisting drinks for the camera. She haunted bars and malls with her sister and another friend. They called themselves the "Three Angels" and puckered their lips into unflattering duck bills. They posed in lush gardens and immaculate homes and shopping malls. If you didn't know they were cleaners and nannies, you would never guess from their profile pages.

I couldn't understand how Pooja had so much money to burn. I worried that she wasn't saving. The flashy lifestyle she flaunted on Facebook struck me as something worse than fakery. It was almost an expression of nihilism—as if she didn't believe there would be a future for herself or her son.

I was also worried about the mood swings documented in her feed. One day Pooja was drinking in a bar long after midnight: "dis party getting hot! feeling happy." But soon she moped in sorrow: "Don't depend on anyone in dis world bcoz even ur shadow leaves wen ur in darkness. 'feeling so lonely' 'GUD NITE' to all my frenz."

Now I saw that the Pooja who came into my house was only a single, fragmentary aspect of a more complicated woman. Her broader existence was beyond my understanding. I felt close to Pooja, and yet I found daily evidence that she was still a stranger, and I found this mystery addictive.

I was privy to constructed selves: the role she performed in my house, and the avatar she built on Facebook. This stranger-woman, this person of flesh and soul, swung between the two like it was nothing. Our family was never mentioned on Facebook. The hours we spent together felt like my entire life, and yet Pooja had enough time and material left over to build an image of an existence that didn't contain us.

Eventually, of course, the spying stung me. I saw a picture of Pooja wearing a quilted navy jacket I'd once bought in Beirut. I loved this coat for its swingy cut, high collar, and oversized buttons, and because it reminded me of traveling alone and ducking into trendy shops on a whim between meetings. Now there it was on the Internet, not fitting Pooja properly.

I closed the computer in annoyance, half stood to march into the kitchen and confront her, then dropped back into my seat. What could I say, *I saw you on Facebook*? Besides, maybe I was wrong. I looked again—yes, I was sure that was my coat. I checked the closet, and there it hung, looking spiffy and innocent of all misadventure. Treachery!

"I was Facebook stalking Pooja (separate and embarrassing conversation)," I messaged a friend, "and saw a picture of her out partying in a bar . . . wearing one of my coats!"

"Ha ha ha," came the reply. "Busted. That is my first real chuckle of the day."

"If that's the worst you saw," continued my wise friend, "it's not so bad."

That night I spilled the story to Tom, expecting an indignation hotter than my own. But, once again, I'd underestimated his empathy for Pooja. He listened quietly, and answered slowly.

"She shouldn't have done that," he said. "And you can confront her, if you want. You wouldn't be out of bounds."

"But you don't think I should." I was incredulous.

"Pooja is poor." This plain truth shut me up.

"What she did was wrong, but very human," he continued. "Are you really going to fire her for it?"

"No."

"If you're not going to fire her, then what do you gain by humiliating her?"

"I know," I said. "But."

"So I guess what I think is, if you want to fire her, I will understand," he concluded. "Really. I will. But if you're not going to fire her, I think you should leave it alone."

I never spoke of the coat again, but the picture rankled. I'd long been stifling the temptation to tell Pooja and Mary to stop dipping into the miniature hotel shampoos and creams I kept in a basket for guests and weekend trips. I resented the petty pilfering that forced me to choose between two unlikable roles: the dim-witted housewife oblivious to the swiping of her stuff, or the small-minded boss who begrudged the domestic staff a few daubs of shampoo. I didn't really care about coats or toiletries, but these things were leftovers from a life I'd lost. Now I was weaker and older. I no longer lived in hotels. My womb had been stretched and emptied. And the women who helped care for my children were plundering the remnants of my past.

My mind churning with all of this, I kept checking Pooja's Facebook page when I was supposed to be working. In another picture, she posed on a park bench in tight jeans and gold flats, cradling a bright pink handbag. A few palm trees were visible behind her, but otherwise the shot was tight. When my eye hit the comments, I started.

"Nice pic," Pooja's sister wrote. "How was ur Hong Kong trip?"

A moment later, she'd commented again: "Plizz send me some of ur lovely pics on Whatsapp."

A few minutes after that, their friend and drinking companion chimed in: "So didi wen r u coming bac yaar we r missing u sooo much u knw na we r three angels . . . like charlie's angels."

Pooja liked all of these comments but replied to none. Soon yet another friend voiced the confusion I was also feeling: "Nice yaar," she wrote, using local slang akin to *dude*. "R u in Hk?"

I found Tom reading in bed, and flopped down.

"Pooja has gone to Hong Kong!" I cried. "Why would Pooja go to Hong Kong?"

I was dismayed and disoriented. It was a Sunday. Pooja had just been at our house the day before, and, as far as I knew, she'd be back the next morning. How long was the flight to Hong Kong? Was it possible to go and come so fast? Pooja must be a prostitute or a drug mule . . .

"What are you talking about?"

Sheepishly I described the findings of my online snooping.

"Pooja's not in Hong Kong," Tom said when I'd finished.

"How do you know?"

"How would she pay for the trip? How would she have a visa? Does Pooja even have a passport?" He snorted. "It's bullshit."

"Then why would she say that on Facebook?"

"How should I know?"

"Aren't you curious?"

"Not really."

"What possible explanation can you imagine?"

"They want somebody to think she's gone to Hong Kong. They're trying to create that impression. It could be any number of things."

"I don't like it."

"Please don't waste your time with this." Tom cast a regretful glance at the book he'd set aside.

"What if she doesn't come tomorrow?"

"She'll be here."

"I'm not so sure."

"I am."

I said nothing.

"Is there anything else?" asked Tom, reaching for his book.

The next day she came. She was right on time.

———

Mary's boyfriend would soon leave India. This wasn't the ending we'd imagined. Mary had expected him to find a loophole in the law or sweep her off to Nigeria for a wedding, but he couldn't solve the problem of his expired visa. She'd been living on his promises for years. Dutifully she'd stood in the lines to procure an Indian passport. But when the time came, he simply boarded an airplane and flew away.

Now it was Mary's turn to cry.

"I told you," she reminded me quietly. "Everybody takes their turn to cry."

And cry she did. I found her weeping in the bathroom, curled on the floor by the washing machine. Watching her, I remembered that Xiao Li had also withdrawn to the washing machine to cry. The sturdy box of clean white angles, the sizzling rush of water and soap; a triumph over the wringing and banging and scraping done by poor women around the world—maybe a machine like that offered some solace.

"Mary," I said.

She stumbled to her feet. I wrapped my arms around her awkwardly.

"It's going to be okay," I said. It was a stupid thing to say. I had no idea whether it was going to be okay. I remembered Mary's panicked outrage when Pooja dumped a man. Mary believed in an absolute truth: Better any man than no man. Now her man was gone, and she'd eventually have to look for another. This time she was not only a widow with kids, but a widow with kids who'd lived with—and been dumped by—an African man. This time she was older and sturdier. All of that would cost her dearly on the Indian dating market, if such a phrase could be applied to a system still dictated by pitiless codes of family and caste and dowries and marriage brokers. Her face was thick from crying, and she pulled away from me as if stung.

"I'm okay."

"Do you want to take a break?"

"No, Madame."

"Are you sure?"

"I'm okay."

Her boyfriend ended up in Houston.

"I think I've been where he is," I told Mary.

I remembered a neighborhood of Nigerian immigrants who'd made their homes in the abandoned infrastructure of down-at-heels shopping centers and cracker-box apartments. I remembered a pungent dish of goat stew in a dimly lit diner on a long-lost Saturday afternoon when the thick salt air crept up the bayous off the Gulf of Mexico. I imagined Mary's boyfriend there, another Nigerian immigrant in Houston. This coincidence felt like another fold in the weave of our household, binding our lives together. Time was coincidence and geography an illusion, or perhaps the other way around.

Mary was alone now, and being alone was her greatest fear. Still she showed up every morning. In between crying jags, she still laughed. Once a door closed or an option disappeared, it was dead to her, and her brain heaved forward, combing through alternate possibilities without perceptible regret or frustration.

I was grateful that my children were growing up in her shadow. I hoped she would rub off on them.

I hoped she would rub off on me, too.

Chapter 23

M a'am," Pooja said very quickly one morning. "My family is coming."

"What?" Couldn't anybody ever, just once, let me drink my first cup of coffee before hurling complex topics in my direction? "Who's coming? Coming where?"

"My son," she said. "And my father."

"That's great! To Delhi?" This didn't sound great at all, especially at seven in the morning.

"Yes, ma'am."

"When?"

"Next week they will come."

"They're coming on the train?" I didn't care how they were coming. It was just something to say while I glared at the stove-top cof- feepot, willing it to boil.

"Yes, ma'am."

"You must be really happy." My cheeks were frozen in the grin. *This grin is too much,* I thought.

"Yes, ma'am." She grinned back, gentle and bashful and crooked of tooth, and my trepidation softened.

Of course, this is good, I scolded myself.

Pooja loved her family. She told stories about them. She cried over them. She showed me their pictures and complained about them and worried over them. She screamed at them, sometimes, on the phone in our kitchen. She eulogized them, other times, as if they were already dead.

But Pooja's life in Delhi was hardly an Indian family ideal. She had taken at least one lover, partied in clubs, gone forth and let the city knock her around. She drank and lost things. She kept breaking her glasses. I supposed that some of that, most of that, must be hidden from her father. And now Pooja would show her life in all its prosaic details—where she bought her food, the house she cleaned for a living, and she'd be forced to see it fresh through their eyes. And they would show themselves, too, rough against the city backdrop, and they would all sleep together in Pooja's tiny rooms in our backyard.

I'd lived away from my own family long enough to know that a single visit can destabilize everything. Visitors raise questions without saying a word—their presence, their eyes, their unspoken thoughts. Pooja might be knocked askew. After the recent traumas of the beating and the drinking, I couldn't stand the idea of Pooja becoming any less stable. And then, too, I didn't know what would be expected of me. They were coming because Pooja's father needed eye surgery. A botched cataract operation back home had left a stray eyelash embedded in his eyeball.

"Take them out to lunch," counseled a friend. "Take them to, like, Pizza Express."

"You think they'd like that?"

"I think so," she said. "It's a nice gesture."

"It might be awkward."

"Definitely, it will be awkward," she agreed. "But afterward everybody will be glad."

This was sensible advice, but I couldn't bring myself to suggest it to Pooja. I worried that she'd find the invitation condescending, but would nevertheless feel obliged to accept. I pictured us all eating mediocre pizza and forcing small talk. I tried to imagine whether my kids would come and, if they did, whether Pooja would help wash their hands and cut up their food. I imagined her son watching her, and imagined myself watching her son watch Pooja. I did not invite Pooja and her family to Pizza Express.

Anyway, Tom had other ideas.

"Let's send Pooja and her family to Agra," he suggested one night as we brushed our teeth.

"What?" I was flummoxed. "Why?"

"Don't you think they would like to see the Taj Mahal?" His tone implied that my question was truly moronic.

"Ummm." My immediate reaction was—no, they would not like to see the Taj Mahal! Fresh off a long and uncomfortable train journey, they'd be plunged into one of the world's most crowded tourist sites to be pestered by hawkers and sold overpriced food that might very well give them diarrhea, all so they could crane their necks for a glimpse of the familiar marble walls.

I had to admit, though, Tom had a sense about these things, and he and Pooja seemed to understand each other. Perhaps he intuited some unsatisfied yearning. Tom enjoys iconic sightseeing more than anybody I've ever known. Museums and monuments were a staple of our courtship and family life. Maybe this was another way Pooja and Tom were alike.

"Tom and I were talking," I told Pooja the next day. "He thought your family might like to see the Taj Mahal."

Her face was carefully empty.

"While they're in town."

She said nothing.

"I mean—we'd pay! We'd be happy to—"

"No, ma'am."

"It's not—I mean—it was Tom's idea—"

"Thank you, ma'am. No, I mean—"

"I know it's a hard trip."

"No, ma'am. It's nice of Sir. It's just, you know, we have to get my father's surgery done. We can't travel."

"Of course."

I was relieved. During this exchange, I'd imagined the uncomfortable logistics of such a trip. I'd have to arrange a car, or book train tickets. I'd have to choose a hotel. I'd have to calculate the cost of entrance tickets and meals, and put cash in an envelope. Every decision would be fraught with awareness of how much we'd spend for our own family as opposed to what we spent on Pooja's family.

"Oh," Tom said disapprovingly when I passed along her regrets. I knew that, in her place, he'd have borne any inconvenience and overlooked every awkward moment—just for the memory of taking his family to the Taj Mahal.

Maybe Pooja wasn't so much like Tom, after all.

————

The day of her family's arrival finally came, and Pooja moved through the rooms restlessly. She scrubbed the frying pan, washed coffee cups, made beds. Then, at last, it was time.

"I'll be back in two hours," she said and headed for the station.

Two hours passed, then three, then four, and still she didn't come back. I picked up the phone and put it down again. *Stop.* Pooja hadn't seen her son in more than a year, and I wanted to interrupt their reunion just so Pooja could steam broccoli and fry chicken for our dinner? *Leave her alone,* I lectured myself. *Be happy for her.*

But she has a job, she has responsibilities, I argued. She was the one who volunteered to come back in two hours. She was blowing her own deadline.

I have work, too. I argued with air.

"Have you called just to check?" Tom asked when I interrupted his work to consult.

"I feel guilty."

"Calling to politely let her know you're still aware that she works for us isn't a bad idea," Tom said.

"You don't think it's unkind?"

"I think it's fine to say, 'Hi, Pooja. I just wanted to check how things are going.'"

"I'm making lunch," Pooja explained giddily when I called. "I'll be back at three."

"Okay," I said coldly.

"Is that all right?"

"Of course!" Now I was embarrassed. Pooja could hear everything—my pettiness, my ambivalence.

"Bye, ma'am," she said. In the background I heard the laughter and clank of family.

————

Pooja's father and son were waiting on the street when I came back from school drop. They stood at a distance, as if they had nothing to do with each other. It was the morning of the surgery, and they were waiting for my car.

Pooja's father was not, as I'd envisioned, a towering man of thick hands and a majestic head. He was short and slight, and his back curved in a subservient stoop. The eye was taped shut, and his head bobbed and rocked as if he were a bird pecking for grain. Pooja's son, Aryan, the small boy of my imagination, towered over his grandfather. He had a long, lean frame, trendy sports clothes, and a hard jaw.

I climbed out of the car, and we all said hello.

"You're okay? Comfortable?" I said.

"Yes, yes."

"Thank you," added Pooja's father, too sincerely for comfort. In the end, we'd paid for the surgery instead of the trip to Agra. The money made everything strange.

The surgery was quick. They were back from the clinic before lunch. Pooja fed Patrick peas and pasta, spooned yogurt into his mouth, and sang his favorite Hindi song about a wooden rocking horse that turns into a real horse and runs away.

In the servants' quarter out back, Aryan looked after his grandfather. It was understood that Pooja had to work.

———

The January sky hung drab and dirty over the city. Winter flowers bloomed in the gardens: brilliant, bitter blossoms of chrysanthemum and marigold. Aryan played soccer in the park, a stretch of slicked mud and scabbing grass. When the sun punctured the clouds our neighbors prowled back and forth, barking into their iPhones and taking vitamins from the faint rays.

Aryan was bored. Our neighborhood was just a place for rich people to live. There was no teahouse; no cheap café; no lively shopping center. Soon he left to stay with his aunt, who worked in a neighboring city full of skyscrapers and shopping malls.

"It's okay." Pooja seemed to mean it. "There's more for him to do there."

I lurked on Facebook as Pooja's sister posted pictures of Aryan's adventures. Mugging at the mall in knockoff Timberlands and skinny jeans. Pushing a cart at the supermarket. Infinite in an amusement hall of mirrors.

Then he came back to Pooja, and she swooned around the kitchen like a teenager in love.

"He's like a little boy," she gushed. "He sits by me. He stays close. He says, 'Mommy, let me take care of you.' He says, 'Mommy, you won't have to work forever.'"

"He missed you," I said. "That's so sweet." I, too, clung to these affectionate anecdotes. I badly wanted to believe their relationship could thrive despite the separation, that it was perfectly fine for Aryan to live with his grandfather in the mountains while Pooja played a bit part in raising my children.

"I'm so happy," Pooja said, and I believed her.

A few days later she was yelling on the phone.

"What's going on?"

"Sorry, ma'am," she said. "It's my sister."

"You're fighting with your sister?"

She grinned sheepishly. "We together had a fight with my father."

"Oh no," I said. "What happened?"

"He's just like that," she said, defiant but evasive. "He got upset the other night. He was yelling at me, 'You're no daughter of mine!' And my sister defended me. So now everybody is upset."

"That sounds bad."

"Yes, ma'am. But it's okay. We're always like that."

"Fighting?"

"Yes, ma'am."

"Oh. Well, I hope it gets better."

"Yes, ma'am."

———

I thought Pooja might crash into another depression after her son left, but instead there was a lingering lightness.

"Aryan was talking to me seriously about his plans," she told me. "He wants to play football. He wants to try out for the teams. If he doesn't make it, he wants to join the army."

"The army!"

"He was saying like that. He was telling me, 'Don't worry, Mommy. I will take care of you.'"

These possibilities glittered in her palm like gathered shells, various and thrilling. Her son the soldier. Her son the student. Her son the soccer star.

"What about you?" I asked. "What do you want to do?"

Sometimes I tried to imagine Pooja in her old age, but the picture never came. I had a vague idea of villages, mountains, grandchildren. I didn't know if these images were realistic.

"I dunno," Pooja said. Her fingers fiddled with our jars of sugar and salt; tea and coffee. "It would be good if I could work overseas. I could save a lot of money then."

"You mean with a family?"

"Something like that."

"Maybe that will happen," I said lightly. I knew we'd never take any of these women out of India. "But your son—"

"That's the problem."

"He's getting bigger now," I pointed out.

"If I could go out for a few years and save some real money, I know what I would do."

"Tell me."

"I'd open a guesthouse back in Darjeeling," she said. "A guesthouse and restaurant. My sister and I always talk about it."

"Fantastic idea," I enthused. "You'd be so good at that."

"You think so?" Pooja said.

"Definitely," I said. "Amazing. You should be in charge of the food."

We are perfectly programmed, we Americans, to pour enthusiasm on every plan that comes our way. We believe decent manners require us to tell one another, constantly, that we can do anything, we deserve better, we must never relinquish our dreams. I have often wondered, during these long years abroad, whether this habit is useful or even kind. Still I am a product of my upbringing.

"I don't know," Pooja demurred. "That's what I'd like to do."

I knew Tom would be interested in this exchange.

"We're not taking Pooja back to America," he said immediately.

"Of course not." What was he even talking about?

"I actually would think it was a great idea—"

"I wouldn't." The hell?

"—but there's no way we're taking an alcoholic back to the U.S."

"There's no way we're taking *anybody* back to the U.S."

"I don't know," Tom mused.

I tucked this conversation away for future argument. I was still thinking about Pooja.

"I was struck by her guesthouse idea."

"It would be great," Tom agreed. "She'd do it just right."

"I think so, too."

"If she can control the drinking."

"Right."

"You know what we could do?"

A rush of happiness opened through my belly. I knew before he said it that, for once, we had exactly the same idea.

"What?" I couldn't bear to be wrong.

"When we finally leave here, we could give her a chunk of cash. It wouldn't take that much to open a place like that here."

"I was thinking *exactly* the same thing," I said, beaming.

"It would be nice to do something for Pooja."

"It could be life changing for her."

"She deserves it."

"And it would be good for us."

"I hear you," Tom said.

"I always think, with every woman, that when we say good-bye I'll give her a lot of money," I said. "I'll make it so, in the end, it was good for her. But somehow we never get that far. Things always fall apart first."

"Well," said Tom. "Let's see how it goes."

"Yeah."

Chapter 24

That spring we experimented with "staycations"—leaving the boys with Mary and checking into a hotel overnight. This, of course, was Tom's idea. I was too neurotic to pretend we had no children, even for a few hours. But in the interest of marital upkeep, I tried. I'd dab on a little makeup and wear something other than jeans, and upon seeing an immaculate king bed in a chamber swaddled in silence, I'd refrain from suggesting we tuck ourselves under the covers immediately and sleep until lunchtime the next day. I tried to relish his-and-hers massages and dinners in lush gardens even though I, for one, was far too tense to experience any recreation.

One fateful Friday night we booked a room at the Imperial Hotel. This iconic landmark is a colonial dreamscape of palm colonnades and art deco pilasters and gilt-framed renditions of gallant Indian soldiers and yet more gallant British soldiers; elephants and temples. The lawn drinks more water than entire Delhi neighborhoods. The partition of India was negotiated at the bar. Tom wanted to go, and I sort of wanted to go, too, at least I wanted to want to go. But I was anxious, and Pooja could tell.

"Ma'am," she said as I packed my smallest suitcase. "I'll sleep in the house."

"That's okay. Mary's sleeping here."

"Mary sleeps so deeply," she said. "If something happens she won't wake up."

"You don't mind?"

"Mary and I will both sleep here," she said. "I'll feel better."

"Me, too."

I smiled indulgently at Pooja's dedication to our kids.

Just before we left for the hotel, I made a crucial strategic mistake. In a last-minute spasm of parental wistfulness, I suggested to Mary that, after we'd finished sleeping late and lingering over breakfast, she could bring the kids over for a dip in the fabulous marble swimming pool. *I'll call you,* I said. I should have known this was a bad idea.

The next morning we were still stupefied in sheets and dreams, thick hotel curtains yanked tight against the dawn, when my phone bellowed.

"What the fuck?" moaned Tom.

"It's Mary."

"Hello?"

"Oh," Mary yelled. "We are here."

"What?" I blinked around the gloomy room. Was I dreaming? Nightmaring? "Where?"

"Kids were too excited."

"You're in the hotel?"

"Kids were too excited, waiting at home. They wanted to come."

"You're—where? In the lobby?"

"Yes, Madame."

"Um."

Tom stared at me. The warning in his eyes was empty. We were trapped.

"I'm coming."

I hung up.

"Tell her to take them home." Tom had the muted hysteria of a prisoner who has exhausted his last appeal.

"I can't. Imagine how crushed they would be."

"Why did she do this?"

"I don't know."

"What did you tell her?"

My complicity, of course, was also in question.

"I told her," I said resentfully, "that I would probably give her a call. Once we got up. To bring the kids for swimming.

"*Later,* I told her," I added.

"She's ruined the whole thing," he grumbled.

"I know."

"The whole point was to get some sleep."

"I know."

———

Dreams uprooted and breakfast invaded, we took the boys swimming and then went home. Everything, including ourselves, looked dingier and drearier after the exquisite hotel. Dust on the stairs. Streaks on the walls. A black bag of trash awaiting pickup on the landing.

In the kitchen Pooja stirred soup, fried chicken dumplings, and smiled to see us. We sat down in the dining room for a family lunch. While the kids ate, my eyes ran idly over the shelves. Skimmed, caught, retraced, and stopped. Somebody had moved the liquor bottles. The Jameson was on the wrong shelf. The Johnnie Walker Black had been dragged forward.

I opened my mouth to call Pooja, but my voice died in my throat because I suddenly remembered the trash bag on the landing. It was a small incongruity that now seemed significant. We never left our trash outside lest stray cats rip the bags and scatter the garbage.

Leaving Tom and the boys chattering and chewing, I walked through the house and out the front door and picked up the trash bag.

Clank.

I gave it a shake.

Clank, clink, clank.

I unknotted the bag and there, nestled among soggy tea leaves and stinking paper towels and wilting cucumber peels, lay two empty bottles of cheap whiskey.

I fetched a trash bag from the kitchen, ignoring Pooja, who puttered over the stove. I slipped the bottles into the bag and, pressing them together so they wouldn't clash, hid them in a little-used cupboard in our bathroom.

I knew it was Pooja. In my mind, she was already fired. But there remained crucial questions. What if strangers came over? What if there were men? And my babies here—I had to know. And that meant I had to get Mary to turn state's evidence.

With trembling hands and quaking heart, I read storybooks to the boys and tucked them in for a nap. By the time I called Mary into the dining room, Pooja had gone home for the afternoon.

"What happened last night," I said coldly.

"No," she laughed nervously. "Nothing," she said quickly.

"Please don't lie."

"No—I was sleeping—Pooja was here—"

"I know something happened."

"I didn't see. Nothing happened. You know I always say my rosary—"

"Who was here?"

"Nobody. Pooja and me."

"Who was drinking?"

"Nobody was drinking."

"Wait."

I returned with the bottles and banged them down on the table. The crash made Mary jump a little, and for a moment I was afraid I'd shattered the glass. That's when I noticed the rage sloshing around inside of me.

"Tell me the truth." I took the bottles out of the bag. "Or I'll fire you."

She looked at the bottles, my face, the bottles again. Anger rushed and poured through my veins.

"I should fire you," I told her. "Whatever happened was your responsibility. I left—*you*—in charge of my kids."

She was quiet. I was also quiet. I was ready to be quiet all afternoon.

"It was Pooja," she finally said.

"Uh, yeah," I sighed. "That much I understand."

She didn't say anything.

"Who was here?"

"Nobody," Mary said. "Only Pooja and her sister."

"They had a party?"

"Not a party. Just Pooja's sister was here."

"Nobody else."

"Yes, before God. You know I am a Christian woman and I can't—"

"If I find out later that somebody else was here—"

"It's not like that."

"And I will find out. The landlord put those cameras on the door—"

"Nobody was here."

"I told you Pooja's sister couldn't be here," I said. "I told both of you."

"If Pooja's sister comes, what can I say?"

"What can you say?" Anger so hot it could sterilize a wound. "You can say, 'Nobody's allowed over. We're babysitting.' And if they insist, you could pick up the phone and call me. That was your responsibility."

"What can I do?" Mary began to cry. "We are ayahs. If I call you then all the others will say I'm bad. I shouldn't do like that."

"You don't work for them. You work for me."

I didn't let on that, in my secret hidden heart, I was not unsympathetic. Mary would remain among these women long after we'd left India. She relied upon them for job leads, housing, or a cash loan if she hit the skids. There was a legitimate, self-protective need to remain a community member in good standing. But I didn't want her to intuit my sympathy. I wanted her to think that, whatever she did, I would find out—and I would avenge.

"I don't want to fire you," I said. "You have been very important to me."

"I don't drink."

"I'm alone here. I don't have anybody I can trust," I said. "When I ask you to come into my house, to help me take care of my children, that trust is sacred."

Tears filmed my eyes. I was deliberately manipulating Mary. I was also speaking with unfiltered honesty. Both were true, both at once. I was showing Mary my buried fears, but I was doing it strategically. I wanted to leverage my vulnerability to make her more trustworthy. To protect our family by bringing her closer to our side.

I was so tired.

And the main problem was still there. I'd have to fire Pooja.

———

The next day was Sunday, Pooja's day off. I considered calling her, but Tom convinced me to leave it alone.

"Wait until Monday morning," he said. "When the kids are gone."

"What if Mary told Pooja what happened?"

"I'd say there's zero chance she *didn't* tell her."

As soon as Pooja walked into the house on Monday, I knew she knew. Without a word or a glance she took her place at the kitchen counter, face to the window and hands slicing fruit as if they belonged to somebody else. I fried eggs and soaked oats in milk. Silently we made breakfast together for the last time.

Tom went to work. Max went to school. Mary arrived and took Patrick to a toddler art class.

"Pooja," I said. "Let's talk."

We sat at the dining room table.

"Did you talk with Mary?"

"Yes, ma'am."

"And?"

"No problem, ma'am. I'll leave."

This was not what I had expected, and it shut me up for a minute. I thought she'd beg for her job, shout in protest, throw things or curse. Her calm indifference was disorienting. When my voice came, it was too high.

"That's it? You'll leave?"

"What can I say? Once the trust is broken it doesn't work anymore."

"Well, did I misunderstand something?"

"I don't know because you talked to Mary," she said. "You didn't talk to me."

"I'm talking to you now."

"You could have called."

So that was it. Crazy as it was, she was angry with me.

"Would it have made any difference?" I asked.

"If it's like that, no."

"You want to tell me what happened on Friday?"

"My sister came."

"I told you your sister couldn't come."

"She was sleeping at my house, and she was bored. She brought me some food, and then she went away and came back with the whiskey. She was drinking, but I wasn't drinking with her."

"Mary said you were."

"Mary was sleeping."

"And you drank my whiskey, too."

"No, ma'am."

"You did, though. You didn't put the bottles back properly."

"Maybe we knocked against them."

"Pooja," I sighed. "This is beneath us."

"Yes, ma'am," she muttered. "Anyway if the trust is gone I don't want to stay here."

My rage was spent. Her feelings were hurt, and I had an irrational sense I'd wronged her.

"Pooja," I said, "do you want to keep your job?"

"Yes, ma'am." For the first time, Pooja looked like she might cry. "Nobody would like to lose their job."

"I planned to fire you, but somehow I don't want to."

I couldn't believe what I was hearing myself say. The wall had broken down between my thoughts and the utterances of my mouth. Suddenly the bottles didn't seem important. Her sister had come, bored, with a little whiskey. Hadn't my own parents and grandparents cheerfully boozed their way through my childhood?

"Okay." Pooja was leery and incredulous, watching me from the tails of her eyes. She would fire herself, I realized, for this infraction. How foolish I felt! Smart enough to figure out what had happened and yet weak enough, delusional enough, to try to change the shape of the truth.

"I'll call you," I said.

I sent her back to the quarter. I called Tom.

"I just talked to Pooja," I said, "and somehow the story doesn't seem quite so bad."

"Oh really?" In the background phones rang, meetings grumbled. I'd called Tom in his den of facts to plead my fantasies. "How so?"

"Well, her sister was just there. And she cooked them dinner, so Pooja let her come over and eat. And then she just kind of brought the whiskey, so Pooja drank with her. But it wasn't Pooja's idea, I mean that's what she said, and for some reason I just had the feeling she was telling the truth. Like it was a misunderstanding. Maybe we're making too much of it."

In the silence that followed, I heard the futility of my argument.

"How is that different from what we already knew?" Tom finally said.

"Well, I mean, intent. I guess."

"It's the same story. Nothing has changed."

"I guess you're right." I was marveling, because it was true. It was exactly the same story. I'd called Tom in a rush, as if new details had come to light. But nothing had changed.

When I called Pooja, I could tell she'd anticipated this result. She knew Tom, and she knew it was over.

"I'm sorry." This time I was crisp and firm. "I couldn't save your job."

———

We gave her a little time to move, and enough money to keep her things in storage until she found a new job. And then it was over; she was gone. It was the second time we'd lost Pooja, but this time there would be no return.

"My thoughts keep turning to Pooja, wondering if she's found a room and how she's doing," I wrote to Tom. "I miss her."

"I hope she does well," he said. "But she made her decisions."

A beat passed, and then he, too, softened.

"I felt sad this morning as well, wondering if she'll see candidates coming in and feel like, for all her work, she's quickly replaceable," he said. "The problem, for me, was that I couldn't imagine her staying and it working out."

"I know." I couldn't disagree. "She had to go."

I'd fired Pooja just when I needed her most: my agent returned the manuscript with suggestions for revisions. I struggled to concentrate, staring at page after page of Track Changes, trying to find the stamina to face these scenes and characters yet again. Worrying, all the time, about Pooja. The draft was starting to remind me of some moth-eaten piece of mangy fur that I'd been stitching and clipping and fluffing for years. I hated the feel and shape of it.

I withdrew from work by watching Pooja's Facebook feed like a soap opera. She made an oblique reference to changing jobs. "If you weren't happy with yesterday, try something different today" read a slogan she copied onto her wall. "DON'T STAY STUCK. DO BETTER."

"time for a change. . . . wish me luck. . . . ." Pooja had written over this picture.

This was, of course, a normal and predictable reflex. She was saving face, covering up the humiliation of getting fired for squalid misconduct. I understood, but I was irritated. I couldn't help thinking we were the "yesterday" that hadn't been good enough.

Later she posted again: "Finally back to Gurgaon. . . . . . . feeling so relaxed, peaceful n happy. . . . yippee!!!!!!!"

She posed on a terrace, lush greenery all around. Wind in her hair, eyes hidden by enormous sunglasses, she scowled at the camera. She was wearing my old shirt: a flowing white peasant blouse with china-blue embroidery. A pretty piece of clothing, but stained. I'd put it aside for donation, but Pooja had snagged it for herself. Something about the sky suggested the sea. But upon inspection, I couldn't see any water. The frame was so tight she could be right here in Delhi. I was always falling for these illusions of hers. I didn't know how far the illusion went. Maybe Pooja had always been some other person. I wanted to think so, now that she was gone. Now I scanned her Facebook page, hoping to see evidence that she was no great loss.

"Hot . . . hot . . . hot. Enthralling . . . enticing . . . Mesmerizing," commented a man in aviator sunglasses.

A minute later, he was back: "Senorita is lookin Creme de la Creme."

"thnx for ur lovely comments," Pooja purred.

"Awesome!!! Enthralling," the man continued.

Maybe Pooja had a new boyfriend.

I turned to Mary for information, but Mary had run dry.

"Have you talked to Pooja?" I tried to sound casual.

"No, Madame."

"You should call her," I said. "I've been wondering how she's doing."

"She didn't pick up my call."

"You think she's mad?"

"I don't know," Mary said, with a crumpled wince of a grin that made me think she did, indeed, know.

"Don't worry," I told her. "She'll get over it."

————

When I invited Mary to move into the backyard quarter, I didn't even consider the possibility that she might not accept. Mary was our most senior employee, and by far the most diligent and loyal. She'd have lived there all along if not for her boyfriend. Now that he was out of the picture and the rooms stood empty, I assumed she'd move immediately. I was already looking forward to the return of an onsite babysitter.

But when I brought it up, Mary balked.

"I don't know." She looked at the floor.

"You don't have to—"

I ran out of words. I was bewildered.

"I mean—" I tried again. "I thought you'd *like* to move in."

"I feel shy."

"Shy?"

Shy implied bodily functions or sex or social timidity, and certainly Mary had never suffered from the latter.

"I'm worried what will the others say."

"What others?"

"The other *didis*."

"What would they say?"

"Pooja is calling people. She says I got her into trouble so I could have the quarter."

"She's telling people that?" I was aghast. "But that's crazy!"

"She thinks I did like that."

"But—you almost got fired lying for her."

"Yes!" Mary's face shone for a moment with the self-righteousness of a maligned witness. "But Pooja is saying I planned everything."

True, the timing was terrible. Mary had just been abandoned by her boyfriend, and there were clean, safe rooms that Mary couldn't have because Pooja was already installed. Then Pooja had gotten fired after Mary had a secret discussion with me.

I knew, too, that Pooja's theory was rooted in something more complicated and ugly: Pooja had eclipsed Mary, and we all knew it. This knowledge twisted its way among us, never spoken but always present. Mary was the faithful employee who'd worked tirelessly for us since we'd come to India. Pooja was a relative newcomer, a mercurial figure prone to drama.

And yet we liked Pooja better. It was as simple and ruthless as that. Pooja had formed relationships that were impossible for Mary to ignore, and equally impossible for her to duplicate. Pooja and I had conversations about things unrelated to the kids or the house. Tom doted on her. Even the baby, technically Mary's charge, was rapt and joyful in Pooja's presence. Her life was turbulent and her decisions unpredictable, but she had some charisma that could not be stifled.

Mary could not pull off such alchemy. Mary bumbled and blabbed and toiled with ceaseless energy so that nobody could forget how dependable and hardworking she was. And we all appreciated her, and felt beholden to her, and wanted good things for her. But in the brutal, illogical law of human relations, where effort earns no reward whatsoever, Pooja was the favorite. I knew it, and Mary knew it, and Pooja knew it, and all three of us knew that the other two also knew, but that it must never be acknowledged lest our fragile balance of personalities collapse.

Pooja might have feared that Mary would strike, but that wasn't Mary's style. She preferred to let the injustice of her second-place status sit among us like a penance, offering it up to household gods and punishing us subtly with her suffering. I was the only one who saw it, but to me it was plain. There existed this Catholic understanding between Mary and me.

I leaned on Mary to take the quarter. I warned her against letting

Pooja's wrath destroy an important opportunity to live in a secure spot and save money. And, at last, she moved in.

After that, their friendship was lost forever. These classmates, these allies, with their impenetrable fortress built barefoot among sofa cushions on our living room floor, in whispered jokes and secrets, picking at their hangnails, hair in their faces—all of that had been torn apart, and it wasn't coming back.

Chapter 25

That summer my agent finally sent a draft of my novel to a few editors. I had enormous expectations. I thought the manuscript would be snapped up and brought forth to acclaim, hardly a word rearranged. It is strange to remember this now, to confess to my own deluded self-regard. But it's true—that's what I expected. I was already picturing the trays of rose macarons and rose-and-pistachio-scented kebabs and rose-infused vodka I'd serve at the all-night party I'd throw to celebrate my forthcoming novel.

It wasn't like that. Of course it wasn't like that. Slowly the replies trickled back. There was praise but also the underlying conviction that the book could not be published as it was. Everyone thought the novel needed to be changed, although there was no consensus on its specific flaws. One editor liked the beginning but not the end; another, the end but not the beginning. One found the structure off-putting; the other thought it was uniquely interesting.

I shouldn't have been surprised. I knew fiction was a gamble. But certain images from the streets of Moscow had clung to the inside of my brain—phrases so jarring I still puzzled over their meaning, loves that had rushed and faded, feelings I had experienced in Russia, so much in Russia, but only in Russia—and I wanted to trace those threads back and knit them together, to turn wisps into substance. I wanted to write literary fiction.

I've always believed there is dignity in risk. There is fun, too, but only—and I was just getting this now—because failure is waiting all the time. That's what makes it interesting; that's where the grace lies. You take your chances knowing you might lose, you might crash, you might go broke.

None of it would be any fun, I lectured myself that summer, *if this weren't always a possibility.* But now I was weakened, and subject to temptation. I could sell a pulpier version. And maybe it would be good, maybe even superior to mine, but it wouldn't be the book I meant to write. I couldn't do that. I couldn't let it be turned into something else. I had to fix the book myself.

"I'd rather keep it unpublished forever than turn it into something I didn't mean for it to be," I told Tom. I wanted to commit this pledge to the record because I was, indeed, tempted to sell it off and move on.

"Good," he agreed. "But I can't believe it's not getting published," he added loyally.

I shrugged. My hurt feelings were drying up, and I recognized the truth of the critiques. I didn't like any of the suggested remedies, but I saw the flaws they sought to fix. The book wasn't ready, I now realized, for an editor. In my desperation to prove that I was still a serious writer in spite of motherhood, I had shoved it forward too soon. I'd ignored my doubts because I was so ravenous to rejoin the wider world. And the book was my only ticket, all I'd tried to do for the past four years. Four years!

Four years, and it wasn't enough. With dull dread I realized that after all the time I'd poured into the project, the project must have yet more time. It was like giving blood only to be asked for more blood still, and then more, and then more. And you think, surely, there can be no more blood, except somehow there is always more blood.

I could face this revision, but not right away. I needed a break from the manuscript, with its tangle of psychological motivations and sprawling plot and surreal Russian backdrops. I couldn't think about it without being washed in the raw emotions of pregnancy and early motherhood. The uneven bursts of work, my crazed insistence on writing when I was too tired to recall basic vocabulary words—the effort had flirted with madness and nearly ruined my brain and yet, in the end, had also salvaged me. The book was a dangerous bridge

I'd picked my way over, and on its faulty structure I'd crossed from a defunct existence as a foreign correspondent into my present self.

Now I couldn't stand the sight of it. I had to leave it alone and do something else.

In truth, the next idea had long since unfolded itself in my brain, intact and inevitable. But the subject was terrifying and also somehow abasing, and it took me a long time to admit, even to myself, that I would go there.

———

"I have this idea," I'd say, tentatively, to a friend here and there. Then I'd mention domestic labor. In the form of a memoir. Myself, and domestic labor.

My self-described "expat" friends in Delhi thought this was hilarious. They loved it, in a nasty sort of way. They didn't understand what I was talking about, really, and so they assumed I was planning to document the mistreatment of maids. We had the habit of collecting and swapping outrageous rumors: which foreigners paid shamelessly low salaries, who made their staff sleep on the kitchen floor, and who kept a much-feared white glove to test the furniture for dust. We'd laughed—because what else could you do?—at the Europeans who were socialists back home but were rumored to have adopted Brahmin standards for their Indian domestic workers in Delhi, forbidding them to drink from the same cups, sit on the same chairs, or use the same toilets as the family. We'd heard all of that and more.

"It'll be a bestseller," my friends said. They were titillated by the suggestion of gossip and embarrassment. They saved salacious anecdotes from other people's homes and presented them for consideration.

I protested, but only mildly. "It's not really going to be like that . . ." I, too, enjoyed the fantasy of exposing the petty sadism. By isolating the worst anecdotes, I could draw a clean line between my virtuous self and the exploiters.

But as my ideas got more articulate, the reaction from acquaintances grew colder. Every time I tried to describe the project, people would interrupt and argue. I never managed to finish talking. When it comes to domestic work and motherhood—believe me, I have learned this—everybody has a point to argue. It was enough to hear that I was writing about my own fate getting intertwined with impoverished working mothers in China and India; that I wanted to write not only about my struggles but about theirs, too—their origins, their paths to domestic work, their childcare arrangements. At that point, the conversation inevitably collapsed. As if the simple exercise of placing myself alongside the nannies was already an affront; as if equating my sons with the children of local domestic help was an unacceptable equivalence.

"Well, just wait a minute—wait a minute," interrupted an American father at a New Delhi cocktail party. "I just want to say—I mean in defense—it's a job. It's a chance for them—"

"No, but I think what she's saying—" interrupted his American wife.

"I'm not condemning—" I interrupted.

"But the thing is, these people, these jobs, I have seen—" he interrupted me again.

"Wait, but she's trying—"

"I *have* a nanny—" I said. As if to protest, I am still one of you! I have not broken rank!

Then they started rambling about the caste system, and soon we all drifted off.

Nearly every parent I knew in New Delhi, with the exception of the nannies themselves (and I even knew of one highly paid nanny who did employ a nanny), hired a nanny. People assumed I was attacking the crucial element that made their lifestyle possible. For working women, it was even more personal: I was implying that the only method they'd found for continuing their work was, in fact, a source of guilt and shame. That wasn't my idea, but people heard it, anyway. Those feelings already ghost around the consciences of women who hire other women to work in their homes. We are all guilty—not quite guilty enough to do something else, but terribly guilty, all the same. And we are determined to avoid the trap of this guilt—we repeat incantations to banish the guilt, and when we sense somebody edging in that direction, we rear up to drive them off.

I was warned not to generalize, even though I was writing about myself. I was browbeaten to include outlying examples—that one super-involved unemployed father, that one unbelievably fulfilled nanny—as if they were mainstream reality. There was a panicky tone to these conversations. As if a few flimsy floorboards kept us all from crashing into the basement, and I was taking an ax to the ground. To suggest this solution for women's work might be less than ideal—heresy. Domestic labor was upward mobility. Leave it alone.

"So we're all just bitches, then," snapped a working mother friend. We were speed-walking together in Lodi Gardens, and suddenly she was striding faster, taking great angry lopes away from me, and I trotted to catch up, spilling conciliatory words.

"*No,*" I panted.

"That's not what this is about," I choked.

"I don't have an answer."

I kept saying that. I didn't have an answer, but I was interested in finding one.

"I assume you've considered this from a Marxist standpoint," crackled a beautiful young woman in a luxurious yellow sari. "Well, you must have, of course."

It was late on a thick monsoon night, at the kind of party I almost never attended anymore. Full of smart young things—journalists, publishers, intellectuals. All read up on absolutely everything and hunting for conversational game. Out for argument, to skin the weak, to make a name for themselves. An ugly room, really, but there I was. And everybody I talked to kept asking whether I knew somebody else, and I never did. And then they would act very surprised and say, "You would love her!" After the tenth time or so I began to smirk, although I knew it added to the ambient ugliness, because, of course, I would not love all these people and it was a silly thing to keep telling strangers—that they would love somebody they have never met.

"Well," I stammered, caught off guard by the lady in yellow and her undergraduate question. I knew I had approximately three seconds to avoid becoming an anecdote in her arsenal—the American writer with the rubbish education.

But all I could see were the faces of Xiao Li, Pooja, and Mary. Village faces, hard-work faces, mother faces. Kitchens, cold mornings, aching backs. Then I remembered Marxist writings on women and work that I had indeed read, earnestly, when I was preparing to cover Moscow. Among other things, they advocated for socialized day care. Well, of course I had considered that—but I didn't need dead German men to come up with that idea.

"Yes, of course," I said quickly. "But my book is not a polemic."

———

One day, around the time when I was reporting on war and political Islam and Middle Eastern politics, I met a prominent editor who said: "I just really love your coverage, the way you write about women and children."

I responded politely, but privately I was baffled. I knew that my stories had been no more concerned with women and children than the articles of my male colleagues. On the one hand, yes, I had documented the effects of war on civilians—but, realistically, all the journalists in the field had done that. To be congratulated for writing about women and children, to be singled out for that, suggested that I had not covered the strategic and geopolitical and tactical aspects of war. I'd covered those angles extensively, but I was remembered for softer pieces. As if I had lingered, all that time, in households. Except I hadn't.

That disorientation came back to me as I sat down to write about domestic workers and the realms of women and children. I couldn't help feeling that I was capitulating. But wasn't this attitude part of the problem? If serious people never wrote deeply about the household, about work and gender and money and race, we couldn't expect things to improve. If the centrality of these domestic chores was consistently denied, then women would just keep on doing all the work. Seeing these women come and go from my house, I'd become curious, then nosy, and finally invasive. I'd stalked Pooja on Facebook, only to realize I couldn't know her by spying.

I didn't want my family to leave behind a trail of forgotten women who once upon a time took care of our children. I didn't want my boys to grow up and say, *I had nannies once. They were like part of the family,* as if the women existed only as a function of ourselves. I wanted to commit a fuller truth to print. Our boys should know there were children we never saw; sacrifices we couldn't make right.

But to do that, I'd have to track down the women I'd lost. I'd have to interview them and ask their permission to write about them. I couldn't predict what I'd find, or how it would change my perception of my own household and my own responsibility. Finding the women, I realized, could be dangerous.

PART THREE

THE WOMEN

Chapter 26

I kept tracking the churn of Pooja's life on Facebook. I followed her moods, watched her face, tried to read between the lines. She'd crow with glee, fall silent for a few days, and then resurface in sorrow.

"Does anyone sell happiness on fb gotta buy some," she wrote one day.

A few days later: "ALONE . . . ALONE . . . ALONE . . ."

One day she wrote to her son: "I m so sorry my baby dat at certain times i m not dere wen U need me d most. MAMMA LOVES U A LOT."

She posted melodramatic cartoons of pretty girls crying and, one day, an anti-abortion meme depicting the hand of a tiny fetus.

I was worried. The pattern of lavish spending, comments from men, and sexy outfits made me wonder whether Pooja had turned to sex work because she couldn't find another job. Considering this possibility, I began to question our reaction to her abuse. For the first time I considered whether, if we'd understood the paucity of Pooja's options, we'd have overlooked the domestic violence. Perhaps I had judged Pooja's plight through eyes that were excessively American—simplistic and idealistic and sheltered from the hard truth of her circumstances.

The same skinny man with aviator sunglasses still covered her every post with obsequious comments. I assumed he was her boyfriend, so naturally I started tracking him, too.

His name was Rupesh. Imagine a Nepali version of Pony Boy who's reached middle age without updating his style. If you can summon this picture, then you are looking at Rupesh. He greased his hair into a pompadour, pegged his jeans, and hacked the sleeves off his sweatshirts. Tight muscles popped from his bones like tennis balls encased in socks. He had a bedraggled moustache and glassy eyes with a high-octane, angry light. He was prone to rambling posts and maudlin poetry.

He didn't come across very well, and neither did Pooja. On the walls of Facebook they proclaimed their love, vented their rage, and humiliated each other with hinted accusations of infidelity. There were sticky love poems, pop song dedications, and fiery breakups.

"D word happiness is deleted from my dictionary," Pooja wrote one day. "It's really not meant for me. To all concerned ppl I hv set ur loved one free."

"I'm sick n tired . . . just waiting for d day wen I close my eyes for eternal sleep," she wrote around the same time. "Waiting for dat day to come."

A few days later Pooja was in a bar with her sister and a near-empty bottle of whiskey. She grinned blurrily. "Birthday bash @ MAN-HATTAN," she wrote. "hv learnt to stay happy."

I sent her a text message. She ignored me. I waited a few weeks and then sent another message. This time she agreed to meet.

———

I wanted to meet Pooja in one of the mall restaurants from her Face-book pictures. I pictured us sipping cocktails in a bright and airless room with perky pop music playing. Drawn close by the alcohol, jarred into frankness by the novelty of sitting together in such a place, we'd talk. I wanted that more than anything: just to finally talk without rules and roles. It had been half a year since she left our house, and anything seemed possible.

But Pooja didn't let me off so easily. She asked to meet at Dilli Haat, a sprawling open-air handicrafts market perched on the edge of a screaming thoroughfare in South Delhi. I'd been there a few times, escorting houseguests who wanted to shop for bargain tablecloths or tapestries. I thought it was an odd place to meet Pooja, whose tastes ran to the brand new and machine manufactured. I wondered whether we'd shop for wind chimes and stoles, or hit the regional food stalls for dumplings and spiced tea. But I had no room to complain about the venue. I'd once held all the power, but now Pooja was in charge.

We met on a Sunday afternoon between Thanksgiving and Christmas. The sky over the city was tinged yellow, and grains of dust stuck to my teeth. I climbed the chalky steps to the craft market entrance and there, right away, was Pooja, stepping forward in a twisted lurch—as if she were reaching for me and trying to escape at the same time.

She looked more street hardened than I remembered, dressed in a camisole and black cardigan, hunched against the cold. Blue eye shadow smudged her lids, and her mouth was painted shocking pink. When I hugged her, I smelled cigarettes and musky perfume. Maybe an undercurrent of stale beer, but I wasn't sure. Her sister loomed over her shoulder.

"Hi, Ricky." I tried to sound bright.

"Hi, ma'am," she replied curtly. "I want to go inside," she told Pooja scornfully. "You two can talk." She vanished into the crowds.

I turned to Pooja. "Should we go? We can get tickets."

To pass the gate you had to buy a ticket. The tickets cost about twenty-five cents.

"No, ma'am," said Pooja. "No reason to go inside."

She wasn't going to spend any money on this meeting, I realized, nor would she allow me to spend any money on her. Not even a quarter. We'd have to hang around in a free public place until Pooja's pride was satisfied.

"I'm really happy to see you." I shifted my weight from foot to foot. "I've missed you."

"Yes, ma'am," she said. "Even me."

"Please don't call me ma'am. You don't work for me anymore."

"Yes, ma'am." She caught herself, laughed, shrugged. "It's okay."

"So—" I glanced around, wondering why she'd picked such an unmanageable meeting spot. "Where can we talk?"

All this time I was evaluating her clothes and posture, desperate to discern what her life had become. Expecting, every moment, that she'd tell me to go to hell. There was something exquisitely delicate between us, and I worried that, if I pushed too hard, it might break. But questions rattled urgently in my skull, and I wanted to spit them out before I lost her again.

"Just here." She nodded toward a low ledge that edged the court-yard. Women perched along its length, wrapping the hair and paint-ing the hands of tourists. We found an empty stretch of red rock and sat there, side by side, staring at the gates of Dilli Haat. Beggar chil-dren approached and tapped on our knees, muttering and mewling. Pooja shooed them away, but not unkindly. She talked to them in a soft voice, and called them *baba*—baby.

"Why did you want to meet here?" I asked her.

She pointed a thumb to the food market across the highway.

"We go there every Sunday, me and Ricky," she said. "We buy pork. Just to have some meat."

"Oh, I see." She hadn't gone out of her way.

"How are Max and Patrick?" For the first time, she smiled.

"They're fine. They still miss you. Max is at the same school. Pat-rick goes to playgroups now."

"I miss them, too," she said.

"You and Patrick always had such a strong bond."

"Yes, ma'am."

"Pooja, really. You don't have to—"

"I can't help it."

"I'm sorry about the way things ended." This was graceless, a blunt blurt, but once I'd started I had to keep going. "I never wanted you to leave, but." There was no way to end that sentence without making things worse.

"I'm also sorry."

"I care about you. As a person. You weren't just a housekeeper who worked for us. I still would like to be in touch with you."

"Me, too."

"So what's going on with you?" I fled the topic of her firing as quickly as I'd pounced on it. "You're working?"

"Yes, ma'am."

It started like that, tentative and strained. She told me about her new job: she was a nanny to infant twins in Gurgaon, just on the outskirts of New Delhi. I was relieved. Her life hadn't changed so much, after all.

"I give them all the love and all the care, but there is something I hold back," Pooja said. "After I left your house, speaking frankly, I was crying for many days. Now I won't bond with them in that way. I am protecting myself from this hurt."

I thought of Pooja's gleeful posts after her firing. There was no time to dwell on this disconnect, though, because now Pooja was telling me that her employers would leave India that spring. She asked me to help her find a new job. I agreed, thinking this was the reason she'd come to meet me.

Then she told me she'd stopped drinking.

"Really?" I studied her shoes. Shiny black flats that came to a sharp point, dulled with streaks of winter dust. Shoes my grandmother would have worn, something you'd find in a church thrift shop. Looking at them made me sad.

"Yes, ma'am. I'm not drinking so much anymore." I noted the equivocation. "I'm not drinking anymore to go to sleep."

"You were drinking to go to sleep?"

"When I was at your house."

"What was going on with you? After Varun left, I mean, I knew you were in bad shape. I could see it—"

"It was bad."

"Tell me."

"I couldn't sleep at all back then. If I slept for half an hour I'd have the feeling that I'd slept for hours and hours. It was strange. I went through a very bad time. I never told you everything that was happening."

Sunday traffic stuttered over a bedraggled overpass. Foreign tourists in their flowing and jangling and khaki India costumes straggled through the gate. I looked at her shoes, my scuffed leather boots, her shoes again.

"When that happened with Varun, I was three months pregnant," she said.

"What?"

"Yes, ma'am."

"You mean that night he beat you up?"

"Yes, ma'am."

"You were pregnant?" I couldn't assimilate this piece of information into the story I'd already built in my mind.

"Yes, ma'am." She laughed, and somehow that laugh—a self-conscious, mirthless, self-deprecating laugh in the middle of a dusty winter afternoon—was easier to understand than any of the words.

"Oh God. I'm sorry. I didn't know."

"It's all right, ma'am. I know."

"So. What happened?"

"I aborted that baby," she said. I suddenly remembered crossing her path when she came out of the bathroom. The sorrowful self-loathing on her face. *Disgusting,* she'd muttered. It was around that time, I realized now.

"You never missed any work. Pooja. You should have told me."

"I didn't want to talk about it," she said. "I just thought, 'Those things are not for me. I shouldn't think about them.'"

Those things. The baby and the man. Those things are not for me.

The truth had come now, but it was still too small. It was an empty frame; I didn't understand it yet. I could have ended the meeting immediately and gone home to mull the fact of Pooja's abortion. But she was still talking. We'd have to flounder forward.

She told me about drinking every night with a friend who also worked in our neighborhood. Both women lived alone in staff quarters. They bought bottles from a maid's husband who peddled black-market liquor.

"Is she still there, your friend?" I asked.

"She left and I left," Pooja said flatly. "Life moved on."

The conversation felt strange the way so many things about our existence in India felt strange—balanced on the edge of a tourist site, in between home and away. We sat quietly for a while. Everything I started to say was wrong, but I didn't want her to go yet. I'd missed her terribly; now I just wanted to sit beside her as long as she'd let me.

"I don't know what to say," I finally said.

"It's all right," she said. "My life is always like this. Now I'm happy."

"I'm glad." I didn't believe her. "You have a boyfriend?"

I had the familiar feeling of pretending I didn't know something I'd learned on social media. Now she laughed hard, curling herself bashfully inward. The man came from a good family, she said. He wanted to give Pooja a business to run—a rooming house for students back in Darjeeling. But they'd met only once in person.

"How did you meet him?"

"He's from my same place," she said, which didn't strike me as a real answer.

"So . . ."

"So, you know, we know each other."

"Mutual friends?"

"Like that."

He still lived in Darjeeling. He wanted her to move back, and she was tempted to go. She wanted to leave Delhi and live closer to her son. But on the other hand, she had only recently escaped one man. And in Delhi she could earn what she called "a handsome salary."

By now the air between us had softened. Gradually we'd turned to face each other. Pale winter hands, fingers twitching in our separate palms as we talked. Pooja asked after friends she remembered from parties and playdates. She asked about my mother and Tom's mother. I asked after her son and father. We both announced that everybody was fine. Then she asked about my book.

"I finished it." This wasn't true but still felt accurate. "Now I'm thinking about something new."

I didn't tell her that she was the new project's muse and main subject. I simply said that I was interested in writing about the lives of domestic workers in Delhi. I had the impression there were many experiences and troubles that employers never intuited, I said, and I wondered about the real lives and stories of these women.

Pooja's face brightened.

"It's true," she said. "We're all just playing parts. There is so much—"

"But how do I get to it? How do I get people to talk to me honestly?"

"I can help," she said. "I have some days off. I know people who will talk to you."

I could imagine it, too. She'd be good at that work. She was skeptical and smart, and she could bring down people's guards. I told her I was still gathering my thoughts. She listed her precise working hours so I'd understand when she'd be available to help.

"Can we meet again?" I asked.

"I'd like to see Max and Patrick," she said.

"They'd like that, too."

"Maybe if you go somewhere, like to the mall or a play center on the weekend, you could call me. Even if I could just see them . . ."

A stab of guilt.

"Of course you can see them. They would like to spend time with you. Let's find a way."

We hugged good-bye. Her sister sauntered over, avoiding my eyes and glaring at Pooja through yellow sunglasses.

"Bye, Ricky," I said.

"Bye," she grumped.

They headed for the pedestrian underpass; they would cross the highway and buy their pork and continue along their way. Lightened by happiness, I drifted back to my car. Pooja was back. Pooja didn't hate me. I'd told Pooja that I cared about her. The burden of guilt I'd been carrying since the previous spring broke into atoms and drifted into the smog of the city. I was forgiven for the firing. That was the first thing: forgiveness.

I squinted into the storefronts and lanes of the food market as I passed, looking for a woman in black, trying to catch one more glimpse of Pooja. But I couldn't see her. She was lost in the crowd.

Chapter 27

I bought a ticket to Beijing and made my plans to see Xiao Li with an absolute lack of excitement. I dragged myself through the packing and logistics. Whenever I pictured the trip, my stomach twisted with anxiety.

It had been four years since, pregnant and professionally adrift, I'd left Beijing. Going back now should have been easy. I was returning, unencumbered by children, to a city I loved. I'd stay with friends and carry out a few simple interviews. I'd already contacted Xiao Li, and she was eager to meet. This was practically a vacation.

And yet I couldn't shake the formless worry. I began to wonder, superstitiously, if I was having a premonition of coming disaster. Maybe I shouldn't go.

No—that was stupid. I had to go. Xiao Li was the beginning of the story, and the story must be gotten.

But disentangling myself from home wasn't easy. It was now obvious that, gradually, I'd become the brain stem of our domestic corpus. Mary knew the kids' routines. Tom was a doting father. But a thousand details and nuances were cataloged solely within my skull. Tom couldn't find the thermometer, and Mary didn't know how to operate it. Nobody had a clue about my elaborate forages through Delhi's markets to keep the household supplied. They didn't know how to get in touch with the pediatrician or classmates' parents. They didn't know how much cash was needed for tae kwon do class or which school uniform to wear on which day. I was the only one who'd ever trimmed the kids' fingernails.

I wrote lists of minutiae, forgetting practically everything and berating myself for allowing this to happen. Resentfully I thought of Tom's reporting trips. He didn't write checklists or brief the nanny or schedule an extra-tantalizing slate of playdates and outings to keep the mournful children distracted. He simply packed a bag and left. When it came to the hourly scramble of school and friends and vitamins and pajamas and meals, Tom was superfluous. A sad position, in a way, but what freedom!

I knew this status quo was my own doing. It began with biology— I'd been pregnant, then breast-feeding. I'd been a physical necessity, which had been a role of exquisite privilege and total destruction. And somehow my rarefied status stayed unchanged even as the babies grew. The habits we'd all adopted—my centrality, the children's dependence, Tom's slight remove—had stuck.

Now I thought: I should have traveled, even unnecessarily, so the boys would understand that women, too, were beings who went. I should have forced Tom's attention onto picayune details. I should have trained Mary more assiduously. I should have traded some measure of control, faced a few more arguments, for a bit of liberation. Instead, what had I done? Maybe I had taught my sons that women stayed back in households while men charged off into the world. Maybe they would grow to disdain women as the dullard companions of a discarded childhood. All of that, all my fault. Enough! It wasn't too late. I was going now. They would stay with Tom, and they would see it could be that way, too.

But if leaving was bad, arriving was worse: when I tried to envision the meeting with Xiao Li, my imagination choked.

Here's the thing, I'd say. *I've been writing about you.*

I pictured myself looking into her face and saying those words, and my stomach flopped.

I need to know more. I have questions.

I'd watched, recorded, and judged. I'd turned Xiao Li from an employee into a character. This meeting didn't feel like journalism; it felt like a confession.

I wrote my children a love letter in oil pastels and left in the middle of the night. I flew east through the darkness and onward to China, where it was already another day.

———

I stayed with friends in our old apartment complex. Same lobby with the uniformed doormen, silk flowers, and imposing faux marble desk. Same elevator with the mirrored doors.

I asked a Chinese friend, a mother from our former baby group, to translate my first call to Xiao Li. I knew there would be an immediate conflict: I wanted to go to Xiao Li's place, and she'd expect to come to me.

I heard her voice: *"Wei?"*

"Xiao Li," I said.

She paused, then exclaimed, *"Ni hao!* Hello!"

"I'm here."

"I know."

"I want to see you!"

"Max is with you?"

"No," I admitted guiltily.

Another pause.

"When can you meet?" she finally asked.

"Anytime. Today?"

"I will come there."

"Can I come to you?" I asked.

Pause.

"You want to come here?" she finally managed.

"Yes. I want to see your daughters. I have presents for them."

Another pause, this one too long.

"My house is very poor," she said in Chinese.

"It's okay." I turned to my friend. "Please tell her I don't care. I just want to see her and the kids. It would mean a lot to go to their house."

Through translation we pushed politely back and forth until, in a flustered defeat, Xiao Li relented.

"Come in the morning, any time after nine," she said. "I'll send you the address."

But a few minutes later, she called back.

"Can you come tonight?"

I heard a man's voice in the background.

"Oh," I said. "Of course."

I assumed her husband had changed the plan so he'd be home, and I was apprehensive. When interviewing women, husbands are frequent spoilers. This is a universal truth from Cleveland to Cairo: In the presence of husbands, women tend to speak less and defer to the man. As for the husband, he often assumes, no matter who or what is asked, that his opinion is the one you really want.

I also thought there was a strong chance Xiao Li's husband would put his foot down against the book—politely but definitely.

But there was no time to worry. I made some panicked calls and managed to hire a Chinese journalist to translate. We took a taxi north as the sun faded away and the city dropped into a spring chill. The taste of recently melted snow mixed with diesel along the highway. Xiao Li sent an SMS: She was standing on the curb, where was I?

We followed the address to a strip mall of shining metal and distressed wood and mellow light glowing from boutiques. Glancing out, I realized that Xiao Li must have chosen the most upscale spot within reasonable distance of her house, and I felt depressed.

"This isn't right." The translator began to argue with the driver.

"No." I stopped her. "I think it's here."

"It looks fancy," the translator said indignantly.

I agreed and my stomach was sinking, but I climbed out of the car.

Xiao Li rushed fast from the darkness, a small girl clinging to her hand. A tidy-looking young man loped behind. I hugged Xiao Li and looked into her face. I'd forgotten the leonine sweep of her facial bones, the piping of her upper nose, her high hairline.

We milled in a commotion of stunted handshakes and introductions. I greeted her husband and kneeled down to talk to her daughter, who grinned against her mother's leg. I introduced the translator as a friend who'd come to help us communicate. Relief came into Xiao Li's eyes. *Then she, too,* I noted, *has been dreading an excruciating evening of decorous, slow-moving Chinglish.*

Then we all had to fuss and invite and protest about where to sit and talk. I knew that because I'd come to them and her husband was present there wasn't even a small chance I'd get to pay. And this knowledge was distressing because I also knew they couldn't afford these cafés. We wound up in a luxurious coffee shop with fireplaces, a wall of windows, and deep leather couches.

"Coffee? Tea?" Xiao Li's husband pressed.

"Just hot water," I said.

Xiao Li giggled. "She loves coffee."

"If I drink coffee so late, I won't sleep."

I watched Xiao Li's husband slide off to the counter. He was not the rough-hewn laborer I'd imagined. The sleeves of his crisp button-down shirt were carefully rolled to show his watch, and his hair was tidily shorn into a crew cut.

Xiao Li and I began the necessary ritual of mutual flattery.

"We've never forgotten you," I said through the translator. "You took such wonderful care of Max, and you were an important part of our lives. I'm so grateful to you."

"You were always very kind to me," she replied. "I never wanted to leave your house, and I knew you didn't want me to go, but I was too pregnant to work and I didn't want to sit around taking a salary."

I was awash all this time with memories. I hadn't anticipated that seeing Xiao Li would unleash intense, visceral flashbacks to early motherhood. The foods we ate, the smells of our rooms, the madness of those long, slipping-away, caffeine-drenched afternoons. That had all been real. Xiao Li's face was proof. But in her face, too, I saw signs of the things that had happened to her since we'd been together.

She'd recently dyed her hair burnt orange, but her bangs were still chopped in a long block across her brow. She still had a taste for flash: her velour blouse was printed with leopard spots, and metal spangles winked on her purse.

"Where's your other daughter?" I asked.

"She's back in Hebei. She had to start primary school."

"I'm sorry not to see her."

Xiao Li's little girl sat on her mother's lap, and I could hardly talk for staring. We'd been pregnant together, and now I had Patrick, and she had this bob-haired child in a frilly dress and thick tights. The girl watched our faces and fiddled with a small toy rabbit. *Little white rabbit,* Xiao Li used to sing to Max. I reached under the table and hauled out the presents.

"Since your sister isn't here, you get first choice."

Stuffed animals and Barbies from India, dolls in glittering saris, with slick hair that smelled of melting candy. Happily the child took the toys.

Xiao Li's husband was back with a mountain of ice cream and waffles and fruit. I took a few mouthfuls, gasped in pleasure, and—afraid the sugar on an empty stomach would make me vomit—muttered something about a diet. This was a mistake. He rushed back to the counter to drop more hard-earned yuan on a platter of fresh fruit.

I swallowed a chunk of watermelon and straightened my back. The small talk was starting to feel itchy and onerous. I'd left my kids and crossed the continent to have one particular conversation with Xiao Li. As I shuffled the words in my mind, I realized that a looseness had come into my muscles and felt a gambler's certainty that the discussion would fall my way.

"I'm working on another book," I began. "It's about women and work. About writing at home and having babies and how women manage to look after their kids while working."

"Very good." Xiao Li looked pleased.

"But I don't just want to write about myself," I told her. "I want to write about you, too."

"Oh?" She giggled politely, as if I'd told a joke, then studied my face.

"You're a working mother, too," I said. "More than I am. I could work because you came and looked after Max. But my question is, what about you?"

"Okay." She smiled a little, then smiled more. "Okay."

"So I'm hoping I can interview you. Not tonight," I added quickly. "But maybe we can meet and I'll take notes and we can talk about everything, about your life."

"Yes," she said happily. "Anytime."

"Great."

"What I think," her husband said, leaning forward. "I think it is very important for women to work. To reach their potential. I think they must be given all support so that they can work and also have children . . ."

His voice droned earnestly. I kept stealing glances at Xiao Li to check her expression, and each time she was waiting to give a reassuring nod or small smile. *I hear you. I see you. I understand.*

———

The next morning Xiao Li and the translator visited the apartment where I was staying. From the living room we had a view across the broad courtyard and into our old apartment, but we were too far away to make out any details. I'd arranged raisin buns and berry muffins on a tray, but Xiao Li ate nothing. She sat very straight and looked at me expectantly.

I opened my laptop. "Tell me about your childhood."

It was as if we'd never met. In a way, we hadn't. Xiao Li described growing up in a village of farmers, a hamlet where all energy and strategy were poured into survival. Her family grew wheat, corn, and rice; tended a few apple and peach trees. Xiao Li went to school, which represented generational progress—her own mother couldn't read or write. China's infamous "one child policy" was in its heyday, but out of sentiment or stubbornness, Xiao Li's parents were remorseless violators. They had four children.

"My mother, I don't know." Xiao Li chuckled. "She just loved babies."

Party officials turned up and threatened to tear the house down. It wasn't an idle threat—the neighbors' home had been razed as punishment for having too many children.

"They took our TV and fined us," Xiao Li said. "We had this really small TV, but they took it. The fines were big, though. We had to borrow money to pay."

Xiao Li was the eldest child, and the only girl. Her schoolwork was spotty, but her younger brother was considered clever enough for university. Unfortunately, this education would cost more money than the family could coax from the dirt.

"I was eighteen when I graduated from high school," Xiao Li said. "I thought I should stop studying and go to work to earn money for him. I didn't want to be a burden."

She said these words flatly—the next event in the story. I was distracted trying to imagine the moment when Xiao Li walked out of village life into the clanging, crashing sprawl of the city.

"I want to say, clearly, that nobody in my family forced me to do this," Xiao Li continued. "My father was working very hard, and I wanted to help. I felt responsible."

In her mind, I realized, she was testifying. She'd decided upon this language in advance. She wanted me to know that her life was rooted in personal choice. This much dignity, at least, was hers.

I was still imagining the moment of contact with Beijing, this city perpetually erasing itself and smashing its past, throwing another spike toward the sky. Xiao Li had a toehold. Her father had come to Beijing to scavenge scraps of iron and steel from building sites and work odd construction jobs. It didn't much matter what he did: any kind of work in Beijing earned more money than farming back home. Xiao Li stayed with her father until she was hired as a waitress in a hot-pot restaurant.

"But wasn't it hard, coming here?"

"I was nervous, but I was also very excited." She shrugged. "I had never seen such big buildings before, such a big city."

Xiao Li moved into a crowded dormitory for restaurant workers. Her hours were exhausting and the salary meager. She worked that job for four years.

"That's a long time," I said.

I imagined the blazing oils and eye-stinging smoke of hot pot, grueling shifts and nasty customers, a grimy cot in a depressing hostel.

"I couldn't afford to be picky." Xiao Li read the distaste on my face. "I didn't go to university, so I felt I couldn't get a better job."

"And then?"

"By then it was time to get married," she said. "I went home."

She paused and then added: "I didn't like it back home."

"Why?"

"I wasn't used to it anymore. I wanted to have a better life, to be able to buy myself little things if I liked."

I liked the way she put it. I recognized the delicious sensation of having a little bit of money for something you don't need. She wanted that freedom so badly she dropped the idea of marriage and went back to work in Beijing. This time, she got a job as a saleslady.

"What were you selling?"

"You know, like, household products."

I imagined mops, dish soap, scissors.

"Like, shoes."

One of those basement stores, then, the dingy too-bright corridors packed with things made so cheaply they didn't seem real, plastics that smelled like engine fumes, brand-new clothes already falling to pieces.

"I liked that job," Xiao Li said, and so I decided to like it, too.

Her brother once arranged an interview in the design firm where he worked, she said. "But when the day came, I didn't go."

"Why?"

"I got nervous. I was afraid I wouldn't be able to do it. I don't know, maybe I wasn't brave enough. Maybe I didn't want to challenge myself."

She paused.

"I still think about that job sometimes."

We sat for a minute.

"This is the same brother you helped send to university?"

"Yes."

"So he finished school?"

"Yes," she said. "He's here now."

"In Beijing?"

"Yes."

"You see him?" This wasn't what I wanted to ask—I was wondering whether he gave her money or had otherwise made her whole, or whether he simply took her labor as his birthright. I wanted to ask whether she resented him and, if not, how she managed to avoid hard feelings.

"Yes," she answered smoothly. "Sometimes I visit him on the weekends."

"That's nice," I said politely.

I had never been so deferential and evasive during an interview. But, then again, I'd never been so painfully conscious of cradling a person's ego in my hands, fragile as a thin glass bulb.

"How did you end up getting married?"

"My husband's classmates set us up. We were both working in Beijing. We went back to my hometown for the wedding banquet, then came back to Beijing and went back to work."

"And then?"

I knew, of course. Everyone knows what comes next, even children chanting nursery rhymes: *First comes love, then comes marriage, then comes—*

"I got pregnant."

She was twenty-seven years old. She quit her job and went back to the village to give birth. A fortune-teller chose an auspicious name for the baby: Rui Jie, meaning "smart" and "clean."

"I wanted to leave the village right away after I finished breast-feeding," Xiao Li said. "But my mother and my mother-in-law said no. They said, 'Stay to bond with her.' I stayed home for a year and a half."

"But then you left—"

"Yes."

"And your daughter—Rui Jie—she stayed with her grandparents?"

"Yes."

"What was that like?"

"I was crying so much. It was so hard," she said. "I hadn't realized how hard it was going to be."

"Tell me."

"I'd call her on the phone, and I could hear that she wasn't recognizing me. The first time I went home to visit her, she didn't recognize me." Xiao Li took a breath, but she didn't cry. She stayed calm and she kept talking. "And I didn't know what to do.

"She was under the care of my mother-in-law. I could see that she was tan, she'd been spending too much time in the sun, but I couldn't complain. I didn't have the right to say anything."

We sat quietly with her sadness between us.

"When did you start doing domestic work?" I finally asked.

"Then," Xiao Li said. "When I came back to Beijing. My sister-in-law told me it would be easier."

"Was it?"

"I liked it. Especially the babies."

"But isn't that hard? Especially when—"

She nodded, understanding.

"Working with other people's children—" She groped. "It's very hard to process all those emotions. I really loved Max a lot, and the girl I took care of before him, too."

She paused.

"Sometimes they reminded me of my own child."

"Oh."

"Not everybody can handle it. I remember one *ayi* told me, 'Every time I hold the baby I think of my own baby, and I just can't do it.' As for me, the only way I can handle it is to think, 'This is my own child.' I pretend it's my baby."

I nodded quickly, squinted into the screen, pretending to study my notes.

"How's your daughter now?" I asked. "How's her heart?"

"It's okay now," Xiao Li said. "We were really worried then. It was a long, hard recovery."

"But she's in school now?"

"Yes."

"How's the school? You like it?"

She sighed. "I don't know." She paused. "I feel like I owe her a lot."

"Why?"

"Because I thought about money and material things, I didn't get a chance to be with her and bond with her," she said. "She is basically a left-behind kid."

In truth, there was no "basically" about it. Xiao Li's daughter was a perfect prototype of China's left-behind kids. Thanks to strict laws denying children the right to schooling outside their home districts, a generation of children is being raised by grandparents while their parents work in faraway cities.

"Even now, we're not very close," Xiao Li went on. "In the long run, I'm afraid it will have a negative effect on her. She kept asking me, 'Why do the other kids have parents picking them up from school, why do I have grandparents?' And then it got worse."

"What do you mean?"

"My in-laws died," she said. "They took care of her since childhood, so my daughter suffered a lot when they died."

"What did you do?"

At first, she said, Rui Jie came to live with her parents in Beijing. But that wasn't going to work, because the girl couldn't go to school in the capital. Next she went to live with Xiao Li's parents, but that was no good, either. She wasn't used to the extreme poverty, and Xiao Li's illiterate mother couldn't help with homework. Rui Jie complained bitterly until, at last, her parents enrolled her in a boarding school. Every eighteen days, the child leaves school for four days and stays with an aunt. The rest of the time, she's incommunicado.

"Now she doesn't have a phone," Xiao Li said. "It's not allowed. If there's an emergency we can contact the headmaster, but that's it."

This sounded terrible, but I tried to keep my face neutral.

"What do you want for your daughter?" I asked. "How do you imagine her adulthood?"

Xiao Li didn't miss a beat.

"I want her to go to university," she said. "I didn't get to go, and it's important for me that she should. I don't really think about the far future, what job she'll do or where she'll live. I just want her to go to college.

"And to stay in the big cities," she added emphatically, and fleetingly I thought about the graphs I'd seen, the global migration en masse into cities that could hardly hold us.

"In big cities there are more jobs," Xiao Li continued. "The quality of life is better. I want her to be in cities."

Rui Jie. The girl who was forever elsewhere. The girl who didn't fit into Xiao Li's work ambitions or my domestic demands. The girl whose rightful allotment of nurturing care I had rented and whose brush with death had been a household inconvenience. The girl who'd been ill and left behind and shunted from place to place. Now she'd vanished back out into the countryside, locked inside a school at the age of ten.

I couldn't ask but, as usual, Xiao Li guessed what I was thinking. She answered with the same phrase she kept using for Rui Jie.

"I feel that I owe her a lot." She paused, and then said it again: "I owe her a lot."

And in my mind, I repeated: *I owe her a lot.*

I wanted to see Xiao Li's village and meet her parents. I wanted to visit her daughter at the boarding school, which I imagined—informed by cursory brushes with institutional China—as a dreary place of cement slabs and barbed wire.

We'd been talking on soft furniture with spring sun pouring in the window. Now I had a mouth full of nerves. I asked her to take me to visit her daughter.

She blinked. The muscles in her jaw twitched.

"Think about it." I couldn't stand the air of suppressed anxiety.

"Okay." Her posture slackened. Right away she said she had to go, and I was glad. My mind was crammed with the things she'd said. Our parting was dry and quick; she slipped out the door with dimples and nods. It was easiest to pretend we'd meet again.

I called her later.

"I really want to come," I said. "It will help me to write this book."

"But I'm going Saturday morning," she said. "You're leaving on Saturday."

I was surprised she'd remembered. Maybe her husband had reminded her.

"That's okay. I'll change my flight."

There was a long pause.

"I'll call you back."

I called the translator. I needed an answer. Xiao Li and I had nuance, but no precision.

"Please try to convince her to let me come," I said. "Either way, find out for sure. She's not giving me a direct response."

The translator called back a few minutes later.

"She doesn't want you to come. She says her uncle died, so it would be weird to come with a foreigner."

"Oh."

"She said you could come back another time and she'll take you."

"Do you think she means it?" I asked. "Or do you think there would be another excuse?"

"To tell you the truth," said the translator slowly. "I'm not sure."

So that was it: I wasn't going to see Xiao Li's village. I wasn't even going to see her room in Beijing. She consented to meet me in spaces she associated with my social position, but only she could pass through those portals. She wouldn't take me back. She'd tell me stories and show me pictures, but she wouldn't let me see for myself. I could assume only that her shame and pride were too potent for her to relinquish that power.

Her avoidance activated old impulses. As a journalist, I'd never taken no as anything but a cue for negotiation. My relationship to Xiao Li, and her shy courtesy, could work to my advantage. I could blunder forward, asking and pestering until she agreed. Otherwise, I could simply show up. She didn't want me there, but she probably wouldn't turn me back.

These thoughts and habits belonged to my past life. I hadn't used them in a long time, and now I was uneasily distracted by their obvious nastiness. My nerves jumped under my skin—I was itching to go, just go, get there and bullshit and figure it out somehow.

But I couldn't do it. I had loved Xiao Li, and she had loved my baby. To write about her was to walk an uncertain line between exploitation and truth. If I bullied my way into the village and pushed through to her daughter, Xiao Li would hate the book. Instead of feeling honored, she'd feel humiliated.

I couldn't do it, and so it was over. I said good-bye.

Chapter 28

I came back to India eager to see Pooja again. China was full of walls and evasions, but Pooja could explain things and wasn't too proud to let herself be seen. I called her up and arranged to meet her in a market near our neighborhood. Thick summer afternoon, drab sky, listless city. Telling Mary, vaguely, that I had a meeting; wondering if she'd hear through their mutual friends that I was seeing Pooja.

I didn't recognize Pooja. I walked right past her in the crowd, even though I was looking for her. She ducked her head, taunting and giggling, into my field of vision, and I stopped and said, "Oh!" and laughed. She was shorter than I'd remembered, and she'd gotten thinner. She'd changed her glasses, again, and gotten a new haircut, again, and a new lipstick color, again. That day she was all swing. Her shirt swung in the wind. Her hair swung as she teased me. She'd pinned a political button to her shirt—raised fist, a slogan for Gorkhaland. She was coming from a street demonstration, and she was weak from hunger strikes.

Pooja always said, *I go from one thing to the next* or *This thing will finish and another will come.* I didn't understand what she meant until I studied how she moved through the world: Pooja immersed herself wholly in one relationship, one interest, one job, and then she ripped the whole thing apart and started something new. Now she'd gone into politics, and politics had changed her. The excitement of a cause had pulled her spine straight and livened her face.

"We'll go to the very end," she said earnestly. "This time we won't stop."

Because of Pooja, I'd been reading about the Gorkhaland movement. The Nepali-speaking people of Darjeeling have tried for more than a century to gain administrative control over their affairs, with little success. India has thirty-six states and union territories, many organized around language, but there is no state for Nepali speakers. Thick with tea plantations and popular with tourists, Darjeeling is run by the Bengali-dominated capital of Calcutta. Still, the dream persists. There have been strikes, assassinations, and low-level militia violence interspersed with periods of calm.

That summer it was all boiling. The government had mandated the Bengali language in the schools of Darjeeling, setting off a fresh round of resistance. Banks, schools, and markets were indefinitely shuttered by a general strike; foreign students were evacuated from Darjeeling's famed boarding schools; street clashes flared; tea leaves rotted on the bushes. In Delhi, Pooja and her friends starved and marched and shouted slogans in protests.

"Why does it matter, whether or not you have a state?" I was trying to understand whether statehood offered concrete benefits or if this was an abstract communal desire.

"Because then we'll have someone who is taking care of us. We'll have our own government," Pooja said. "You see how we're treated."

I thought I knew what she meant: Pooja often complained that Nepalis were mocked by other Indians as "chinky" and dismissed as drunks and prostitutes. I couldn't see how a new administration would undo ugly ethnic stereotypes, but Pooja was convinced that statehood would boost her community's status. She also believed a state would have changed her personal trajectory.

"There would have been so many jobs and opportunities," she said. "I wouldn't have had to leave my son like that. I would have stayed with my family."

The strange thing was that, in spite of her conviction, she was hopeless. She was sure the strike would fail, and that statehood would not be granted. The hunger, the inconvenience, the shuttered schools, the violence—it was all in vain. And yet she did it; she wanted to do it. Eagerly she gave her summer over to a lost cause.

"They go into hiding," she grumbled about the party leadership. "How many times did Gandhi and Mandela go to prison? You have to face your fate. Hiding, you don't get anything."

"You should be the leader." I meant it.

"If I talk like this, they'll kill me." She shrugged. "Everybody worships those party leaders."

That was the same day I asked to include her in my book. She accepted smoothly and naturally, like she'd scooped up a fallen apple without breaking stride. We were sitting in a bar that smelled of sour beer and peanut shells. A soccer game bleated on television. Nothing shifted between us with the revelation that she would be a character in my book. Only knowledge slid, smooth and thin as water.

"How's Aryan?" I asked.

"I don't know. That's the problem. With this strike, they shut down the networks in Darjeeling."

"The government?"

"Yes, ma'am. I can't reach my father or my son. I don't know if they're all right. It's making me crazy."

"What will you do?"

"I'm going," she said, as if it were nothing.

"What? What about your job?"

"Ricky will do it."

"Your bosses don't mind?"

"They don't mind."

"She's not working now?"

"No, ma'am."

"When?"

"I have to see the tickets. Maybe Wednesday, Thursday . . ."

"Can I go with you?"

"I don't mind, ma'am, but for you it might be uncomfortable."

"Why?"

"Like, I'll take the train to Siliguri, but you should go to Darjeeling. You want to see my house, right? You want to see the village and my family?"

Pooja knew exactly what I needed. Of course she did. A hop of happiness in my ribs.

"Right. Yes."

"But to Darjeeling the transport is closed. So maybe my aunt can help me go in an ambulance. Or maybe I have to walk at night. It's like that—"

"I don't mind."

"I don't know if it's safe."

"I don't mind. I mean—unless it makes it more dangerous for you—"

"It's not like that, for me I don't care—"

Back and forth, polite and deferential. Eventually we agreed that Pooja would go alone. Maybe the strike would end, or maybe she'd find a way for us to travel together. Otherwise we'd hike together into the mountains. We had the beginnings of a plan.

She'd leave in a few days. I drove out to Gurgaon to interview her before she left. Darkness was clotting the sky as I rode south over roads buried by monsoon floods, past buildings dark with blackouts. People stood up to their ankles in the brooks of the roadsides, not bothering to hide from the rain. I was headed to Gurgaon, the urban appendage where the daydreams of India's elite harden into steel and concrete and corporate logos. Delhi is low to earth and falling apart. Gurgaon is ambitious unto the heavens.

Pooja and her sister were waiting for me outside the compound where Pooja worked. I was apprehensive about Ricky, but she grinned and called, "Hi, ma'am," as she climbed into the front seat. All was forgiven, then. We drove to the mall while the sky spat down.

In a dim brewpub the sisters ordered beer and jostled to tell their story, interrupting and passing looks. They were obviously pleased to have a chance to discuss their quarrelsome, boisterous, love-soaked, unlucky family. Typing notes on my laptop, I made no effort to organize the conversation. I wanted to see where they'd go on their own; to notice what they'd repeat and avoid.

The first thing Pooja said: "My dad and my mom were in love."

They were about to reveal the desperate cash poverty that had stalked their family for decades, but they wanted me first to understand that their mother had accepted these material deprivations in the service of her love. Their mother had grown up rich and their father was poor, and she'd married him although her parents cast her out and moved away from the village in shame. She raised her daughters to believe she never regretted this choice for a moment, and that theirs was a dignified poverty because it was freely chosen over a birthright of privilege.

"She was always happy with my dad," Pooja said. "She said, 'Whatever I did, I loved him.'"

The daughters thrilled to this story. Love was their first point of pride. *My dad and my mom were in love.*

Next, they boasted about their father. He fought in the war with Bangladesh. He broke his nose boxing. He was a driver for the Soviet consulate in Calcutta.

"Our dad got medals," Pooja said. "When he drinks, he tells stories about the war and how he survived."

"Our father will never tell his age," Ricky interjected. "He's been saying he's sixty-five for ten years." The sisters fell together, helpless with laughter.

I still remembered the explanation Pooja had given from the start: She'd run away with a man when she was still a girl. Everything else flowed from this original flight.

"Tell me about that," I said.

Ricky shut up and watched Pooja, startled eyes spiked with mascara. At the time of Pooja's undoing, Ricky was still a child. Now Pooja talked alone: She was a schoolgirl when she caught the attention of a village man named Babin. He wrote her a love letter, which she ignored. One day the man's sister waylaid Pooja as she walked home from a school picnic. *Babin is waiting for you,* the sister said. And so Pooja went to the man's house. She was fifteen years old.

"For two hours we sat. He didn't talk and I didn't talk," said Pooja. "There was some connection."

The randomness of this story made it familiar to me. Happenings slip and snarl illogically in this world; we do things we can't explain. I could imagine Pooja sitting with a strange man in the gathering darkness, speechless and thrumming with hormones. Night came too quickly, and Pooja wanted to go home. Babin offered to walk her, but instead he took her to a relative's house and raped her.

That she was raped is a legal and objective truth, but Pooja doesn't see it that way. In her mind, she ran away with Babin. For Pooja it was not a question of consent—which, in her mind, she gave—but of permanence. In the hills, sex was marriage, and marriage was eternal. But she was so naive she didn't understand, at first, that the intercourse she'd experienced was the act that made you married.

"We were together three days. At first I didn't even know that I was married. Then I understood that 'Okay, now he's going to be my husband,'" Pooja said. "Now there was no point in going back."

"Why?" I asked.

Ricky chortled.

"You know, everyone in the village would talk," Pooja said.

"Were you scared?"

"I was a little bit scared and shy. I wasn't crying, but I was scared. 'I can't go back home.' That feeling was there."

"Mommy was crying so much," Ricky said suddenly.

"You remember?"

"I remember. Dad came, and he was crying, too."

"My father came home from Calcutta," Pooja explained.

"Why?"

"Because I was an underage minor," Pooja said. "He called the police."

The more I heard about Pooja's father, the more I liked him.

"Did they find you?"

"The police didn't, no," Pooja said. "But my father did."

"How?"

"Through some sources. You know, people are related. People talk."

"Were you still in the village?"

"No, by then we were at the border. We were about to go to Nepal so nobody would find us. His brother gave us money. And then my dad showed up."

"Oh God. What happened?"

"My dad gave me one tight slap and said, 'Will you come?' He said, 'Are you coming home?' I said, 'Yes.'"

"That's crazy," I said. "What was in your mind?"

"I don't know if I really understood what was happening."

I tried to remember being fifteen. The memories were woolly, as if years passed when I was half asleep or too cold to think straight. Adolescence was a fever pressure that thinned the lights and watered down thought. Feeling took over, unfamiliar emotions that blew plum dark over the sky like storm clouds. The moods and sensations, tumbling and flowing, making everything wild. To get married in that state—my God!

Pooja's father took her to Calcutta for a month, hoping she'd forget Babin. Finally he brought her back to the village with a stern warning: "He said, 'You have to study, study, study. That's your job. You don't have to look here, there, or anywhere.'"

Pooja tried, and her parents tried, but the extended family took no pity on her. Her grandmother led the charge, insisting noisily and publicly that Pooja was married and had therefore lost her place in the family. On the festival of Dussehra, Pooja approached the matriarch with the rest of her cousins, hoping for the blessing of a daub of rice paste on her forehead. "No," her grandmother said, rebuffing her in front of everybody. "She no longer belongs to our family."

"I was a shame on the family. I was the only one who ran away like that," Pooja said. "My cousins never used to speak to me nicely."

In the end, Pooja gave up. Her old life was gone, and although her father wanted her to endure her family's mistreatment long enough to finish her education, the rejection was too painful to bear. She ran away a second time with Babin, and this time they made it to Nepal. They stayed there for a year, until her mother sent a message that she was forgiven.

So Pooja and Babin came home and settled back down in their village. Pooja taught school and Babin tried to become a professional singer but failed, and so instead he drank cheap whiskey and felt sorry for himself. Years passed like that: Pooja worked to support Babin, and Babin drank.

"He got depressed and he got into alcohol," Pooja said. "Now I understand that. I didn't have the brains to understand at the time."

I started to protest, but she kept talking.

"He would drink every morning," she said. "He became an alcoholic."

As miserable as this existence sounded to me, Pooja was nonchalant. In the trajectory of her life, marriage had been one of the better stretches: she was close to her family and, despite the troubles of drink and money, there was love.

Seven years into their marriage, two things happened at once: Pooja got pregnant, and Babin came down with a fever. His malady was never diagnosed. Pooja was six months pregnant when she became a widow.

"What was that like?" I asked.

"He went away. He was no more," she said simply. "That period was like—I was in the middle of nowhere. He had been my support. He was not supporting me financially, but he was supporting me emotionally."

By tradition, Pooja and her baby should have stayed with her in-laws. But she found no solace there. On the contrary—they angrily blamed her for failing to nurse Babin back to health, and demanded that she agree to turn over the baby to be raised by one of Babin's brothers.

"What did you say?" I was so immersed in this story I almost forgot to type notes.

"I said, 'I waited seven years to get pregnant. I'll never give my baby to anyone,'" Pooja said. "That was my thing: 'I am a good mother.'"

"And they accepted that?"

"Not really. They were very mean to me. They'd keep me separate and talk in the other room."

"Horrible." In Pooja's life, I realized, the first cruelties came not from the world, but from the family, in the household—the household again.

"But my dad came," Pooja said, and yet again I felt a rush of gratitude for this father. "He said, 'She's not a burden to me. I can take her back.'"

Pooja went back to her father's house, broke and grieving and about to give birth. She wanted badly to deliver her baby in the hospital but couldn't see a way to pay the bill. To pass the time, she began playing low-stakes hands of gin rummy with the women of the village. She won every time.

"God was great at that time," she told me. "My luck—I don't know. I think that God favors me somehow."

I wondered whether the women had deliberately thrown the games. Maybe this had been a way to take pity on the desperate widow. I didn't ask; it seemed rude to question Pooja's long-cherished story of providential caretaking. By the time she went into labor she'd stashed enough money to pay for her own delivery and to help an unknown woman pay for hers—this charity over the objections of Ricky, who still rolled her eyes at the memory years later.

Pooja named her baby Aryan, which means "noble." He was a sickly child whose medications sharpened the problem of money. A neighbor babysat for free while Pooja taught school, and her father drove a taxi for a nearby hotel, but there was never enough cash. The family struggled to pay for food and school supplies.

Pooja tried leaving Aryan at home and migrating to Nepal and then Calcutta, where salaries were higher—but that meant leaving Aryan in the care of Ricky, who was still a child herself. The boy grew so sick he wound up in the hospital, and Pooja came home again.

"I never knew it was so bad for you," I said.

This was an understatement: these stories were hitting me like a rebuke. It was dawning on me that Pooja had deliberately downplayed her poverty out of pride, and that we'd both saved face by pretending we came from roughly the same sort of background.

Sometimes, of course, the pretense had cracked. One particularly damp monsoon season, I'd discovered black mold spreading across a spare pillow, and handed it to Pooja to throw away. But instead she'd squinted at the spots and said lightly—too lightly—"I think I can fix it, ma'am. I'll take it," and carried it up to the roof to dry out in the sun. That memory came back to me now.

"We faced very hard times," Pooja agreed, interrupting my thoughts.

"That's why we still have bad feelings with the other family members," Ricky said. "Because they knew, but they didn't do anything."

Her eyes filled with tears. I had never seen this side of Ricky—tough, brash, bawdy Ricky, and all this sorrow welling underneath.

"We were so desperate, you know? They could have just invited us to eat. But they never did."

"That would be hard to forgive," I agreed.

"Now they ask us," Ricky said indignantly. "Now that we have enough money, they want us to come. But it's like—where were you before?"

"We keep to ourselves," Pooja said firmly. "We are nice, we chat, we visit, but underneath, we keep to ourselves."

"I don't go," said Ricky, who always pushes further. "Now I won't accept their food. They should have asked us before."

"I hear you," I said.

"We did so much struggling to survive. We needed school fees for me and Aryan," Ricky said. "I didn't have money for the books. The teacher would tell me, go out. I'd have to walk out with everybody staring."

The indignity flared fresh in her eyes.

"I'd come home so angry. Sometimes we didn't have the money even to buy a pencil and eraser. And Aryan would lose his eraser—" Ricky paused. "I'll tell you the truth. I would even hit him. I'd be so angry with him."

I concentrated on keeping my face empty. I tried to arrange my features into a simulacrum of compassion. She had been a girl, too, I reminded myself, a child, and life can be so mad—but still—I glanced at Pooja, but Pooja's head was tilted toward Ricky. She already knew, then, she had heard this before.

"So that's when you came to Delhi," I said to Pooja.

"Yes. I was feeling so bad. Aryan was little and he needed his mom," Pooja said. "But there was no option."

She came to Delhi, stayed with an uncle, and went to work for a British family who paid her five thousand rupees a month—about seventy-eight dollars at the current exchange rate. The move was painful but life-saving: this seemingly meager sum was enough to bridge the gap from just barely surviving to financial stability.

"We celebrated," Ricky remembered. "I still remember—everybody bought new clothes on Dussehra and we were so happy. I saw that happiness on Aryan's face."

The topic of Delhi reminded the sisters of another pet subject: Varun, the abusive boyfriend who'd upended my own family's status quo and who, I now learned, had been tormenting Pooja for more than a decade.

Pooja first met Varun in her early days in Delhi. Back then he was sweet and solicitous. He helped her find a better job, and quietly trained her in cooking and service.

"After a year, he started to change," Pooja said. "He started saying, 'Have you slept with Sir?' I was saying, 'What are you talking about?'"

Soon, she said, "he was beating me every day." Varun isolated Pooja from her family, lashing out if she gave time and attention to anybody else. He was even jealous of her son.

"Aryan hated him," Pooja said. Ricky nodded in confirmation. They all hated him. But Pooja stayed.

"I always thought, if I give him a chance, maybe he will change," she said. "I was always saying, 'One day things will be all right.' I wasted years of my life. I was like a puppet. He had control in his hand.

"Now," she added, "I've learned a lesson."

"I can't believe you were abused so long," I said. "I used to worry that I ruined your life by making you choose between your job and Varun. But now I feel like that was for the best, anyway."

"Yes," said Pooja.

"If only you got rid of him before," Ricky said, rudely.

The more we talked about Varun, the lower Pooja shrank into her seat and the taller Ricky swelled with indignation.

"Another thing I always wondered about." I wanted to change the subject. "How was it for Aryan, knowing you were taking care of other kids?"

"He came to visit," Pooja said. "But I couldn't give him much time."

"How did he handle it?"

"When he was eight, he had some knowledge. He'd say, 'I'm your son. Why do you keep that girl on your lap?'"

"Oh God." Just hearing this was like a needle in my heart. "What did you say?"

"I said, 'I have to love her also. I work for her, and she is also a little child. When you're not here I look after her, and she loves me a lot. She is like my child, too. But after all you are my child.'"

"Did he understand?" I asked.

"Slowly, as he grew, he understood."

"But how is it now?"

"I feel sometimes that because I was not in connection with him for a long time, maybe that led him to be more quiet and reserved. I think so. His communications with me are very limited." She nodded at Ricky. "He plays with her. He never plays with me. He talks with Ricky about everything. About girlfriends, everything. But with me, I say, 'Who is she?' 'She's my friend,' and that's it."

Pooja spoke plain and straight. She didn't try to make it pretty.

"He stays at home. He doesn't go out. His friends come looking for him, but he likes to stay in the dark. He pulls the curtains," Pooja said. "Maybe I didn't give him so much attention. There were times when he needed me and I wasn't there. But I was not selfish. I gave ten years of my life to somebody who was ruthless. I spoiled my life with my own hands."

The thought of Aryan led to the thought of money. The thought of money led back to Aryan. These are the two strands that bind Pooja's life. Sometimes Aryan asks his mother, plainly, to live with him. But Pooja can't figure out how to make it work. She can't afford schools in the city, and she can't earn enough money back in the village.

"Staying away from my son, the guilt is always there," she said. "Even my dad, when he gets angry, he says, 'What did you do for your son?' I feel very bad then. And I cry. My dad says, 'You saw only your life.'"

This struck me as both cruel and unfair, but I didn't protest. I bit my tongue and wrote it down.

———

It was late; it had gotten late. I paid the check, and we spilled out into the mall, past the shuttered shops and empty cafés. My legs were unsteady. Standing up, pushing away from the table, was like waking up from a dream.

Rambling through the dimmed mall, I asked about Pooja's boyfriend. Their Facebook activity had fallen quiet, and I was wondering whether they'd broken up.

"He's waiting," Pooja said. His family wanted the couple to get married as soon as possible. The boyfriend's elderly mother was ill, and the family wanted Pooja to nurse her. Another man and a new life were waiting. Pooja could step into it—but she hesitated.

"Now he says everything right. He wants to take care of Aryan. We will all live together. I won't have any problems," she said. "Men always say like that at first. But I want to know, what will he be saying later? That's my thing."

"You're right," I said.

"Let's take selfies," Ricky suddenly suggested.

"But you know," Pooja said as we wrapped arms around shoulders and grinned. "None of our people know we are working in these jobs."

"What?" This was the most surprising detail I'd heard all night. "What do they think you're doing?"

"I dunno, ma'am," Pooja said. "A call center."

"They think you work at a call center?"

"Yes. Only my father and son know the truth."

"But why?"

"They'd laugh at us. These aren't respectable jobs."

"They see we have money, and they think we have great jobs," Ricky said. "If they knew the truth they would make fun of us."

"Does your boyfriend know?"

"No way," Pooja said flatly. "His family—they hire servants themselves. If they knew I had worked like that, in people's houses, they would never let him marry me."

I imagined the stress of sustaining this fiction, and stiffened with vicarious panic.

"Won't they find out? Aren't people from home also working here?"

"Yes, but they face the same problem."

"Really?"

"Yes. Our group of friends—none of our families know what kind of work we do in Delhi."

I dropped the sisters off and drove back toward home, head awash in the stories I'd heard. I wondered whether Aryan was depressed. I remembered how Pooja shrank next to her sister when they talked about Varun, as if her mistakes had cost her the right to stand up for herself.

The car slid down rain-silvered roads, past steaming puddles and creaking, hand-painted cargo trucks massed on the city's border, long-haul drivers waiting for midnight to bring their goods into the capital. Looking out the window, I had the illusion that Gurgaon was not a real place but some ultramodern stage set. The mall had been bright and crowded with people, but the only impression it left was one of emptiness—the great naked panes of glass, caverns of manufactured materials, grinding escalators, and the cold breath of air-conditioning. All that stuff assembled and stitched cheap by people like Pooja, branded and marketed and imported by people like me, bought by God knows who, and God knows why. These things for sale were props and ephemera. The mall was just a great gleaming empty cube meant to contain our miseries. A distraction that became a trap.

Chapter 29

A few weeks later Pooja knocked on the door of my hotel room. I'd flown to Siliguri, a crowded, restless trade and transit hub in the Himalayan foothills. In what struck me as a surprisingly libertine arrangement, Pooja was staying there with her boyfriend and his family, trying to decide what to do next.

I hugged Pooja, and as we stepped apart, she swept her eyes over the room. Shabby blankets covered the bed, plastic flowers collected dust, and mold spots stained the walls.

"I was surprised you stayed here," she said.

"I know somebody who knows the manager." I shrugged. "Supposedly he has some really good drivers—Nepali drivers—to get us to your village through the strike."

She mentioned another hotel. "That one is nice. Next time you stay there."

"I don't mind." How little Pooja knew of me! She had no sense of the many cheap and dirty and dangerous places I'd occupied before coming to India and sliding into the formal role of "ma'am."

I had no tea or snacks, so I poured glasses of purified water. In the window the summer-white sky flushed pink with coming night. A highway screamed past, a metallic hurricane of cargo trucks and buses.

"Remember that time you argued with Aryan on his birthday because he wanted to come here for a movie?" This memory had suddenly come to me: Pooja shouting into her phone in the kitchen.

Pooja laughed. "I always tell him, 'Don't go to Siliguri.' There are so many drugs. Dealers look for boys like him."

"What kind of drugs?"

"Brown sugar."

"Heroin?"

"I don't know. They call it brown sugar."

"It's brown? They shoot it?" I pretended to inject my arm.

"Yes."

"Heroin."

"That's the thing with my boyfriend," she said abruptly. "He's a drug addict."

"Oh no." But I wasn't really surprised. I'd noticed a reference to NA on his Facebook page.

"But now he went to rehab. He hasn't done it in seven months."

She studied my face as she spoke. As if she expected me to tell her, with certainty, whether this recovery could stick.

"He goes to these NA meetings," she added when I didn't say anything. "But he used drugs for twenty-eight years."

"That's good," I said doubtfully. "They say those meetings can really work."

"I told you, his family has a lot of money. So, if he doesn't stay clean, his inheritance will go into a trust." She looked at me again, and again I sensed an eagerness for my verdict, as if I could tell her whether the financial motivation would be enough to keep him clean.

"Addicts have to want to stop for themselves," I finally offered. "That's what everyone says."

"I'm afraid he'll start again."

"What does he say?"

"He had a lot of emotional pain. His mother was always busy . . ."

Disinterested in the psychological topography of this troublesome-sounding boyfriend, I asked about the bruises on her arms. Pooja explained that she'd gotten banged around helping to hoist Rupesh's mother—and her wheelchair—up four flights of stairs. Speaking of which, they had a big flat in a stylish neighborhood, and that was only one of their many properties—

As she chattered about his family's wealth, I stared at the jellyfish of congealed blood suspended under her skin. Had somebody hurt her, was she using needles? Her explanation was plausible. I suspected I was making too much of the bruises because they were there, visible, unlike the many hours and days of her life that were hidden from me. Still, I couldn't stop staring.

"Do you bruise easily?"

"Yes," she said. "Let's get some air."

I immediately guessed she'd steer us toward a shopping mall, and she did. In the food court she sipped a Pepsi and I drank a rose milkshake and Pooja talked about Rupesh: Meeting him in a dumpling shop and flirting on Facebook. His failed marriage and the child he'd left behind. Mostly she talked about his money. She wanted the money, of course, but she wasn't sure she loved him. No, that wasn't right—she loved him, but she didn't trust him. No, not that she didn't trust him, exactly, but she didn't trust men, in general. I tried to concentrate, but I was drowsy from traveling. "I need to go to bed," I finally said.

We rode like tourists together through the hot night, bending and gawking as we jostled in an auto-rickshaw. Siliguri is a town crammed with people elbowing one another aside on their way to somewhere else. Its roads spin off to Nepal, Bangladesh, Bhutan, and China. We passed tall square buildings layered with floor after floor of shops, gaudy and compact and glowing in the night, stacked up toward blotted stars. There was something thrilling about all that market, all the far-flung geography that converged in a knot of highway and commerce here, the trading of things and money, bodies of sellers and buyers bending and quivering like candle flames in their many chambers.

"It's like Calcutta, isn't it?" Pooja shouted over the din. I knew what she meant. I remembered a kaleidoscope of raised highways, tireless crowds, colors cut into shards, the faces and jumble of life.

"Yes." But then I remembered again and added, "But Calcutta is more."

"Yes. Calcutta is more."

Then the auto-rickshaw crashed with a crunch into a parked motorcycle, and Pooja shouted, "Oy," in her big throaty voice. The motorcycle's owner peeled himself from the crowd, squinting blood-shot eyes in a face like raw beef. He was a drunk man with drunk friends. They screamed at the driver, grabbed the roof, and slammed the rickshaw from side to side in a sickening rock. I gripped the seats and braced for the moment when somebody would notice me, the white person in the backseat, and their anger would come my way in a burst of bright pain. Pooja just sat there impassively; she might have been waiting for a bus. At last the driver pushed the men back and peeled down the road. Only then did conversation erupt.

"These people are crazy!" Pooja called into my ear. "They park anywhere, and then you give them a little bump and they want to kill you."

"Weren't you scared?" I asked Pooja.

"No," she said. "I would have given him one tight slap. If he had hit that driver, I would have climbed out and beaten him."

I could imagine this. She would have waded down into the darkness and taken on the drunks. From Pooja, I expected nothing less.

———

The next day we drove to a neighborhood of tightly packed alleyways and tiny shops.

"You see, there's a nursing home there." Pooja pointed out a gate. "Families come and go, but there's nowhere to eat. I was thinking . . ."

A metal shutter clamped tight over one of the shops. No bigger than a closet, but it was enough, and the rent was cheap. If Pooja bought burners and cooking gas, she could start a business selling simple, fresh Indian food.

"People are always wandering around here looking for something to eat."

"It's a great idea."

"The problem is, my money is stuck in the bank with the strike," she said. "I have to see. Can I get my money, or no?"

"Pooja," I sighed. "This is all such a mess."

"It's always like that."

Heavy morning rains thinned to drizzle. Pooja frowned out the taxi window.

"I don't like Siliguri. It's like—" She made a face. "These women come down from the mountains and think they're hidden here. They have boyfriends. They go on Facebook and they chat, they make dates, they meet."

I didn't point out this was exactly how she'd met Rupesh.

"I don't like this Facebook," she continued. "When I see women— these ladies—they have no dignity."

"And they are so stupid. They come to Siliguri, and they think they are in Hollywood."

I laughed and repeated her words, watching cows doze with bellies in mud, sunburned men with toothpick legs propped onto rusted bicycles.

"I feel insecure," she said abruptly. "I don't trust him."

"Your boyfriend?"

"Yes. I get so worried when he's going on Facebook."

"Really?" It seemed to me they were both on Facebook constantly.

"Yes, we always have a big fight."

We watched the wet city move past the windows.

"He asks me, 'Are you going to marry me?' He asks me that all the time. I say, 'I don't know.'" She was almost singing, her tone swinging and falling. "He says, 'Then what are you doing here?' I tell him, 'I don't know.'"

The lazy intimacy in her voice made me want to turn away, as if I'd opened a door on them in bed.

"He says, 'It's not good for you to stay like this. Later what will happen to you? People will know, and if we don't get married, they'll talk.'"

"It's true," I said. "You should decide."

"I know. Maybe I'm being selfish."

"Selfish how?"

"If I marry him I won't have any more financial problems."

"You can still have other problems. If he starts using drugs again you'll have a huge problem."

"His cousins tell me, 'We won't make you face it alone. If he relapses we will be there for you.'"

We stopped at a supermarket to buy food for Pooja's family. Supply lines to Darjeeling had been cut for months; people were trading vegetables and tea and running out of everything. We piled the cart with mustard oil, sugar, flour, rice, red lentils, tea. Pooja added crackling pouches of salty snacks and cookies and a large bottle of Coke.

"With these things, my son will be happy." She put the junk food onto the belt. "He's easy like that. He doesn't expect anything big."

I paid, and then we loaded the bags into the taxi and drove until she suddenly told the driver to turn.

"Is this your house?"

"Not *my* house," she corrected me sharply. "I only stay here."

A barefoot guard slept on a bedraggled sofa in a walled car park, stomach hanging from a fading undershirt. He slit his eyes, not bothering to lift himself.

"Will you come up?" This was more order than invitation.

"Is it okay?"

"I told him you're coming."

"But I feel nervous to meet him." If Pooja's boyfriend didn't know she was a domestic worker, then who was I supposed to be? What if I accidentally got her caught in a lie and blew up her chance to marry into a rich family?

"He's also nervous." Pooja hustled toward the stairs, and I trailed reluctantly behind. "He says, 'I'm looking unhealthy, I'm thin.' When he was on drugs he was never afraid to talk to anyone. But now he became timid."

We were already climbing the marble staircase. Rusted stains of betel leaf streaked the corners, and the walls were scrawled with crayon, but something about the building suggested a faded grandeur.

"I tell him, 'You can't hide,'" Pooja puffed as she climbed. "'You wanted to be with me, so be with me.'"

She rang the doorbell, and I silently clocked the fact that she didn't have a key. A maid opened the door and disappeared with a subservient shuffle.

Rupesh came out smiling and sheepish, a slight man dressed in a tight black T-shirt and jeans. A line of dark rot ran along his gums, giving the illusion that his teeth were floating, suspended by nothing.

"Beautiful piano," I said.

"He has so many pianos," Pooja said. "How many do you have?"

"Seven."

"Seven," she repeated.

"In Kurseong?" I remembered Pooja saying the family had more property there.

"Yes."

"How nice."

Superficial rejoinders. Long pauses. Pooja told the maid to bring me a glass of water. I asked after Rupesh's mother.

"Come say hello," Pooja said.

"I don't want to bother her." I was alarmed.

"She'll be happy."

Reluctantly I followed Pooja to a bedroom where an emaciated old woman sprawled on her quilt in a nightgown. She moved her head and croaked.

"Hi," I sing-songed. "Hello." Big smile.

She croaked again.

I brought my hands together in namaste and ducked back out of sight.

Sitting next to Rupesh, I sneaked glances at the tattoos crawling down his arms. He mumbled uneasily and spoke in a thick accent. I kept asking him to repeat things. Pooja watched from across the room.

"Want to see the place where he went to rehab?" she called, her laugh clattering rudely among us.

We froze. She wanted to drag his addiction into the open. She feared it, and so she wanted to neuter it with discussion. Neither I nor Rupesh shared this desire.

"Oh, is the rehab in our direction?" I asked mildly.

"Yes, yes," he echoed my tone.

"Oh, okay."

"How long have you been in Delhi?" he offered after a pause.

"Four years," I said, and scrambled to change the subject before he could ask how I knew Pooja. "Before that we were in Beijing."

Pooja was no help. She watched us flounder with an insouciant grin, daring us to wreck her world. She was the only one with any-thing to lose, but she didn't care. She never cared! I don't think I've ever known anybody with a stronger gut than this widowed village maid with her Coke-bottle glasses and fingernails filed to points.

We made it through the visit. Rupesh didn't ask. Either he was truly as incurious as Pooja supposed or, as I was starting to suspect, he already knew. Maybe he sensed a truth he didn't wish to confirm. Maybe he feared spoiling his romantic dreams. Or maybe he was sim-ply oblivious. I didn't think so, but sometimes it's hard to tell.

———

The road was a thread wrapped around the cones of hills, spinning higher, cutting into the edge where earth became nothing. Low sun-rise rays cut through mist over tea fields; a clan of monkeys scram-bled across a bridge; mountain rivers tumbled toward the sea. The taxi climbed into the foothills, and the valley fell below. The strike had emptied this highway of tourists and trade. All up the mountain people jogged and rambled over asphalt oddly drained of the usual cargo trucks, buses, and braying cars. As we neared Pooja's village, she peered intently into the crowds. Aryan was somewhere along the road. He'd gotten up before dawn to run; he was training for a marathon.

"I can't see him," Pooja fretted.

"Maybe he went the other way."

"No." She turned to me. "How are you feeling?"

"Fine."

"Don't look down. Only look forward. If you look down you may get sick."

She spoke in metaphors without trying; she could have been talk-ing about life itself.

"You need to have a big heart to drive in the hills—Aryan!" she suddenly shouted, and thumped the driver's arm. Cranking down the window, she hollered his name: The car was still rolling, but she was already climbing out.

A tall, lean boy peeled himself from a knot of teenagers and loped over. Pooja and her son beamed at each other and intertwined their fingers, turning their hands in the morning light. They said a few words, nodded, and then Pooja jumped back into the car.

"He will come," she said, and we drove on.

Pooja's father puttered in the road by his house, scraping up leaves and trash with a pair of thin wooden paddles. He strode toward the car, robust and delighted and natty, even, in black sweats and smart black-framed spectacles. I couldn't recognize the shrunken, sickly man I'd met in Delhi. He led us inside, and we sat down to chat, slowly and irrelevantly, in careful English.

He left the front door open, leaking in the outdoor smells of fresh broken leaves and melting ice. His family had lived in this house, hammered together from planks gone mellow with age and painted bright blue, as long as anybody could remember. The front room held a carefully made bed, a cramped sofa, and an ancient television. Hindu gods smiled with closed lips from the walls, and thin red curtains allowed a sheen of sun. The floor was swept clean, pictures and teacups and plates carefully arranged on shelves. The house smelled pleasantly of kerosene and cigarette smoke and tea.

"Only my sister and I clean." Pooja scowled at a thin layer of dust on the lidded teacups. "Otherwise it's two men living here in a mess."

"It seems very clean," I protested.

"Only *we* dust."

"Can I smoke?" her father asked.

"It's your house," I said. "Anyway I like the smell."

I accepted a cup of tea and asked him about working for the Soviets in Calcutta. We traded a few lines of Russian. Pooja was abstracted, sitting by the door and craning to peer down the road.

"Here he comes," she finally said.

Aryan ducked through the door and bent his thick crop of hair first to his mother and then to me, bending toward our feet. I laid my hand on his head as she had done, flustered but pleased, too, to be included.

Mother and son did not kiss or embrace; they hardly touched. They sat across the room and stared into each other's faces, and between them tenderness billowed like the juice of dried tea into water.

Aryan couldn't sit still. His legs bounced and jigged on the balls of his feet. His hands crawled over the bedcovers like crabs. He pantomimed brushing his teeth, and ducked through the curtain to the kitchen.

"He's shy," Pooja said.

"He needs some time," his grandfather said.

People kept pausing in the open door. Neighbors, cousins, friends—all of the above, usually. They grinned and shook their heads as if to say, *Of course Pooja would come during the strike.*

"If you want to write the story about how I took care of my son," Pooja told me, "you need to write about everybody in this town. They all contributed one way or the other."

"This is Kalpana," she announced when the lady across the street appeared, palms pressed together. "I told you about her."

I remembered—the neighbor who'd minded a newborn Aryan those first months while Pooja taught school. She'd fed him cookies during school hours because Pooja couldn't slip away often enough to satisfy his newborn appetite.

Kalpana wore a housedress and cardigan; her long hair was tugged back from a weather-beaten face. All the time I'd been sitting in Pooja's house, I'd been watching idly as she brushed the eaves with a long-handled duster, swept the floors, and sloshed around with washing water. "Her house is right there."

"Yes," Pooja said.

"In my imagination, everything was farther away."

The village was a brief scattering of houses strung along a single mountain road. The road was the spinal column, heart, and brain of the village; the most lively and unpredictable thing in town. A mountain pass older than pavement; the villagers say, writhing through the Himalayas from India to China. Children played on its banks. Old people sat around and watched it flow.

There was just one road, but that road had two sides. One side edged off the hillside into heaven. The other was choked from behind, smashed up against the rising mountain.

Pooja's mother had come from the heavenly side of the road. Her family had a house and shops that hung over the valley, open to air.

Pooja's father came from the choked side of the road, and that was where the family remained. The house was just two small rooms attached to a dim, moist kitchen and a small prayer closet to hold the souls of the ancestors. Because she had married out of her father's house, Pooja was not allowed inside this shrine.

"There is no bathroom," Pooja told me. It was a confession. "We go in the back. This is uncomfortable for us."

"I imagine so," I agreed.

Jungle grew thick on the hill out back. "That's why snakes come inside," Pooja said.

I knew we were both thinking of the story she used to tell me, giggling to see me shudder. A snake had once crawled into her father's house and onto her sleeping body. She felt it slide across her chest, the bones knitting and kneading. Blindly she grabbed the animal and threw it; her father shoved it into the road. It was four feet long, they said, and poisonous. The next morning they looked for signs of the snake but found nothing. In Hindu philosophy, snakes are laden with seemingly conflicting meaning—fertility, timelessness, desire, infinity, creation, destruction. Killing a snake is considered spiritually dangerous.

Remembering, I shuddered again—but was distracted by the sight of teenagers trooping down the road with backpacks.

"School is open?" I was confused.

"Just coaching," Aryan said quickly.

Pooja turned to follow my gaze.

"Coaching like sports?"

"So they don't fall behind," Pooja said coldly, turning back to scowl at her son. "So they pass their exams."

Aryan bounced his knees a few times and then stretched his arms showily overhead.

"Aryan doesn't want to go?" I guessed.

He grinned quickly. "No."

"You don't like school?"

"I hate it," he said.

Pooja glared. Aryan smirked and showed his palms in innocence.

Abruptly Pooja suggested we go out. She walked in the middle of the road, flanked by me and her son. All around us sang a chorus of falling water, dozens of streams flowing past the village, under the road and onward. Swooning notes of old Bollywood scratched from open windows. Birds screamed and clucked in the thick growth. I gulped great lungfuls of mountain air, clean and cold after the long swelter of a Delhi summer, and tried to imagine how Pooja had left this pristine mountain perch for the squalor and sin of the Indian capital.

Pooja introduced me to everybody we met, to countless cousins and uncles and aunts and friends, and never failed to mention that I was writing a book and that she, Pooja, was going to be featured. She was related to virtually everybody in town.

"Where do you play football?" I asked Aryan.

"There." He pointed up the hillside. "There's a playing field."

"Can we go?"

Pooja and her son exchanged looks.

"No," he said.

"Two people died there," she said. "Just before the strike."

"Died how?"

"Electricity. A wire," Pooja said.

"One man was on top of the other," Aryan said. "They were burned. Their faces—"

"They think he tried to pull the wire off but then he got killed, too," Pooja said.

"God."

"But then the strike started and nobody came to check," Pooja said. "So now we don't go."

Life in this village was full of casual death. I'd been hearing the stories all morning: The girl buried in a landslide on her way to second grade. The aunt who went off the side of the mountain in a car. The cousin who died of sepsis infection after an endoscopy. Fire departments and hospitals were too far away to make much difference. These families had made their homes between loose earth and sky; they had to take their chances.

The road curved, tracing a wrinkle in the mountain, and a deep ravine yawned open. A waterfall, choked with trash, coursed in muddy shadows.

"They say bad spirits are here," Pooja said.

"Why?"

"Some deaths were here—"

"Suicide," Aryan interjected.

"Suicide," Pooja agreed. "We don't come at night. It's not allowed."

"People jump?" I peered over the edge. The slope didn't look steep enough; you might only break a leg or arm.

"I don't know," said Pooja in a voice that made me think she knew. "One girl died here. And then another girl was walking here, and she saw the dead girl. She told people that. She was scared. And then she died, herself. And then we stopped walking here at night."

We were all quiet for a while.

"I know these things sound crazy," Pooja finally said. "But if you live here, if you know the people, you believe."

At the temple gate I rang the bell as I passed, copying Pooja and Aryan, brilliant prayer flags brushing my hand. We hiked uphill through dense growths of bamboo, fern, and pine until the trail led out into a clearing. A small, squat temple; crisscrossed prayer flags; a few wooden benches.

"Whatever you ask here, somehow you get it," Pooja said.

Every year people came from miles around for the temple festival, she said. They slaughtered chickens and goats and feasted for hours. Afterward the temple was polluted by blood.

"Always, the next day, rain comes to wash it and make it pure again," Pooja told me. "This is true. Every year, always, it rains the next day."

I believed her. Standing at the temple, with wind in my ears and incense smoldering on the altar and the earth piling up toward heaven, I believed everything she said.

Pooja and Aryan approached the temple gates and prayed. They touched the tiles painted with Hindu gods. They touched the gate itself. They didn't look at each other. Then they stepped away.

I prayed, too, partly because I didn't have anything else to do and partly because I believed Pooja when she said my prayers would be granted.

We hiked back down to the road, leaving the transcendental atmosphere of the temple behind. By now I had fallen into the village; I fantasized about staying. But surely it must be terrible sometimes—choked with dust from groaning traffic; frigid cold in the winter. Pooja interrupted my musings by pointing out the house of Aryan's girlfriend.

"She's really your girlfriend?" I asked.

"No," Aryan said.

"Yes," Pooja corrected. "I have seen the messages."

Aryan grumbled and hunched his shoulders and blushed. "It's okay," Pooja said. "You have an understanding mother."

"She's older than him." She turned to me. "Nineteen. Can you believe it? I spoke to her on the phone. I said, 'You know this boy is very young. He's too young for you.'"

"What did she say?"

"'We are only friends, Auntie.'" Pooja's voice was a lilting imitation.

Aryan stared at the road under his feet, the corners of his mouth tightening, submerged laughter around his eyes. He hated the conversation and relished it, both at once. We discussed teenage love. Pooja was dismissive.

"I got married when I was a young teenager. I didn't know what I was doing," Pooja said. "Of course, I got Aryan. But still it ruined my life."

Right in front of him she said that: *It ruined my life.* I turned my head in time to see him flinch. But he said nothing. He walked along listening to me and Pooja discuss his age and his feelings, and he said nothing. He was an athlete; he could have left us behind. But he was trained to politeness. He matched our pace.

At the next cousin's house, over plates of macaroni and egg fried with chili, Pooja began to dig into Aryan again. He was repeating a year. He wanted to drop out.

"What does he want to do instead?" Realizing I'd adopted the family habit of discussing Aryan as if he weren't there, I turned to him. "What do you want to do?"

"Only football." He grinned.

"Only football." Pooja spat the word like a bitter peppercorn. "Only games. He's not studying. One day I'll kill myself if he doesn't study."

"Why?" I hated hearing this phrase.

"All these years I've been struggling. I want him to understand why I left him—it was because I wanted to give him a good life," Pooja cried indignantly. "He thinks making money is easy. He hasn't seen how I suffered for everything he has. I have gone very, very low. And the fact is, I am getting old."

"Why is he repeating class ten?" I asked. "Why are you repeating class ten?"

"He messed up his exams!" Pooja yelled before he could answer. "He doesn't understand me."

"He's lazy," Pooja's aunt agreed.

Aryan yawned elaborately, shimmied his shoulders, and grinned a puckish grin. The women of his family gazed at him adoringly.

As we walked up the road Aryan began to sing. "Rock-a-bye, baby, rock-a-bye." He glanced over, and Pooja joined the chorus. This was a radio hit then, a pop song about a single mother who sacrifices and suffers so her son can have a better life. They looked at each other and looked away and sang a few more bars.

I was getting anxious about the road. We'd slipped through at dawn, before the militias were awake and stirring, but I thought we were starting to push our luck. The militias had recently been setting cars on fire for breaking the strike. It was time to leave.

"Do you want to stay?" I asked Pooja.

"I'll come with you," she said. "I have things to do, too."

Before we left, Poonan and her father ducked into the kitchen. He caught my eye and rubbed his thumb and finger together. "We have to talk about business," he said and chuckled.

When they came back, Aryan and his grandfather followed us to the road and stood watching as we climbed into the taxi.

"Pooja, you're always like this," giggled a cousin. "You come like the wind, and you go like the wind."

Nobody hugged. Everybody smiled.

Aryan stood waving until we couldn't see him anymore.

We drove back down through fog that poured into the green valley like milk filling a cup. Vines of morning glory; clean, thin waterfalls; banana trees flashing past. We drove all the way down, out of the hills, past army barracks and fields of rice and tea, where women paced the plantation rows under vibrant parasols. We didn't stop, and we barely spoke until we reached a coffee shop on the edge of Siliguri.

We ordered the coffee I'd been craving since dawn, and my notebook was out and there was a calm, naked mood, as if we would now, at last, come to the meat of things. Pooja's mind was full of her son, her father, her past, her choices. She'd come back down the mountain because here in Siliguri were the things she might choose—the man, the food stall, props of a future unformed. Pooja in the middle, pausing.

"I will die soon," she announced. "I'm tired of everything."

That's how she began. That was her first declaration upon leaving her father's house. She continued for a while, talking in vague and melodramatic terms about her despair, and I murmured things like, "Don't say that."

Then she began to discuss the details. Her boyfriend had recently sold some property for about $150,000. He took Pooja along when he finalized the sale. He put the money into the bank and told Pooja they could live comfortably off the 7 percent interest.

"Why don't you do it?"

Pooja shrugged. Rupesh was dangling money. He'd offered her $1,500 to open her food stall. She'd declined.

"I tell him, 'I'll ask anyone in the world, but not you.' He says, 'Why are you so egotistical?' But I don't want his money. And I don't want to hear the later part: 'I gave you this and this, don't forget it.'"

"You're scared."

"I learned a lot from Varun."

"I remember when you first came to my house, you looked different," I said. "Your hair was just hanging and you wore those baggy clothes."

"Whenever I dressed up, Varun got so angry he ripped the clothes off my body." She pretended to claw her own chest. "But I thought, 'Whatever he is, he's the one.' Now I realize: Acceptance is very bad."

Pooja's thoughts paced rings around the same topics: Son, boyfriend, father. Money, shop, jobs. To marry, to work, to move, to stay? She repeated herself, and yet it was not repetitive, because each time she returned to a subject she opened it wider and spoke more clearly.

Her friend had told her about a nanny job in Dubai paying seven hundred dollars a month. With that job, she could save enough money to build a house with an indoor toilet.

The mention of Dubai made me skeptical.

"Who's this friend, how do you know him?"

"It's a lady."

"How much do you trust her?"

She changed the subject.

"I'm worried about Aryan. I want to keep him with me," she said. "He's not seeing my difficult part. I want him to understand: 'My mom is working a lot and I need to stand on my feet.'"

"I think you're being hard on him," I said. "He's a good boy. He will understand, but he's still young."

"When I was his age I was already married."

"But you don't want that for him."

She stared into her coffee cup.

"I should be closer to him," she said quietly. "I left him when he was three and a half years old."

"But what else could you do?"

I sounded angry, and, in fact, I was. I'd lost patience with Pooja getting lashed by everyone, including herself, for going to work. The only other viable choice had been to give away her son. She'd sweated and survived; she'd saved her family. Must she also be pilloried?

"I left him when he needed me most," she said. "How many times he must have wanted to hug me and cry. It hurts me to think about it. He must have been in pain."

She stopped talking for a while, and then she told me, again, that she would die soon. Sometimes she couldn't breathe. The feeling came over her, and she had to stick her head out the window and gulp for air.

"Like a lid comes on top of me," she said.

I told her about anxiety attacks. "You're under a lot of stress."

"I finally want to tell you the whole story," she said, and took a breath.

"I told you before"—she looked straight at me—"I was pregnant when that happened with Varun."

"Yes." So she did remember telling me—neither of us had mentioned it again, and I'd wondered.

"He wouldn't accept that the baby was his," she said.

"That's what you were fighting about that night?"

"Yes."

"Oh." Surely he didn't think that skinny delivery boy—

"When he left I was three months pregnant. I didn't know what to do. I couldn't face the doctor's questions. *Where is your husband?*"

"They would ask that?"

"Sure." She gave me a pointed look, as if this were a stupid question, then continued:

"I was thinking about killing this baby. My child. How can I do that? My child is trying to live inside of me, how can I kill him? I felt a terrible guilt just for thinking about it. I didn't know what to do.

"Mary said, 'Don't worry.' She knew a pill that would abort the baby up to the third month. She said, 'How many months are you?' I said, 'Like that. Three months.'"

Pooja looked at my face. "It was risky," she said and nodded, agreeing with what she thought she'd read there. But my thoughts were elsewhere:

"Mary," I repeated, surprised and not surprised.

"She said, 'Give me a thousand rupees and I'll bring you the medicine,'" Pooja continued. "She brought two pills. She said, 'Take one today and another after two days. Then it will come out.' She told me to pray to Mother Teresa, to pray very hard that I wasn't committing a sin."

"Oh God." *Mary!* Even abetting an abortion, she couldn't drop the ostentatious piousness. She'd pressured Pooja, a vulnerable Hindu, to pray to a Catholic saint lest she go to hell.

"I took the first pill. It was there, in your house. But nothing happened. Two days later I took the second pill and still nothing happened. I sat in my room all night and prayed. I was so scared. 'It's not coming out, what will I do now?' Finally, at three in the morning, it came out in the most horrible way. In a pool of blood. I was in so much pain. I cleaned everything. I came to work in the morning."

"Oh God," I said again.

"I hated myself for doing that. I never wanted to kill my baby like that."

So that was the story, then. That was the whole story. But Pooja was still talking.

"After that, I began partying hard. I worked all day at your house.

I'd start drinking from a bottle in my bag as soon as I left. I'd go to my sister. I would drink and dance like a crazy person, until I fell down dead. I spent so much money just to escape from this pain. In the end of the night they'd just throw me into an auto like I was dead, and send me back to Delhi."

"So you were drinking even more than we knew," I said, and contained in this thought was an absolution I offered to myself. *I was right, then, to fire you.*

"Yes, ma'am," she said simply. "It was bad."

"I can't believe this all happened." But that wasn't true. I could believe it. What I meant was: It is insane that, although all of this took place in my house, I would never have known.

I stared up at the flat plaster lid of the ceiling and blinked a few times. I wanted to say something to Pooja. What could I say?

Hey Pooja, let's go somewhere and cry until we can't cry anymore.

Hey Pooja, getting into your life is like giving myself to an ocean that is washing me out to sea, and in a way I wanted to go there, but then again maybe not.

Hey Pooja, I have to go.

We both have to go.

Hey Pooja, we have to go now.

Pooja had finally given me the thing I'd been looking for all these months. She had finally given me some truth.

She had been in our household and we had shared life, and yet so much of Pooja's trouble had been hidden from me. Now I saw her. I saw her full spread of contradictions and complications. Many women in her position would hide their problems out of pride or privacy, or even with a canny understanding that their employers are not, in their heart of hearts, eager to confront the depressing reality of the lives of the domestic staff.

But how could I evaluate the ethics of these arrangements—let alone write a book about them—without understanding what had been endured under my roof? Whatever Pooja's troubles, I had a certain responsibility for them. I'd taken her into my house, and forced her to kick out her partner. I had benefited from her weaker circumstances in some ways, and in other ways, I had created them. At least now I knew. She had given me the crucial piece of information I had lacked.

There was always an easier story to tell ourselves: Pooja is drinking. Then: Pooja is becoming a drunk.

Then: Pooja must be fired. Pooja has been fired.

Finally: Pooja was here once, but now she is gone.

Now I didn't need these stories because I had some truth. Now there was this person, this woman, this mother. And she had told me what she had done and what had happened to her.

But with the knowing came fear. She had said: *Soon I will be dead.* She kept saying that. I was afraid she was clearing out her soul. I was afraid she'd brought me home to hear her final confession.

I felt the danger. With Pooja, I always felt the danger. I felt the pain of her, the mistakes of her. The way things fell to her in the world. Her gift of winning and her genius for losing.

On the other hand, it was not my job to save her now. I couldn't even if I tried. The trade of cash for labor was long past. We lived in separate houses. I couldn't save her from drug addiction or another bad marriage. It wasn't my job, and it wasn't even my right. Pooja had her own gravity and her own plans. Her life was flowing and so was mine, and I had coasted with her for a time, but then we'd parted. Insofar as I knew what I was doing, so did she.

Pooja stayed with me until it was time to go to the airport, and then she rode in the taxi and dropped me at the curb. I hugged her and thanked her and sent her back to town in the taxi. Not to her flat, as she'd reminded me, but to the flat where she stayed. Back to Rupesh and the vagaries of her life. And I flew back to my own life, which used to contain Pooja but now, to my lingering sorrow, did not.

Chapter 30

It was a Saturday afternoon, and the kitchen was empty. Mary kept interrupting.

"I'm working on this project about women and—"

"Okay, okay."

"—work and childcare—"

"Okay. Yes. Okay."

"Wait, just listen, because what I'm trying to—"

"Okay."

"I want to write about you," I blurted in exasperation.

"Oh yes, okay."

"Just listen. Okay?"

"Okay." She laughed.

"So I wanted to write about—like—I'm able to work because you're here, taking care of my kids. But who's taking care of your kids? See? That's what I want to—"

"In the village we don't have nannies," she interrupted.

"Right." Had we begun an interview on the spot?

"The children walk around from place to place. Everyone is taking care. They know who is taking care."

She was picking up speed.

"We don't have doctors and medicine. It's not like that. In the village, you don't get sick. Oh, there!"

She pointed her finger toward the window. I bent to follow, expecting to see something drastic—a wild monkey on the roof, an airplane tumbling from the sky, a robber scaling the wall. But there was only the familiar dusk landscape of rooftops and trees cut stark against a fading summer sky.

"What?"

"There." She jabbed again. "On the terrace. That roof—not roof—like straw—"

"The thatching?" The neighboring roof terrace was shaded by thatched palm.

"Yes, that one. We have that on our houses."

"Right."

"That's how we give birth."

We were both quiet for a moment. Then I said, "What?"

"We have to hold on to that so our legs hang straight down. And they put a bedsheet below. And the baby falls out very easily. The baby is caught by the sheet."

"You have to hang on to the roof?"

"Yes."

"While you're in labor?"

"Yes."

"But what—how can you hang on? There's so much pain. How can you concentrate to hang on to a roof?"

"We do like that."

"Somebody must hold you up."

"They hold on to your legs."

"I see. Women do that?"

"Yes. Men cannot come there."

"Even the father?"

"Yes. No. The father is not there."

"I've heard of hanging on to a tree trunk. Like stretching up to keep your body straight. But what you're describing—I've never heard of that."

"Even I did like that."

"You told me you delivered in the hospital."

"Only my son. Because then we were in the city. My daughter, I delivered like that."

"It's very interesting."

"So, we have to be like that. We have to be strong. That's why, for us, if children are walking around, it's better. That's how they will learn. Otherwise they will be too soft. It's all right to be a little bit soft"—she pointed in the area of her lungs—"but not too much. It's better to be strong."

"I don't think you are soft."

She laughed. "No."

And then, as if there were nothing more to say, Mary packed up her phone and water bottles and walked out the door for the weekend.

I sighed. It was exactly the sort of stilted and at-cross-purposes dialogue Mary and I always had. I'd formally asked to interview and write about her. Mary had derailed the conversation with one of her amazing—and amazingly irrelevant—anecdotes. She'd rambled inconclusively and then abruptly left. I wasn't sure she'd heard the fundamental thing I'd wanted to communicate. I wasn't sure we were capable of understanding each other at all.

————

I opened the laptop and looked at Mary over the screen. She grinned uneasily and hissed through her teeth at the formality of this arrangement.

"Mary," I said. "Where are you from?"

This was an open mystery. When a Bhutanese family had moved into our neighborhood, we'd discovered that Mary couldn't speak Dzongkha, and Mary had stopped talking so confidently about Bhutan. Instead she'd mentioned Burmese heritage, a home in Assam, a city on the Bhutanese border.

Now Mary told me that her parents had been in Bhutan. That's how she put it: "My parents were there in Bhutan." They were among a group of Nepali refugees expelled from Bhutan in the 1970s, she said. They wound up in Matigara, in northern India, where her father was hired as a driver by Jesuit missionaries. Mary was naming the nuns and describing their good deeds when, abruptly, the conversation took a sharp turn.

"My mother was Mexican, actually," she said.

One of those long, empty beats passed between us. The improbability of this statement was so total, the fact that she'd never mentioned it before so bizarre, that at first I couldn't think of anything to say.

"How is that possible?" I finally asked.

"She was traveling. She was doing some business in Bhutan. She met my father."

"What was her business?"

"I don't know."

"You don't know why she came to Bhutan?"

"No."

"Was she backpacking?"

"No. Traveling. Some work."

"And she met your father?"

"She didn't have the paper to go back to Mexico. She learned the language. Nobody could recognize her."

"What do you mean, she didn't have the paper?"

"It happens to many people. They lose their papers."

"You mean she lost her passport?"

"Like that."

"But she could have gone to the Mexican embassy. You don't just get stuck."

"It happens."

I couldn't agree that it happened. You didn't lose your passport on the other side of the planet and then simply shrug and marry a Nepali refugee and learn the language and spend the rest of your life pretending to be Indian or Bhutanese. But how could I press this point when I was, in effect, denying Mary's origins?

"I mean . . ." I studied Mary's face. "You look Mexican. You really do."

"We all have the same face."

"Do you remember her?"

"Yes."

"What was she like?"

"She was my mother. Very nice."

"And then they died?"

"On the same day. They were going to China for some work. The plane crashed. I was eight."

These details never varied. About her parents, Mary always said: *They died on the same day.* And then: *I was eight.* The plane crash was mentioned as an aside, if at all. The first time we discussed her parents, Mary had said: "They died in a crash," and I'd assumed it was a car accident.

"You don't know why they were going to China?"

"No."

"Where did the plane crash?"

"In China, maybe."

"Do you remember the day they died?"

"Yes."

"Tell me about it."

"We were little," she said vaguely, and then skipped ahead. "We were like strays after my parents died. But these missionaries, they adopt a lot of families. So, it didn't make that much difference."

Mary was the youngest of four or three children, depending on whether she counted an older sister named Lamia. A wealthy Bhutanese family adopted Lamia when she was ten, Mary said, and took her back to—

"Sweden—no Switzerland—I think Switzerland—yes, Switzerland," Mary said.

I'd already learned that such equivocation from Mary could mean Germany or Canada or Swaziland. This geographical uncertainty was in my mind, along with the knowledge that girls of this relatively advanced age rarely get adopted. Lamia came back to India sometimes, Mary said. They were grown women, but Mary still spoke of her sister as a ward of foreign guardians.

"She's become very rich, but the ones who adopted her, they don't want her to go back to her people," Mary said.

One of Mary's brothers joined the Indian army and died under circumstances she couldn't or wouldn't explain. Her other brother entered the Catholic priesthood and became principal of a missionary school in the hills. But he was gay, and eventually he left the church.

"He just gave up. He said there's a lot of injustice among the priests, inside the hostels," Mary said. "He faced a lot of problems."

"What kind of problems?"

"I don't know," she said, and changed the subject.

———

There is some uncanny connection between Mary and Pooja. If you believe in Buddhist principles, you'd say they have a karmic link. Otherwise, it's a crazy coincidence. Their lives flow on parallel paths in this land of a billion souls, touching every few years then stretching apart again.

Pooja and her sister remembered Mary as a class leader in the convent school, an alpha personality from the orphanage next door. "To be honest, she was a mean-type girl," Pooja said. They didn't keep in touch.

Years later, when Pooja came to Delhi and stayed with her uncle, their paths crossed again. The uncle kept a girlfriend on the side. The girlfriend, Pooja told me, was Mary.

Pooja didn't recognize her old schoolmate at the time. The girlfriend, of course, didn't visit the house. Pooja heard plenty of family gossip, but Mary was a common name.

It was on that first day of unexpected reunion in our living room, chattering excitedly in Nepali, that Pooja and Mary uncovered this coincidence, Pooja told me.

"Mary said, 'Don't tell her about your uncle,'" Pooja told me. "And I said, 'Okay.'"

Now that their friendship was beyond salvage, Pooja and I sometimes discussed the mysteries of Mary. Pooja, like me, had puzzled over Mary's tangled past and her contradictory stories.

The Mary described by Pooja was crafty, manipulative, and highly secretive. She was a notorious borrower of money. "Whenever she got her salary, everybody came to collect."

Neither of us could understand where Mary spent her money. She wore my hand-me-downs until they fell apart. She didn't have a smartphone. She hadn't traveled in five years. She ate simply and didn't seem to drink.

"I'd ask her," Pooja said. "But she never really explained."

"What's your theory?" I wanted to hear all of Pooja's thoughts about Mary. I felt duplicitous, discussing Mary behind her back, but I was so eager for information I stifled the misgivings.

"I thought about it." Pooja raised empty hands. "But I never understood."

"You think she was giving to charity?"

"Maybe." Her voice was doubtful.

It was Pooja who told me about Mary's sideline as a self-styled healer whose pills and advice were sought by other domestic workers. This revelation was appalling—I'd often witnessed Mary's biomedical ignorance. Twice she'd poisoned herself—her head swollen like a balloon, vomiting for days—with toxic doses of random pills prescribed by shady "doctors." The night I'd rushed home because Patrick had thrown up while she was babysitting, I found her feeding him yogurt and thumping his back. She believed eating raw citrus peels prevented intestinal worms. She thought mustard oil and prayer cured almost everything.

Whenever she returned from a doctor visit she'd thrust into my hands a packet of lab reports and prescriptions. We paid for her medical care, so this was partly a presentation of receipts, but it was more than that—she wanted me to examine the paperwork and evaluate her health. She wanted to involve me in the condition of her body. And I always slipped away because it felt too feudalistic; it implied a scope of control over Mary's person that I couldn't accept.

"I don't know how to read X-rays," I'd stammered the first time.

It took me years of living in India to understand that, to Mary, my efforts to draw a respectful boundary must have looked like callous indifference.

And then there was the story of Pooja's abortion. Intellectually I understood that Pooja had faced a terrible predicament and that Mary had saved her. But something about the way Pooja told the story refracted Mary into a weird and shadowy figure, brandishing her tinctures and spells.

And yet—that nightmare image wasn't true, and it wasn't fair. When everybody else was oblivious or quailing, Mary had been steadfast. She was not afraid to go into the darkness. She'd dirty her hands, and she'd even—by her own definition—pollute her soul. She'd accept the hard assignment; she'd take the sin. Mary would do what needed to be done.

————

Mary loved to talk about her childhood with the missionaries. She grew up in spartan lodgings, one of a band of girls whose parents had died or abandoned their newborns.

"I don't know, people say it's hard, but for us—we really enjoyed," she told me. "You don't feel stress. Your friends are there. You have playing time, singing time, church time, study time. You know?"

The orphans lived in hostels and studied in the missionary schools dotting the foothills of the Himalayas. Later they were steered into vocational training: nursing, stitching, teaching.

"Life was very precious with those missionaries," Mary said. "We felt it was better than other people who live with parents."

"Wasn't it hard for you at first?" I asked. "I just imagine, for a little girl, it would be painful to lose your parents and go into an orphanage."

Mary shook her head. It had all been fine, she insisted. Not just fine, but better. Mary's life had been better and had made her stronger than ordinary people.

"They take you in and make you forget," she said. "The missionaries love you more than parents."

Mary had a gift with children, and so she worked in schools. She traveled to remote villages for mission work. She grew up and left high school and met a young science teacher—"a very brilliant man"—who also worked with the church.

"He was Christian?" I asked.

"His family was Hindu, but he converted."

"His family worked in the tea plantations?"

"Yes. He was from a very good family. A poor family, but a very nice, simple family."

One day, tittering in anticipation of my reaction, she showed me a photograph of her wedding day.

"Wow," I exclaimed. "You were beautiful."

In the picture Mary stood among her new in-laws, willowy and unbelievably pretty, smiling that same broad, calm smile from an exquisite version of her face. Her wedding gown had a high neck and long sleeves, like something from the nineteenth century.

"And then?" I couldn't stop staring at this familiar but unknown bride in the photograph.

"We had a small house. He was teaching school," Mary said. "I was at home."

It was hard for me to imagine Mary as a housewife in a cottage. The whole setup sounded too cramped, too ordinary, to contain her personality. But that had been a long time ago, and perhaps Mary had been a simpler person in her youth. I always had the suspicion that Mary's troubles had forced her to grow into the outsized woman we knew, that she'd flourished under adversity like a wild plant blocked from growing up—by sprouting fresh shoots and unfurling new leaves. Mary was like that; an overgrown person.

"How was it for you, getting married?" I asked.

"Only after marriage did reality start," she said. "Then I understood how hard it is. Then I understood what is life."

"Why was it hard?" I was thinking, as she talked, that this was the first time any of the women had described a lifestyle that did not sound depressing or precarious—and it was also the first time any of them had characterized something as difficult. Growing up as a charity case in Indian orphanages had been idyllic, but living as a middle-class housewife was hard? It was all backward, and yet I could see her sincerity, so I tried to follow.

"I don't know. I felt alone even though my husband was there," Mary said. "From the beginning of life, I was always in a group. Then I was in my house, and suddenly I was alone."

For Mary, then, marriage did not represent an escape from barren institutions, but rather the loss of the collective lifestyle she knew—and her first contact with a world no longer filtered and censored by a protective screen of nuns and clergy. I was starting to have a dim understanding. Mary had no experience with family life, and she'd disliked her only taste of running her own household. But if she so disdained households, how come she was the person I'd hired to run mine?

"But then you had Gladys . . ." I prompted her.

"Yes. There was this Canadian priest, he was in charge of us." I let this strange description pass. "He said, 'Name her Gladys.' So we did."

"What was it like for you to become a mother?"

"It was strange."

"Strange?"

"I don't know. It's easy to take care of other children, but when it's your own, it's hard."

"Really?" I studied her face. Mary rarely admitted to failing or floundering. Now she looked abstracted, as if she were still trying to work out the meaning of those years that had been so unlike the rest of her life.

"So what did you do?"

"You know, I just decided, I'll do what those missionaries taught us. When my husband came home from work, I'd give him the baby and just go out to the streets."

"Why?"

"Just to help people." She shrugged. "There are always so many people who are in trouble."

She brought lost souls home to drink tea, she said, and dedicated a room in her house to hard-luck cases so they could have a place to sleep. She'd take girls out of prostitution and deliver them to hostels run by nuns.

"On Sundays they'd come to visit me as if I'm their mother," she said. "The sisters always said, 'If you see someone is in trouble, even if you don't like the person, just sit and listen to their problem. Your kind words may help them. Even if your enemy comes to your door, invite him in to drink water.' They trained us well."

Listening to her, I remembered a conversation from years earlier. Mary had mentioned some drifter from church who was crashing on her floor between jobs.

"I always let people sleep in my place," she'd said.

This had struck me as a terrible idea. "But aren't you afraid you'll get robbed, or worse?"

She'd looked at me blankly for a few beats.

"I don't have anything," she'd finally said.

Soon after her first baby was born, Mary was pregnant again. She was still in the hospital recovering from the birth of her son when her husband died in a motorbike crash.

Once again, Mary was an orphan adrift, but this time she was a mother, too.

———

One day Mary brought pictures. They were glossy snapshots of family members posing somewhere public and ornamental—an airport or a courthouse, something like that. I took them in my hands, but I didn't know what I was seeing.

"When were these taken?" I asked.

"A long time ago. Before I was born."

"Really?"

My subconscious detected something discordant, but I couldn't identify the source of my doubt. Why did I have the feeling the pictures were taken around the 1990s? Was I picking up on some vehicle in the background, something about the clothes or hair? Maybe it was the quality of the photographs, which were glossy and relatively high resolution. I couldn't figure it out.

"Who is that?" I pointed to a jowly man whose olive-drab military uniform was studded with medals and insignia.

"My father," Mary answered.

"Oh!" I exclaimed. "He looks like you."

He did indeed, but this enthusiasm was rote. I was silently puzzling over the picture.

"He was in the military?" I added.

"Yes."

She'd never said that before. Or had she? I wished there was a tactful way to duck into the study and consult my notes. The uniform bore an embroidered name tag on the breast. I pulled the photo closer and squinted: TORRES.

"Why does it say Torres?"

"It's my mother's name."

"But why was he using your mother's name?"

"You know, people get false papers. I think they were trying to get false papers so they could go and live there."

"You mean go and live in Mexico?"

"Yes, they were trying to do that. But they died in that plane crash."

"But *where* was the plane crash?" I'd been sitting up past midnight to comb through aviation records online, but still hadn't found any crash that involved India and China during a three-year stretch around the time when Mary was eight. There were a few domestic crashes in both countries, and theoretically several of those flights could have been connections her parents had taken, although none of them seemed geographically probable. But I couldn't be sure, since her details were so perpetually vague. I didn't know the routing or the time of the year; where they'd started or where they were headed.

"I think in China."

I held the snapshots and tried to understand the link between fake papers and a uniform; the purpose of taking a wife's name; when Mary's father could have been in the army; whether he'd fought for India or Bhutan; whether the uniform was fake and, if so, to what end? I stretched my imagination for a plausible story—just a hypothesis!— that could contain all the pieces of information.

"My parents were in trade," Mary said suddenly, interrupting this befuddled reverie.

The day before she had told me she didn't know what her parents did.

"Trade of what?"

"I don't know."

I have a close friend from Bhutan. I ran Mary's story past her.

"That doesn't sound right at all." My friend's voice was full of marvel. "The country was so closed back then. We didn't have backpackers and things like that. It wasn't like Afghanistan."

"So you don't think a woman could have come from Mexico and ended up staying?"

"It's such a small country," she replied. "And it was so quiet and closed back then. I just feel like people would have known. Like it would have been in the news, you know? If a Mexican woman stayed and got married like that?"

"So you think it's impossible?"

"Look, anything is possible," she said. "But it's so unlikely. I'd say it's, like, ninety-nine percent that story can't be right."

"Huh."

"Unless," she said, "there are some details we're missing."

"Right." That was always the problem.

I toyed with the pieces. Latin America. Himalayas. Trade. Were Mary's parents drug traffickers? Human traffickers? Was her mother a Mexican gangster queen, an international fugitive who'd gone into hiding in this most unlikely of places, a refugee camp in Bhutan?

I was starting to feel like I was going crazy.

———

I told my mother about my struggles to uncover Mary's past. My mother didn't say much, but I could tell she disapproved.

"Do you really want to take her stories away from her?" she finally asked.

"No," I admitted. "I don't."

———

I asked Mary, again, how she wound up in domestic work.

"Actually my brother is the one who brought me to Delhi," she said.

"What? Which brother?"

"The priest."

"You told me before you came with an agent."

"Actually we all came together."

I'd lived for years with the story she first told me: Mary had been forced to hand her children over to her mother-in-law and trafficked off to Delhi. But now Mary was about to demolish that version of events.

"When my husband died, I was the one who told my mother-in-law, 'I'll work, you take a rest, be with the children,'" she said. "People in the village were very scared. They hear about the city, what they do with girls. But my mother-in-law said, 'You are very strong, more than my son.'"

I didn't remind Mary of everything she'd said before—her dutiful deference to a steely mother-in-law, and the wretched turns of fate that had forced her so low. Now Mary was the dashing hero who patted the old lady on the hand and charged fearlessly into the world. This, I had to agree, was a more bracing way to think of oneself.

Mary explained that, by the time her husband died, her brother (the defrocked gay priest) had gone to work in Delhi for a fabulously wealthy businessman whose name, to her plain disappointment, I didn't recognize. In this new story, when Mary boarded the train with the agent, her brother followed like a guardian angel.

"He said, 'I'll sit near you in the train. Don't tell her I'm your brother,'" Mary said. "Some of these women, you know, they sell the girls. He said, 'I'll just watch. Let me see if you are safe. Don't say anything.'"

But the broker was not a nefarious pimp. She herself worked as a maid. Mary described her as a decent lady who earned a little money on the side bringing young women to the city. They disembarked in Delhi, and she sneaked Mary and two other women into her own quarter to sleep off the trip. The next morning Mary was taken to work as a maid for a Punjabi-Canadian woman who was visiting relatives in Delhi.

"The broker lady said, 'You stay with her for four months and learn Hindi.'"

"You didn't speak Hindi before?"

"No. In school it was English, Nepali—"

"You learned in four months?"

"Yes, it wasn't hard. Hindi and Nepali are similar."

Mary mentioned that she still sees that broker sometimes.

"She's old now. I feel pity," she said. "I give her some money. Life is not easy."

"How long did you have to pay her?" I asked. "Back then, I mean."

"One month only."

"Really? Before you said you paid her for two years."

"My mother-in-law paid her."

"Why?"

"This same broker took all my relatives. My mother-in-law paid her once a month for six months."

"So, six months."

"Yes."

"But last time you told me longer."

"No, it was not like that."

Whenever I tried to confront Mary with a conflicting story, she adopted a calm, glazed smile and stared at me like there was something I wasn't grasping. She never got ruffled and she never, not once, allowed herself to be dragged into a discussion of what I considered the fundamental question: why her versions of events changed so radically and whether she even believed in truth and untruth. She'd chuckle and repeat her current version of the facts. The older versions were dead. She wouldn't be lured into confirming or denying that she'd changed her story.

"Do you remember telling me two years?"

"No. I don't know."

"But you did."

"It was not two years."

"But why did you say that?"

"I don't know."

We sat quietly. I stared at my notes. Words. Dates. Nonsense. I didn't know what to say anymore. I've interviewed thousands of people: drug addicts, trauma victims, convicted killers, children, psychiatric patients. Sometimes they lied; sometimes they were confused or delusional. None of them had ever changed their stories like Mary.

"Actually, my brother got me away from that broker," she said suddenly.

"What? Which brother?" I imagined all the notes of all our interviews hurled into air, gliding off on breezes.

"The same one. The priest."

"What did he do?"

"I don't know. He talked to her. Then I didn't have to pay her anymore."

"Okay."

Whenever I said "okay" to Mary, I had the feeling I'd stolen her line.

———

Maybe I should have dug down to the bottom of Mary's identity. As a reporter, I saw obvious avenues for exploration. But I left them alone. *If I find her story, if I put together the truth about her past, would that be a gift or an assault?*

Mary in my house, with my children, day after day. Mary puffed and blustered; sang and muttered. Mary was a kite vanishing into the sky, reeling out farther and then farther still. She invented a character, created a part, and then she couldn't resist playing, improvising lines, adding gestures and embellishments. She was a work of her own imagination.

This was Mary telling me about a little girl who called her "mother." That girl is grown now, but she had once been a child who lived next door—next to what door?—never mind, just some door in Mary's past. The girl was beaten and neglected by a heartless stepmother. She crouched outside waiting for Mary to come from work.

"She slept with me at night. I took care of her," Mary said. "She's married now, but she still calls me mother. She was closer to me than my own children."

This was Mary complaining that she couldn't get tickets for the WWE Supershow.

"You like wrestling?" My imagination couldn't find this image. Where did Mary watch wrestling, when, with whom?

"I love that WWE," she said serenely. "It's my favorite."

This was Mary in the park, swaggering and swinging in wide trousers, men's cap pulled down low over her forehead, tossing wisecracks back and forth with the gardeners and drivers, beads of candied tobacco in her cheek, the corner of her mouth tugged high in a lopsided smirk. Mary holding court over the men, Mary unafraid, spitting slang like a street-corner crime boss.

This was Mary telling me stories about going out to poor neighborhoods by the airport, saving young women from forced prostitution. There is always this theme with her—prostitution, the saving of girls, the brutality of men. How far could one woman travel, how many characters could be contained in a single life?

"I'm a social worker," she said.

"Hmm." I considered this possibility: that Mary earned her salary in my house but, by vocation, in spirit, she still considered herself a missionary.

"I know you think I'm an agent," she said suddenly, and she was right. I'd often had the feeling that Mary ran a side business placing women into domestic jobs. It's become a truism among my friends that Mary can always fill a household job vacancy. But every time I ask, she denies taking a profit.

"It does seem that way," I agreed.

"But it's not like that," Mary said. "I'm a social worker."

"Okay," I said. "I believe you."

It was true. In that moment, looking into her face by daylight, I believed her.

I believe her still.

Chapter 31

I'm not sure whether Mary is aware of her tortured relationship to truth. When I've tried to discuss with her, broadly, her tendency to blur facts, she's interrupted with testimonies to her Catholicism. "I don't do like that," she says. "I'm a Christian woman, I can't do that."

I assume that, as a young orphan in bleak circumstance, she was frequently lied to by adults and older siblings and even herself. Fantasy and comforting obfuscations intermingled in a very young brain; maybe they changed, forever, the way she interacts with reality. Mary's parents, siblings, and husband are dead or vanished. She was left to the missionaries; left to her own devices. She told herself this was the best thing that could possibly have happened. She has built, with a strength I find literally marvelous, an entire life and system of forbearance from the myth that she was lucky to have been an Indian orphan. Mary is geared for survival, not reckoning.

That's not the half of it. Mary brushes the kids' teeth shoddily and heaps too much cake onto their plates and feuds with other nannies. She gossips and mangles stories. She has broadcast things I've said privately—sometimes accurately, and sometimes not, and don't ask me which is worse.

I guess some people would have fired her or at least chewed her out for these indiscretions, but those same people would, no doubt, employ some other nanny who I'd dismiss for another cause. These relationships are subjective and personal; there is no perfect formula.

Mary has taken her place as a flawed character among all the other flawed characters in our household. She's the devil I know, and that's part of it, but it's more: I trust her with my children. I trust that she is street-smart, and that she will protect them. Mary is the one who twists the truth. She's the one who annoys me the most. She's the one who stayed in our house the longest. She's the one I trust.

"These jobs aren't easy," she told me once. "You have to be very strong. To stay in a house like that, to work like that."

She was talking about somebody else—our driver's wife—who'd gone to work in a big Indian household and was crying and clashing with the various personalities among the staff of servants. She was explaining to me why she, Mary, could survive the crucible of domestic work.

"I left my family behind. I left my life," she said. "That's why I can stand it."

I agreed. I'd long since come to the paradoxical conclusion that Mary was an ideal household employee because she had no real regard for households and therefore no desire for one of her own. She came free and unattached—give her money, she'd stay and work.

She'd convinced herself that parents were superfluous, and so she didn't torture herself for leaving her children behind. Her children wouldn't be too soft. They'd be strong. It was all for the best.

One year Mary's teenage daughter came to stay with her during an extended break from university. Mary enrolled the girl in an evening computer course on the other side of Delhi. Homework assignments requiring a computer drove her into cybercafes in dodgy neighborhoods. Tom was so appalled by the dangers of this arrangement that we bought the girl a laptop so she could work at home. Mary was grateful, but bemused.

"Aren't you worried about sending her across Delhi alone on the bus?" I asked Mary.

"It's good, only," she replied lightly. "That's how she'll learn."

Mary was the dream worker for a dystopian world. She was an institutional product; a migrant without yearnings. Her lack of guilt or emotional conflict made it easier for me, and for my family. If Mary didn't mind, why should we?

A gun for hire; a mercenary mother. Mary was a guilt-free tool of some lucky woman's advancement—mine, as it turns out.

————

Of course, it wasn't only me; it wasn't only us. There are so many other mothers like me. There are so many other mothers like Xiao Li, Mary, and Pooja.

The same story echoes around the globe. It's the story of every woman who becomes a mother and still wants to earn her pay. How can we succeed at jobs when there is so much work at home? How can we raise our children when we are so busy with our jobs? (Or, as women like me prefer to say, our *careers*. The career is a very useful abstraction, I've learned, since you can continue to have a career even when you don't have a job.) Our minds go to the same places—our partners, and when they fail us, who can we hire, and if we can't afford to hire, then who can we otherwise press into service, what grandmother or aunt or neighbor?

I could fill an entire book with numbers, parades of facts all marching in the same direction.

The statistics tell us what we already know—women are doing most of the work, even in America. It's not an ambiguous truth. I can locate no data suggesting otherwise. In 2015, the U.S. Department of Labor found that American women spend twice as much time cooking and cleaning as men, and three times as much time doing laundry.

Into this global truth of women doing all the work flows the solution of hiring domestic workers: the International Labour Organization believes there are as many as one hundred million domestic workers in the world, and their ranks swell every day. Who are these workers? They are mostly (80 percent) women, and many of them (17 percent) are migrants.

The numbers tell a story of global income inequality, spikes in migration, rural decimation, and the explosion of increasingly dysfunctional urban centers. People abandon their dying villages to find work. They get to the cities and wind up working in other people's households. These women migrant workers are crucial because they solve a conundrum: middle-class and wealthy women demand a place in the job market—or at least a measure of leisure commensurate with their social ranking—but their male partners don't want to do more housework.

So they hire another woman, and, in many cases, they hire a woman from someplace else. From Latin America, if they live in the United States. From impoverished villages, if they live in a big city in Asia. From Africa, if they live in Italy. From the Philippines, if they live practically anywhere at all.

People sometimes talk about poor women as if they were another product that should be moved to market, like underwear from Bangladesh or mobile phones from China. One day a thirtysomething American woman I know—single, white, unmarried, successful, city-dwelling—posted an article on Facebook about how shockingly difficult it is to raise babies. "That's why we need to import cheap nannies!" one of her friends replied.

I never hear anybody point out the plainest truth: that this model for women's emancipation depends, itself, upon a permanent underclass of impoverished women.

But of course these stories are not only about women—they also scream the reality of men who manage to duck not only the labor itself, but the surrounding guilt and recrimination. All those well-meaning men who say progressive things in public and then retreat into private to coast blissfully on the disproportionate toil of women.

In the end, the answer is the men. They have to do the work. They have to do the damn work! Why do we tie ourselves in knots to avoid saying this one simple truth? It's a daily and repetitive and eternal truth, and it's a dangerous truth, because if we press this point we can blow our households to pieces, we can take our families apart, we can spoil our great love affairs. This demand is enough to destroy almost everything we hold dear. So we shut up and do the work.

No single task is ever worth the argument. Scrub a toilet, wash a few dishes, respond to the note from the teacher, talk to another mother, buy the supplies. Don't make a big deal out of everything. Don't make a big deal out of anything. Never mind that, writ large, all these minor chores are the reason we remain stuck in this depressing hole of pointless conversations and stifled accomplishment. Never mind that we are still, after all these waves of feminism and intramural arguments among the various strains of womanhood, treated like a natural resource that can be guiltlessly plundered. Never mind that the kids are watching. If you mind you might go crazy.

Cooking and cleaning and childcare are everything. They are the ultimate truth. They underpin and enable everything we do. The perpetual allocation of this most crucial and inevitable work along gender lines sets up women for failure and men for success. It saps the energy and burdens the brains of half the population.

And yet honest discussion of housework is still treated as a taboo.

For all her advice about holding one's place at work, this is a realm that Sheryl Sandberg has mostly managed to sidestep. Instead of addressing directly the employment of domestic workers in her home, she has pointed out that men aren't asked that question. By implication, since men aren't asked, she shouldn't have to answer. And she's half right—men aren't asked that question. But this is a dodge. Men ought to be asked. Everyone ought to be asked. Who's cooking the food, who's minding the kids, who's scrubbing the toilets?

How do you manage to be out in the world, and if you are here, who is there?

———

We'll be leaving India soon. Our time is running out. I have the feeling Mary senses our departure, that she can read our family the way sailors read the tides and skies. She's seen this cycle before.

Just as Tom was negotiating his next job, Mary got sick. She burned with fever; she threw up; she couldn't control her bowels.

She kept offering weakly to come to work, and I kept ordering her to stay home. I sent water and packets of rehydration salts back to her room. I called her every day and tried to convince her to go to a doctor. Every day she declined.

I didn't push. I had other problems. The housekeeper was sick, too, so I scurried around cleaning and cooking and washing the clothes and shopping for food. I was taking care of Patrick, who'd also come down with a virus. I knew that Mary's daughter was staying with her, and I figured that was enough—another adult, albeit a young adult, keeping watch. Mary asked for diarrhea medicine, which I sent. But the days slid past, and she wasn't getting better.

Meanwhile, I was in barely suppressed agony. My book edits were due, and those two weeks were supposed to be a stretch of intense work. I begged Tom to take a few days off, even one day, even half a day. He insisted that he couldn't; he had deadlines of his own. I wrote groggily after the kids went to bed. When Tom was home on the weekend I holed up in cafés with my laptop. I needed childcare. I needed Mary.

I was keenly aware that I'd been tripped up, yet again, by the very things I was writing about. How easily Mary and I had changed from two women whose needs synced up neatly (my need for childcare, Mary's need for money) into two women with desperate problems they couldn't solve for each other. It happened just like that, overnight, with no warning or backup plan for either of us.

A week after Mary first fell ill, I was walking home from a long Saturday of work in coffeehouses. Winter soot blew in drifts over the city; a faint wind stirred the leaves like a comb through hair. I was coming around the corner to our house when I heard a quiet voice: "Hello, Madame."

I jumped a bit, and there was Mary, limping along with a sack dangling heavily from her wrist. Her face was grayish and bloated.

"Mary! How are you feeling?"

"Better." She spoke softly, like a small girl. "I could walk a little so I went to buy bananas and cucumbers."

"Are you still having diarrhea?"

"Yes, too much."

"Okay, so the bananas are good, but don't eat those cucumbers. Cucumbers are a diuretic. They will make you worse."

"I called a chemist," she said, using the common Indian term for pharmacist. "He said to eat bananas and cucumbers."

"Yeah, but listen, he's wrong. Bananas, yes; cucumbers, no." I was trying to help. I sounded aggressive.

She half nodded and dropped her eyes.

"You look terrible," I said.

"I couldn't walk until today. I kept having accidents in my pants.

The neighbors complained because the smell from my toilet was so bad. They thought there was a dead rat. Then I told them, no, I'm sick, so they made us clean the bathroom and the drain because, you know, they said, 'We will all get sick.'"

"Oh my God." This was much bleaker than I'd imagined. "Why did you want to come to work today?"

"I thought . . ." She trailed off.

"Mary," I said. "You are not going to lose your job. Okay? But please don't come until you can eat normal food."

"Okay."

"Why wouldn't you go to a doctor?"

"I didn't think I could come down the stairs."

"You didn't think you could get out of the house?"

"I thought, I will die here. My head was spinning. I could hardly sit for toilet."

"But you kept saying you were getting better and you didn't need a doctor. That's not the same thing." I reeled with the familiar mingling of tenderness and frustration. "We could have helped you down. You are supposed to let me know what's going on!"

"Sorry, Madame."

"No, it's not— Listen. I think you need to go to the hospital. Go home and rest, okay? I'll call you."

I walked home in a daze, mulling the gravity of Mary's condition. I'd assumed she'd been suffering from a particularly tenacious stomach bug, nothing out of the ordinary. Now I realized we'd been lucky she hadn't died.

Mary always led me to believe that Delhi brimmed with friends and relatives and church acquaintances, that she had a rich and deep support system. But I could see for myself that, in her time of need, she'd been alone. She'd thought she might die, and nobody had come.

I should have checked on her, I thought now. I should have overcome my reluctance to involve myself in Mary's private matters. I didn't want to infantilize her; I didn't want to slide into some kind of neo-feudalism. I'd imagined how I'd feel if I called in sick only to have my boss show up at my door. But now it was clear to me that I'd been responsible for Mary, like it or not, and by local standards I'd shirked my duties. In the unspoken, let alone unwritten, contract of our employment relationship, it had been my job to take charge.

And yet this made no sense at all. I was in no position to take care of Mary. This difficulty was built into our relationship: her moments of crisis were guaranteed to find me overwhelmed by the loss of childcare and logistical support.

I'd already cataloged the downside of depending upon impoverished women, but never had the limitations of employment in my house been more obvious. Just as Mary was not a day care and couldn't guarantee a steady flow of childcare, I was not a company that could offer benefits and insurance and broader social protection. I didn't have a human resources department. We were just two people who'd tried to cobble together an arrangement that was mutually beneficial.

When it came right down to it, we were each on our own.

That's why ad hoc domestic labor is, ultimately, a bunk system. It's a jerry-rigged, flaw-riddled compromise that will never live up to its promise of upward mobility for one woman and personalized childcare for another.

I sent Mary to the hospital. And, after a few days of antibiotics and decent medical care, she'd mostly recovered.

I was left shaken. Mary and I had been in different chambers of the same household. We'd needed each other, but we couldn't help or even see each other. So we'd languished in parallel, together but separate, needing and not receiving, trapped in the rooms we had chosen with the hopes of brighter circumstances.

And I kept thinking, there has to be something better.

———

Mary has changed in the years since she came to our house. Her body is thicker and slower. Her face is more round and weathered. Her eyes are failing; she can no longer read stories to the kids unless the print is big. Her knees and back are stiff. She limps.

The children have grown, too. They are tall and talkative. They have plans of their own. I can see that our claim to them will expire. They are separate souls; they will belong to nobody but themselves.

Lately it seems as if this era of life, this intense and messy and sleepless stretch, has run itself out. Neither of my babies is a baby anymore. There are bits of time in the day that weren't there before, and every month those bits of time are a bit more substantial. I'm less tired. Things seem possible again. The idea of a job in an office or a newsroom no longer sounds like a crazy pipe dream, but something I should perhaps consider.

Mary fills the school hours with housecleaning and laundry. She calls the electrician and plumber and grocery delivery. She is no longer the sacrosanct guardian of tiny children. Lately I sometimes come upon Mary simply sitting there—a melancholy sight that would have been unimaginable a few years ago—not out of laziness but because there is truly nothing for her to do.

If we weren't leaving anyway, we'd look for a way to break up amicably. We should set her free, really, so that she can find a family with babies to take care of. That would be better.

At least once a day, either Mary or I points out some milestone— the children's growth, a forthcoming holiday, the change of season. And then Mary says: "So quickly, time is passing." She says this every single day, and every day she sounds utterly surprised and rueful. Lately our house feels like an ongoing memorial service. But I think that is because Mary is still here. She is a remnant of a life we've outgrown.

I know we'll never really leave Mary. I know we never exactly left Xiao Li or Pooja, either. We couldn't, even if we tried. Their influence lives inside our children; they left their mark on our family.

One day Patrick was fretting about graduating to a new preschool class.

"I don't *want* new teachers," he bawled. "I want my *old* teachers!"

Max turned to him, smooth as stone.

"I used to feel that way, too," he said firmly. "But you just have to move on."

I caught my breath. I couldn't believe this advice—ruthless and yet optimistic, slicing to the heart of the problem—was coming from my five-year-old. And then I thought, *That's Mary.* Max will never realize where he got this brisk and positive method of tackling the world, but I can recognize its roots.

I have regrets about Mary that are hard to name. I paid her well. I tried to treat her well. I helped her when I could. Still, I can't shake the feeling that I bought something from her that should not be for sale. Her life force. Her energy.

Now that it's all over, I wonder what we traded and what we took. Mary got money for her children's school fees and her in-laws' surgeries. I got some time to work.

My children were the lucky ones. They made no trade; it was all benefit. They soaked up the love and attention of extra caretakers. They were exposed to languages and cultures and tastes and sounds. They learned new ways of moving through the world, other ways of being alive, personalities alien to their parents' psychology.

The children of Mary and Pooja and Xiao Li had to trade like grown-ups, and their trade was the most brutal of all: they got money, but they grew up without mothers.

Our family is leaving them behind now, we are leaving all of this. We'll take the time and the love, which have made us stronger, more successful, more enriched than we were before. We'll leave the cash we spent, and we won't miss it.

Now it seems to me that it was always a transaction of energy—of the finite supply of energy that flows out and cannot be refilled. Physical strength, mental fortitude, emotional endurance. Women have, for generations, drained that energy at home. I wanted to have my kids and save some energy for other work, and so I turned to Mary and the others. I had the chance to buy my energy back from the family at a rate I could afford to pay.

And it helped. Help does help; that should never be denied. During those first few years, when babies are small and physical needs relentless, help makes such an enormous difference that it is impossible to discuss it coherently. The difference is not subtle; it's night and day. It is life changing.

I still get irritated with Mary sometimes; it races over my skin like a fast-spreading rash. Sometimes I think we should fire her. Other times I am flooded with that familiar devotion, and I think we should take her along with us.

But, if I'm honest, I know we won't do either. We'll simply leave, and that will be the end.

Acknowledgments

A funny thing about this book about women: It would not exist without the invisible love and work of countless women.

My brilliant friends from our Delhi writing collective, Sonam Dukpa-Jhalani and Jyoti Pande Lavakare, read early drafts of these chapters with rigorous criticism tempered, somehow, with love and encouragement. My agent, Kathy Robbins, and my editor, Kristine Puopolo, were immediate believers in the idea of this book and worked exhaustively to push it forward. My own mother, who has guided me through both parenthood and writing, generously gave her blessing to write about sensitive family history.

I am enormously grateful to all of my thoughtful, funny, sharp friends who also happen to be mothers—many of whom were enlisted to read parts of this book or discuss the subject. Most memorably, and in no particular order, Alissa Sheth, Genevieve Connors, Barbara Demick (whose influence is woven throughout this book, but especially the prologue), Sana Sood, Uli Putz, Jamie Tarabay, Medha Kochhar Singh, Ellen Barry, Elizabeth Kennedy, Nilofer Azad, Amy Lazarides, and Lyndee Prickitt. Kehinde Komolafe, Elaine Wong, Holly Williams, Stephanie Kleine-Ahlbrandt, Arpan Munier, and Tara Wilkinson, who I joked was the muse of this book (and who was, in a way, the muse of this book) also left their marks on these pages. I'm forever thankful to the Beijing baby group moms, especially Jennifer Ma, with whom I had a joyful—and supremely helpful—reunion when I went back to China for research. Elaine and Paul hosted me during that trip and fortified me with late-night conversation and Japanese whiskey. I am also grateful to the Delhi writing group—Anuradha, Jan, Sujatha, Manju, Amy, Mala, Gopika, et al.—for readings and dinners that brought such a strong sense of community, inspiration, and support.

Tommy Yang and Nicole Liu, my friends and former colleagues from the *Los Angeles Times* in Beijing, also provided me with invaluable assistance in China. Duc Nguyen helped me brainstorm subtitles. My sincere gratitude also goes to the smart and patient people at Doubleday and the Robbins Office for their work on behalf of this book.

I'd be lost without Tom, who has always encouraged my work in every conceivable way and who did not flinch at the prospect of an honest (but inherently biased) account of our most fraught and challenging days. I can't begin to express my gratitude and love.

And, finally, my most true and enormous thanks and admiration to the women in this book. Xiao Li, Pooja, and Mary will forever give me strength and push me forward to do what needs to be done. They have been brave in every possible way, and they have taught me more than they'd ever guess. I bow down; I touch their feet.

ABOUT THE AUTHOR

Megan K. Stack is the author of *Every Man in This Village Is a Liar,* a finalist for the 2010 National Book Award. As a war correspondent for the *Los Angeles Times,* she reported from dozens of countries and was posted to Jerusalem, Cairo, Moscow, and Beijing. She was a finalist for the 2007 Pulitzer Prize in international reporting.